Architects of Anthropology in India

Architects of Anthropology in India

(Volume - I)

Edited by

Sarthak Sengupta

GYAN

Published, 2021

Published by

Gyan Publishing House
5, Ansari Road
Daryaganj, New Delhi-110002
Phone: 011-47034999, 9811692060
www.gyanbooks.com
E-mail: books@gyanbooks.com

Printed at: Gyan Press, Delhi.

Cataloging in Publication Data—DK
Courtesy: D.K. Agencies (P) Ltd. <docinfo@dkagencies.com>

Architects of anthropology in India / edited by Sarthak Sengupta.
volumes cm
Contributed articles.
Includes bibliographical references.
ISBN 9788121220439

1. Anthropologists—India—Biography. 2. Anthropology—India.
I. Sengupta, Sarthak, 1955- editor.

LCC GN20.A73 2021 | DDC 301.092254 23

Dedicated to

the sacred memory of

Late ***Dr. Murari Mohan Sengupta****,*

my uncle, whose hallowed life has been a source of constant inspiration to my professional and academic pursuits.

Contents

Preface

In India, anthropology was introduced by Sir William Jones, who established the Royal Asiatic Society of Bengal at Calcutta in 1774 to study Nature and Man. However, the teaching of Anthropology in Indian Universities introduced in the University of Calcutta in 1918 as part of the curriculum of Ancient History and Culture and as a holistic study of humankind began in the same University in 1920 when it was given the status of an independent subject for study at the post-graduate level leading to a postgraduate degree. Thereafter, a separate Department of Anthropology was established in 1921. The year 2020, thus, marks the glorious completion of hundred years of teaching of Anthropology in India, and such an important landmark calls for a remembrance.

It is most striking about the discipline is that it is still deficient in having a documented volume on its history and development. It is a matter of great concern that a hundred-year-old academic discipline at the level of postgraduate teaching, which is devoted to the study of the biological and cultural evolution of human beings covering millions of years, could not reconstruct its history. The doyens of anthropology, how through the utmost devotion for the discipline and their obsession to imprint its huge implication in understanding the life of the humans, diligently persisted teaching and research of anthropology in India that deserve proper documentation highlighting a truthful and interpretive assessment of their contributions. Thus, we decided to celebrate this auspicious occasion deliberating upon the contributions of the founding stalwarts of the discipline who break new ground in the field of anthropological research in India. In this treatise, a modest attempt has been made to prepare a repository documenting the life and research contribution of those doyens who are no more with us.

I shall consider my efforts to be amply rewarded if this volume in any manner arouses interest and encourage the budding anthropologist of India.

Dibrugarh, 6th December 2020 **Sarthak Sengupta**

Acknowledgements

The editor of *Architects of Anthropology in India* record with a deep sense of appreciation towards the intellectual existence shown by all the contributors to this volume who not only responded to our invitation with promptness and grace but some of them also participated in the colloquium with great enthusiasm organised to mark the Centenary Celebration of Post Graduate teaching of Anthropology in India at Department of Anthropology, Dibrugarh University in March 2020. They made sincere efforts contributing their mite in the form of write-up within the stipulated date for incorporation in this volume and truly without their kind academic support this compilation would never be possible.

Gyan Publishing House, New Delhi has earned our sincere appreciation and made us indebted through their initiative in bringing out the volume in a minimum possible time.

I would also like to extend my greetings to Mr. Manimugdha Bhuyan of the Department of Anthropology, Dibrugarh University for designing the jacket. Thanks are also due to Prof (Retd). Ranjana Roy and Dr. Debasis Mondal of University of Calcutta, Kolkata; Prof. (Retd) P. K. Chattopadhyay of Punjabi University; Prof. (Retd) Barun Mukhopadhyay of Indian Statistical Institute, Kolkata; Prof. S.R. Mondal and Prof. Sanjay Roy, North Bengal University, and Dr. Naba Kumar Duary of Anthropological Survey of India, Kolkata who arranged few photographs to use in the jacket.

Last but not the least, I thank my wife Kabita, sons Sushruta and Samrat, daughter-in-law Surovee, and granddaughter Shinjinee for their loving support while I worked for the volume.

Dibrugarh, 6th December 2020 **Sarthak Sengupta**

List of Contributors

Abhijit Guha, Formerly Professor, Department of Anthropology, Vidyasagar University, Paschim Medinipur, West Bengal,721102.

Akhono Sakhrie, Assistant Professor, Department of Anthropology, Dibrugarh University, Dibrugarh, Assam, 786004.

Anannya Gogoi, Assistant Professor, Department of Sociology, Dibrugarh University, Dibrugarh, Assam, 786004.

Arindita Goswami, Assistant Professor, Department of Anthropology, Dibrugarh University, Dibrugarh, Assam, 786004.

Dali Dutta, Department of Anthropology, Dibrugarh University, Dibrugarh, Assam, 786004.

Gautam Kumar Kshatriya, Formerly Professor, Department of Anthropology, University of Delhi, Delhi, India, 700007.

Geetanjali Devi, Assistant Professor, Department of Anthropology, Dibrugarh University, Dibrugarh, Assam, 786004.

Geetika Ranjan, Professor, Department of Anthropology, North-Eastern Hill University, Umshing, Mawkynroh, Shillong, Meghalaya, 793022.

Junali Kropi, Assistant Professor, Department of Anthropology, Dibrugarh University, Dibrugarh, Assam, 786004.

Juri Borah, Assistant Professor, Department of Anthropology, G C College, Silchar, Assam, 788004.

Jyoti Prasad Saikia, Professor, Department of Sociology, Dibrugarh University, Dibrugarh, Assam, 786004.

Manisha Rabidas, Rajiv Gandhi Junior Fellow (NSFSC), Department of Anthropology, Dibrugarh University, Dibrugarh, Assam, 786004.

N. K. Das, Formerly Deputy Director, Anthropological Survey of India, Government of India, Kolkata, West Bengal, 700016.

Prasanta Kumar Chattopadhyay, Formerly Professor of Forensic Science, Punjabi University, Patiala, Punjab, 147002.

Rajat Kanti Das, Formerly Professor, Department of Anthropology, Vidyasagar University, Paschim Medinipur, West Bengal,721102.

Rajatsubhra Mukhopadhyay, Formerly Professor, Department of Sociology, North Bengal University, Darjeeling, West Bengal, 734013.

Ranjana Roy, Formerly UGC Emeritus Fellow, Department of Anthropology, University of Calcutta, 35 Ballygunje Circular Road, Kolkata, West Bengal, 700019.

Sekh Rahim Mondal, Formerly Professor, Department of Anthropology, University of North Bengal, Raja Rammohanpur, Darjeeling, West Bengal, 734013.

Subhadra Mitra Channa, Formerly Professor, Department of Anthropology, University of Delhi, Delhi, India, 700007.

Subho Ray, Professor, Department of Anthropology, University of Calcutta, 35 Ballygunje Circular Road, Kolkata, West Bengal, 700019.

Sukanya Sharma, Professor, Department of Humanities, Indian Institute of Technology, Guwahati, Assam,781039.

1

L.K. Anantha Krishna Iyer

Manisha Rabidas

Diwan Bahadur Dr. Lakshminarayanapuram Krishna Ananthakrishna Iyer was the pioneer of the younger biological subjects with special mention of his contribution to the field of anthropology during its formative stage in pre-independent India. He is best known for his strenuous and pioneering work among the tribes in the western part of the then Madras province. During the pre-independent era, in South India, anthropology primarily was so intermingled with the works of Dr. Iyer that it was nicknamed *'Ananthropology'*.

Ananthakrishna Iyer was born in 1861 to an orthodox Brahmin family in Palakkad (Palghat) in the Malabar district (now Kerala) of the Madras presidency of British India. He was the eldest among the four sons and two daughters sired by L.N. Krishna Iyer. His earlier education went along with the introduction of a new educational system in India. He finished his matriculation from a local high school at Palghat, which is now called Victoria College. After his early education, he moved to Calicut and enrolled himself for an undergraduate course at Kerala Vidyasala (now Zamorin's College). There, he met Mr. Cecil M. Barrow whom he later found as a colleague in Victoria College at Palghat. After completing his First Arts examination, he chose Natural Science as his main subject along with Philosophy, Psychology and History as a requisite of the main subject under the academia of the Madras Christian College in 1883. During this time, he had the opportunity to develop a friendship with Dr. William Miller. Dr. Miller was a missionary Principal who had tremendously helped in the line of higher education in India. Anantha Krishna Iyer, however, could not collect his degree at the end of graduation.

At the very beginning of his career, he was hit by continual misfortunes. His graduation was interrupted when his family was caught in a debt wherein he took the entire responsibility. He lost his first wife, Srimathi Meenakshi, and a few years later, also, his second wife, Srimathi Subbalakshmi. His second wife blessed him with a daughter and two sons. After much persuasion of his family, he was married to Srimathi Gangai Ammal who blessed him with two sons and three daughters. Because he was debt-ridden and had a large family to look after, he decided to join as a Surveyor in the Revenue Settlement Office, Department of Madras at Ootacamund (now Ooty) in the year 1888.

After two years in service, he discontinued the job and settled in 1890 as a teacher at Palghat in his *alma mater*, the Victoria College. Mr. Barrow was in charge of the office of Principal. Iyer continued to disseminate knowledge there for seven years (1890-97) and during this very period, he successfully obtained his graduate degree and also a diploma in Licentiate in teaching. He had another appointment as an Assistant Science teacher in Maharaja College, Ernakulam (1897), and remained there in service for the next twenty-three years. During this period, he qualified as an Inspector of Schools and his academic service took a turning point when he was appointed the Superintendent of Ethnography in the Cochin state in addition to full-time employment at school. With all these qualities and experiences garnered over the years, he took part in the systematic ethnographical survey of India (1902) which was set foot by the late Sir Herbert Risley as a sequel to the Census of 1901. His aptitude and expertise helped him develop a State museum, Zoological gardens, and an Industrial Bureau in 1914. His retirement from the Cochin state as an official was announced in the year 1924. His extraordinary and valuable service conferred on him the title of *Rao Bahadur* by the Government of India in 1921.

Anantha Krishna Iyer had experienced a wide variety of career opportunities in his professional path, switching seamlessly from one engagement to another. During these switches, he gradually formed a skill to identify and observe men's disposition. This experience helped him develop his professional cognition in the line of research which later cultivated and had come into light through his pioneering ethnographic masterworks on the indigenous tribes and castes. This had an anthropological invoking in him. While he was working on the ethnological survey, he successfully published his first book *'The Cochin Tribes and Castes'* which had come in two volumes published in the years 1908 and 1912 respectively which stirred much interest among the scholars of the anthropological world. Dr. John Beddoe and M. Bougle extolled these two volumes as to the first-rate substance and how the author had bolstered them with facts.

With his popularity arising as a self-taught anthropologist in the scientific world, Ananthakrishna Iyer was elected as the President of the Anthropology/Ethnography Section at the grand foundation event of the Indian Science Congress held at the premises of the Asiatic Society, Calcutta in 1914 with Sir Asutosh Mukherjee, the then Vice-Chancellor of the University of Calcutta (1906 - 1921) as its President. Dr. Iyer's striking repute was soon brought to the notice of Sir Asutosh Mukherjee who was organising the Post-Graduate Departments of the University and was actively looking for young dedicated scholars at that time. He met Dr. Iyer at the Congress and invited him to the Calcutta University to deliver a course of lectures on Anthropology. In 1921, at the end of the course lectures, Mukherjee announced the appointment of Dr. Iyer in the country's first formal Department of Anthropology at the University of Calcutta. The same year, he was made the Head of the Department and also the Chairman of the Board of Anthropology. He stayed there until his retirement in 1932. In between this engagement, in 1924, he was also invited by the Mysore state government to succeed as the Superintendent of the Mysore Ethnographic Survey after the sudden demise of Mr. H. B. Nanjundayya. Since the time he held this reputable post, began the most important works of his life which displayed his limitless skills and expertise in ethnographical research. After his working session at the University of Calcutta, he would return to Mysore during every vacation to undertake long exploratory field trips. As part of the survey, after he finished his work in 1936, four volumes along with an appendix providing a descriptive account of the population of the Mysore state was published. Anantha Krishna Iyer was invited as Reader in the University of Madras in the year 1916. He planned for a third volume on the Cochin series dedicating it for an entire anthropometric study but was postponed midway due to his other groundbreaking research on the Syrian Christians. This was published by the Cochin Government Press in 1924. Apart from the voluminous yet valuable publications of his books on the tribes and castes of Cochin and Mysore, Syrian Christians, several papers have also been contributed by him in the journals *Man, Man in India, Journal of the Asiatic Society of Bengal,* etc.

Impressed by his vast field knowledge, he received invitations to deliver lectures at different universities in Europe. He was seventy-two at the time when he boarded a ship with his youngest son, Mr. L. A. Natesan on April 23, 1934, for the next five months. He visited several reputed universities and institutions imparting diversified knowledge on tribes of India and acquainting them to the outer world. He spoke on 'Black Magic in India' at the University of Rome. At the Institute of Anthropology of the University of Florence, he delivered a lecture on 'Primitive culture in Southern India'. He spoke at the Anthropological Institute and School of Indology at Paris and thereafter, delivered lectures in front of a learned audience at various distinguished universities in Oxford, Austria, and Germany. One primary reason for his European visit was to attend an international conference of Anthropological and Ethnological Sciences in London, a first of its kind, which was to be held in July in the same year of his visit. His tireless and valuable contribution in the field of Anthropology and Ethnology was well recognised by the organisation of the Congress and therefore he was elected to the Honourary committee. At the conference, Ananthakrishna Iyer presented a paper on 'The Agricultural Basis of Religion in India'. Soon after the conference was over, he boarded for his journey back and reached India at the end of August, the same year. Following his trip, he took up enthusiastically the ethnographic survey of Coorg. The fieldwork was done in collaboration with Professor Lidio Cipriani invited from the University of Florence at the end of 1934 which continued till the summer of 1935.

Ananthakrishna Iyer was a self-taught anthropologist. Though he had no formal training in Anthropology, in particular, he held the view to popularise the study of anthropology. He was the founding member of the Indian Science Congress and later continued to attend almost all of its annual sessions, except a few. He remained the President of the Anthropological/Ethnological section of the Congress five times. In 1934, Professor Ananthakrishna Iyer was also a Foundational Fellow for the Indian Academy of Sciences (Bangalore) and the National Institute of Sciences. Following his vast ethnographical knowledge and feats, he was recognised as a reputed scholar both nationally and internationally. He was a Corresponding Member of the Royal Anthropological Institute of Great Britain and Ireland and the Bureau of American Ethnology, Washington. The President of France elected him as the *Officer D'Academie*. He was also awarded an Honourary Doctorate of Medicine and Surgery by the University of Breslau in Germany (1935); Honourary Fellow of the Anthropological Societies of Firenze, Vienna, and Koln and Asiatic Society, Vienna, etc. In the year 1935, he was conferred the title *Diwan Bahadur* by the Government of India.

His indefatigable spirit in the activity of fieldwork continued till he breathed his last in the year 1937. He left behind him to mourn his death Mrs. Iyer, four sons, and four daughters, all of them happily settled in life. Iyer's son, L.A. Krishna Iyer, and his grandson, L.K. Balaratnam both followed the same pathway of anthropology.

Books

- Iyer, L. K. Ananthakrishna. 1908. *The Cochin Tribes and Castes*. Vol. I. Cochin Government Press, Ernakulam; pp. 366, 44 photographs.
- Iyer, L. K. Ananthakrishna. 1912. *The Cochin Tribes and Castes*. Vol. II. Cochin Government Press, Ernakulam; pp. 504, 81 photographs.
- Ethnology of South India, a contribution to the Encyclopedia of South India, 1920.
- Iyer, L. K. Ananthakrishna. 1924. *Syrian Christians of Malabar, Cochin, and Travancore*. Cochin Government Press, Ernakulam, pp. 340, 44 photographs.
- Lectures on Ethnography. Calcutta University Press, 1926; pp. 277, 44 photographs.
- Iyer, L. K. Ananthakrishna. 1935. *Mysore Tribes and Castes*. Vol. I. Mysore Government Press; pp. 550, 60 photographs.

- Iyer, L. K. Ananthakrishna. 1928. *Mysore Tribes and Caste*. Vol. II. Mysore Government Press; pp. 578, 78 photographs.
- Iyer, L. K. Ananthakrishna. 1930. *Mysore Tribes and Castes*. Vol. III. Mysore Government Press; pp. 615, 75 photographs.
- Iyer, L. K. Ananthakrishna. 1931. *Mysore Tribes and Castes*. Vol. IV. Mysore Government Press; pp. 550, 75 photographs.
- Iyer, L. K. Ananthakrishna. 1936. *Mysore Tribes and Castes*, Appendix, Mysore Government Press pp. 70.

Biography

- Ramdas, LA. 1988. L. K. Ananthakrishna Iyer. N. K. Bose Memorial Foundation, Varanasi.
- Chakrabarti, SB. 2012. 'Remembering L. K. Ananthakrishna Iyer: An Icon in Indian Ethnography'. *Journal of the Indian Anthropological Society*, 47, 3: 237-241.

2

Rai Bahadur Sarat Chandra Roy

Dali Dutta

Sarat Chandra Roy was born on 4th Nov. 1871 in a village of Khulna district in East Bengal (now in Bangladesh). His father was Purna Chandra Roy, who was a member of the Bengal Judicial Service, and his mother Smt. Rajlakshmi Devi was a devout housewife. From the City Collegiate School in Calcutta, he passed Matriculation in 1888 and obtained a B.A. degree with Honours in English from the General Assembly Institute (Scottish Church College) in 1892. He completed a Master's degree from the University of Calcutta in 1893. After that, he proceeded for a B.L. degree which he achieved in 1895 from Ripon College, Calcutta. He departed from this earth in 1942.

S.C. Roy had worked for some time as a Headmaster at the Mymensingh High School, and later as a Principal at the GEL Mission High School in Ranchi. Later he left teaching and started practice in the District Court of 24-Paraganas (Alipore, Calcutta) from 1897 but he shifted to Ranchi within one year, and there he could successfully build up his professional career and earned a good reputation in Court. He was the Founder Fellow of the National Institute of Sciences in India and Patna. He was the first Curator of the Patna Museum and was appointed by the then Governor Edward Gait. In the legislative council of Bihar and Orissa, he secured his seat for successive terms. Roy was also a member of Simon's Commission. In the subsequent years, he devotes his time to the journal *Man in India* and other journals, writing and lecturing at the Anthropology Department of the University of Calcutta, and serving as a Reader at Patna University.

Anthropological studies

In any Indian University, he was the first Indian who delivered a course of lectures on Anthropology and the first to make an effort to publish a quarterly journal for anthropology. He founded the '*Man in India'* journal in Anthropology (1921); still, the serving of this journal is progress to the students and scholars of Anthropology. Sri Roy staunches himself solemnly in the anthropological and related ethnological studies in India. His studies allocate the base of anthropological knowledge of the tribal population of Bihar and adjacent areas. Just the beginning of the twentieth century, he first studied the Munda tribe of Chota Nagpur. His findings began to be published in the journal namely 'The modern review' right from the year 1907. However, the first book came to the arena in 1912 with the title *'The Mundas and their Country'*. Before publishing his 1st book in the year 1912, Roy took 12 years of meticulous research, he devoted his three weeks to do the legal practices and the remaining week of a month constant to move and inquiry for understanding the tribal ways of life.

This was succeeded by several important monographs- '*The Oraons of Chota Nagpur*' (1915), '*The Birhors'* (1925), '*Oraon Religion and Customs*' (1927), '*The Hill Bhuiyas of Orissa*' (1935), and '*The Kharias*' (1937). The sphere of S.C. Roy's interest was very broad. He wrote on diverse topics namely, caste, Hindu religion, racial migration, cultural ethnography, and so on. While he considered studying a particular tribe, he tried to cover some prime characteristic features of their life like arts and crafts, traditions and customs, etc. which were important for ethnology. His monographs were aimed at compact information of the life of tribes as "universal categories of culture". He received appreciation due to his dedicated services to the field of Anthropology. He was awarded the *'Kaiser-i-Hind'* Silver medal (1913) and the title of 'Rai Bahadur' (1919). He has also made an appreciable contribution to the field of Physical Anthropology and Prehistoric Archaeology. Based on Readership Lectures given in Patna University between January and March 1920, the book namely,

Principles and Methods of Physical Anthropology was published in the same year. He made a significant contribution to Prehistoric Archaeology by excavating the Asura site in the year 1915 (situated on the eastern bank of river Tajna in district Ranchi). In this site, he found stone temples and sculptures, cinerary urns, and columns of sculptural atone which were attributed to the Asura people. Sarat Chandra Roy was one of the explorers of anthropological studies in India, although he had no academic degree in anthropology. In 1920, he was elected as an Honourary Member of the Folklore Society of London. He was the only Indian who was rewarded with such an honour. In the same year, he became the President of the Anthropological Section of the Indian Science Congress. In the years 1932 and 1933, he was also elected as the President for the Section of Anthropology and Folklore of the All India Oriental Conference respectively. He was also a member of the Council d'Honour of the International Congress of Anthropological and Ethnological Sciences.

S.C. Roy firstly studied the Munda tribe of Chota Nagpur. He had conducted the study on their customs, beliefs, traditions, life-ways, and dialect. In his book *Munda and their Country,* he outlined the origin of the tribe utilising folklore, language, and prehistoric pieces of evidence. He discussed their history and their land systems in great detail. His book *The Oraon of Chota Nagpur* describes the social organisation of the tribe. He also mentioned the prevalence of youth dormitory, the village panchayat, and the Paraha system and explained the function of the dormitory in the social and economic life of the Oraon. He learned both Mundari and Kurukh dialect spoken by Oraons, in less than 6 months to communicate with the tribals he met.

His book *Oraon Religion and Customs* showed the effect of acculturation and rapid cultural contact among the Oraons, as seen in the Bhagat movement. He also contributes information about various reform movements among the Oraon. His book *Hill Bhuiya of Orissa* (1935) provides a comparative account of plain and hill Bhuiyas. Besides several monographs, he wrote several research papers on the life and culture of various tribes such as totemism among the Asur and Pahira of Chota Nagpur. He also worked on kinship systems and human sacrifice in various tribes of Northeast India. These works were praised by the esteemed anthropologists of that time like J.G. Frazer,

W.H.R. Rivers, R.R. Marett, and R.B. Dixon. S.C. Roy contributed to restoring the integrated character of Anthropology in India. Initially, his writing was much impacted by historical facts but soon he started analyzing various factors that animated the studies. Altogether he had more than a hundred original papers and seven books in English. Also, he wrote seventeen articles in Bengali, sixteen of which were published in the Bengali magazine '*Prabasi*'. He not only made a valuable contribution to the study of human society and culture; he tried to popularise the subject of anthropology among the general readers. Because of these vigorous investigations, he is considered the 'Father of Indian Ethnography'.

The residential bungalow possessed by S.C. Roy is not only housed his collection of over four thousand books but it is also a repository of objects, tools, weapons, household goods, and whatever else he could retrieve throughout his visit to tribal villages. One of the rooms is decorated with customary weapons on the wall. One of the major attractiveness of the collection is the stone and copper weapons and tools of different kinds, shapes, and sizes. A variety of bows and arrows, broomsticks, bamboo baskets, sickles, armor, and axe. It was considered to be the best personal library-cum-museum related to anthropology and sociology. He collected stones and statues from Khunti and Orissa. But he never tried to either assist himself or make a killing by selling his assemblages. After his demise, his daughter looks after his bungalow, but when she expired as if the bungalow lost its matriarch. Now, the grandson of S.C. Roy looks after the collection. Practically, the museum is closed.

In sweet memory of S.C. Roy, the Indian Anthropological Association, in collaboration with the University of Ranchi and Council of Social and Cultural Research, Bihar releases a book on the contribution of S.C. Roy to Indian Anthropology (1971).

Books and Monographs

1. 1912. *The Mundas and their Country*, City Book Society, Calcutta.
2. 1915. *The Oraons of the Chota Nagpur: Their History, Economic Life and Social Organisation,* City Bar Library, Ranchi.
3. 1925. *The Birhors: Little Known Jungle Tribe of Chota Nagpur,* Man in India Office, Ranchi.

4. 1928. *Oraon Religion and Customs*, Edition Indian, Calcutta Temple Press.
5. 1935. *The Hill Bhuiyas of Orissa*, Man in India Office, Ranchi.
6. 1937. *The Kharias* Vol. 1 & 2, Man in India Office, Ranchi.

Contribution in Journals

2014. 'Magic and witchcraft on the Choto Nagpur plateau: A study in the philosophy of the primitive life', *Journal of the Royal Anthropological Institute*, 44:324-350.

1915. 'The corn-spirit and the tree spirit in Choto Nagpur', *Journal of Bihar and Orissa Research Society*, 1:1.

1915. 'Orientation of gravestones and houses in Choto Nagpur', *Journal of Bihar and Orissa Research Society* 1,2:277-280.

1915. 'Probable traces of totem worship among the Oraon', *Journal of Bihar and Orissa Research Society* 1,1: 53-56.

1915. 'Birth and childhood ceremonies among the Oraons', *Journal of Bihar and Orissa Research Society*, 1,1:31-46.

1916. 'Devine myths of the Mundas', *Journal of Bihar and Orissa Research Society*, 2,2:201-214.

1916. 'Totemisms among the Birhors', *Journal of Bihar and Orissa Research Society*, 2,2:250-254.

1916. ' A general account of the Birhors', *Journal of Bihar and Orissa Research Society*, 2,4:457-467.

1917. 'A note on totemism among the Asur', *Journal of Bihar and Orissa Research Society*, 3,4:567-571.

1918. 'Marriage customs of the Birhors', *Journal of Bihar and Orissa Research Society*, 4,1:62-90.

1918. 'Birth, childhood and puberty ceremonies of the Birhors', *Journal of Bihar and Orissa Research Society*, 4,2:214-231.

1918. ' Death and funeral customs of the Birhors', *Journal of Bihar and Orissa Research Society*, 4,3:307-321.

1918. 'Religion of the Birhors', *Journal of Bihar and Orissa Research Society*, 4,4:455-482.

1919. ' Birth, childhood, and puberty and death customs of the Parbi Bhuiyas', *Journal of Bihar and Orissa Research Society,* 5,4:618-619.

1921. 'Ethnographic notes and querries (on primitive economics, sociology, religion, and magic), *Man in India,* 1,1:66-72.

1921. 'Anthropological researches in India', *Man in India*, 1,1:11-56.

1921. 'Ethnographic notes and querries (on primitive economics, arts and crafts, sociology, religion, magic and notes on castes and tribes), *Man in India,* 1,2:164-165.

1921. 'A new religious movement among the Oraons', *Man in India*, 1,4: 266-321.

1922. 'Ethnographic notes and querries (on beliefs, customs, myths of the Birhor tribes), *Man in India*, 2, 1 & 2:111-112.

1922. 'Gonds of the Oraons', *Man in India*, 2:137-157.

1923. 'Exorcism in Chotanagpur', *Journal of Bihar and Orissa Research Society*, 9,1:118-139.

1924. 'Magical practices, omens and dreams among the Birhors', *Journal of Bihar and Orissa Research Society*, 10,3:209-220.

1925. 'Totemism and religion', *Journal of Bihar and Orissa Research Society*, 11,2:162-176.

1926. 'The Oraon feast and sal flower', *Journal of Bihar and Orissa Research Society*, 12,3:216-242.

1926. 'Exorcism among the Oraon of Palamau district', *Journal of Bihar and Orissa Research Society*, 12,4:477-497.

1927. 'The bull-roarer in India', *Journal of Bihar and Orissa Research Society*, 13:54-61.

1928. 'Primitive religion in Chota Nagpur', *Journal of Bihar and Orissa Research Society*, 14:65-74.

1930. 'Studies in Indian Anthropology', *Presidential Address, Sixth All India Oriental Congress*, Patna, 1930.

1931. 'The effects on the aborigines of Chota Nagpur and their contact with western civilisation' *Journal of Bihar and Orissa Research Society*, 17,4:378-380.

1931. 'The jungle tribes of Bihar', *Journal of Bihar and Orissa Research Society*, 5,1:

1932. 'The study of folklore and tradition in India', *Journal of Bihar and Orissa Research Society*, 18,3-4:353-381.

1936. 'The aborigines of Chota Nagpur: Their proper status in the reformed constitution', *Indian Nation*, pp. 21-25.

1937. 'The study of anthropology from the Indian viewpoint', *Journal of Bihar and Orissa Research Society*, 10-8,37: 243-256. And also in *Man in India*, 16,1:81-93.

1938. 'The Indian outlook on anthropology', *Man*, 146-150.

1938. 'The importance of anthropological studies in India', *New Review*.

References

Cohen Ronald, 1971, *S.C. Roy Centenary Celebration, Newsletter*, American Anthropological Association, Washington.

Sengupta, S. 2008, 'Recasting the Oraons and the 'Tribe': Sarat Chandra Roy's Anthropology', in P. Uberoi (Ed): *Anthropology in the East*, Seagull Books, Calcutta.

Srivastava, Vinay Kumar, and Chaudhury Sukant K. 2009. 'Anthropological studies of Indian tribes', in Yogesh *et al* (Ed): *Sociology and Social Anthropology in India*, p. 52, Indian Council of Social Science Research, New Delhi.

Upadhyay, Vijay S and Pandey Gaya, 1993. 'Indian Anthropologists-Sarat Chandra Roy: The Father of Indian Ethnography (1871-1942)', p. 395. in *History of Anthropological Thought*, Concept Publishing Company, New Delhi.

3

Bhupendranath Datta

Abhijit Guha

Introduction

The name of Bhupendranath Datta is not found in the standard encyclopedic books of anthropology in India. For example, the name, contributions, and life sketch of Bhupendranath Datta did not find a place in *Bibliographies of Eminent Indian Anthropologists* (with life sketches) by Ray (1974). Only in a recent period research attention to Bhupendranath Datta's anthropological and sociological contributions are being found in the Indian scholarly journals (Mukhopadhyay, 2019). The question is who was Bhupendranath Datta? What were his anthropological contributions? Were his contributions so insignificant in Indian anthropology that he did not deserve discussion in the history of Indian anthropology?

Life and works

In a valuable and unique Bengali biographical dictionary named *Samsad Bangali Charitabhidhan* (revised fifth edition 2010) published by *Sahitya Samsad*, we get a short description of the life and works of Bhupendranath Datta. He was born on 4th April 1880 in Calcutta and died on 25th December 1961 in the same city and was the youngest brother of Swami Vivekananda. Bhupendranath passed the then school leaving Entrance Examination from Calcutta Metropolitan School and joined the Bengal Revolutionary Organisation. Notably, at this young age, he became editor of the famous revolutionary weekly *Jugantar* and was sent to rigorous imprisonment for one year by the then British government for writing against the colonial rule. After being released from jail he went out of the country in disguise under the name of Basanta Kumar Brahmachari at Belur Math with the help of Sister Nivedita (Dasgupta, 2018). Then he reached USA and earned his undergraduate degree from New York University in 1912 and then took a Masters degree in sociology from the famous Ivy League Brown University in 1914. Then after the beginning of the First World War, he reached Germany and joined the illustrious anti-British Berlin Committee organised by the Indians in exile and he was also the Secretary of this organisation during 1916-18 (Mukhopadhyay, 2019). But what was most remarkable in the career of this outstanding intellectual was that along with his revolutionary activities, he continued his study and research in sociology and anthropology in India. Bhupendranath earned his Ph.D. degree in anthropology in the year 1923 from the famous Hamburg University of Germany and became a member of the German Anthropological Society and German Asiatic Society (Mukhopadhyay, 2019). His scholarship was not limited to his specialised area in biological anthropology in which he did his doctorate but was as vast as to include sociology, history, law, philosophy, statistics, and literature. He wrote books and articles in Bengali, English, German, Hindi, and Iranian languages. Some of his remarkable books were *Bharater Ditiya Swadhinatar Sangram* (Datta,1949), *Bharatiyo Samaj Padhyati* (1958), *Amar Amerikar Abhijnata* (1933), *Baishnab Sahitye Samajtatta* (1945), Banglar Itihas (1963), *Dialectics of Hindu Ritualism* (1950), *Hindu Law of Inheritance* (1957), *Dialectics of Land Economics of India* (1952) and *Swami Vivekananda: Patriot-Prophet—a study* (1954).

The scholarly articles published by Bhupendranath make an impressive list. His papers were published in *Man in India*, *The Sankhya*, *Modern Review, Journal of the Department of Letters*, *Calcutta Review, Bihar Orissa Research Society Journal,* and *Anthropos*. He was the first author of a paper on 'A note on the foot and stature correlation of certain Bengal castes and tribes' with P.C. Mahalanobis in *The Sankhya* in 1938 (Dutta and Mahalanobis, 1918).

Bhupendranath Datta was also a true political activist and a worker fighting for the cause of the Indian peasantry. He should also be regarded as one of the pioneering nationalist anthropologists in India (Guha, 2019a). In 1921, Datta went to Moscow to join the Communist International founded by V.I. Lenin. Bhupendranath presented his research paper on the political condition of colonial India to Lenin. Lenin gave a reply to Datta and requested him to collect data on the peasant organisations in India. As early as the mid-1930s he was directly involved with the peasant movements in India and was the president of the *Krishaksabha* of Bengal as well as the All-India Trade Union Congress. During this period he joined the Quit India movement of Mahatma Gandhi and was jailed by the British government (Samsad Bangali Charitabidhan, 2010).

Unlike present-day 'specialised' anthropologists Bhupendranath was equally strong in the two major subfields of the subject, namely, physical anthropology and social-cultural anthropology. We find quite a good number of scientific articles in various national and international journals by Datta including *Man in India*, one of the oldest professional journal of anthropology founded by Sarat Chandra Roy in 1921. I will here briefly discuss his two remarkable articles published in *Man in India* in 1935 and 1942. The title of the 1935 article is *Ethnological Notes on Some of the Castes of West Bengal*. It should be noted that the anthropologists of this period were mainly studying tribes rather than castes. Secondly, he looked at castes from a dynamic and changing perspective which was also new for the anthropologists of his time (Datta, 1950). The fact that the same caste could take up different appearances and functions under the influence of changing political and economic conditions were not overlooked by Bhupendranath Datta. For example, like a modern anthropologist, Datta observed the Bhumij community of Bankura in the following manner.

> The word "Bhumij" means indigenous... The Bhumij of Bankura formerly had been the ghatwals of the Raja of Vishnupur; that is to say, they used to serve as his militia and to watch and defend the passes which led to the state of Vishnupur. In place of their service, they used to get land rent-free for their maintenance and used to live well. But with the disappearance of the Vishnupur State and the expropriation of their lands by the East India Company, these people have fallen off from their position (Datta, 1935a:219).

Bhupendranath's second article of *Man in India* entitled *Origin and Development of Indian Social Polity* written as early as 1942 was also significant because in that long article his proposition was "Evolution of the society and status of the castes should be evaluated according to the economic and political condition of the state". Accordingly, he explained that caste has no biological basis and one of the most interesting subsections of the article is "Class-struggle in ancient India" in which Datta elaborately demonstrated how the origin and transformation of the caste system took place through the myriad conflicts and struggles among the different social classes revealed in the stories of the epics of India (Datta, 1942). Strangely, this kind of original idea on the caste system which was published in the pioneering research journal of India was overlooked by the later-day anthropologists of India (Bose, 1965). Nirmal Kumar Bose just mentioned Bhupendranath Datta's name in his article published in *The Economic Weekly* but did not attempt to understand Datta's unique approach in Indian anthropology, which dealt with caste from a Marxist point of view (Bose, 1965:1337-1340).

Datta's book *Dialectics of Hindu Ritualism* written after his caste article dealt with the political economy of Hindu religious institutions. It was one of the early Marxist sociological expositions of the Hindu religion (Datta, 1950). It would, however, be wrong to view Bhupendranath as a rigid and dogmatic intellectual. In his next book *Hindu Law of Inheritance (An Anthropological Study)* published in 1957, he mentioned categorically.

> Strangely, it was found out that some of the earlier writers of Indian legal history have based their writings on the hypotheses of Morgan and Maine. But while reading the history of the cultural evolution of India, we must not forget that the present-day anthropologists say that civilisation never had a unilineal development the world over. It is even admitted by Frederick Engels that the later-day anthropologists are not accepting the dictum of Morgan. Humanity never had a stereotyped evolution in its career of advancement. This we must bear in mind when we apply ourselves to Indian history (Datta, 1957: ii).

This book contains a detailed discussion on the two ancient systems of law which governed inheritance in India, viz. *Mitakshara* and *Dayabhag* from a historical perspective. The book revealed the erudition of its author as regards Sanskritic literature and law books which threw up a challenge to Sir Henry Maine's theory on the existence of village communities in India based on principles of communal or joint ownership of agricultural land. Suffice it to say that till today the syllabi of anthropology and sociology in Indian universities contain heavy dosage on the contributions of Maine, Morgan, and Marx but ironically not a single word on the original inputs of Bhupendranath Datta on the laws of property inheritance in ancient India.

His contributions in the subfield of physical anthropology were no less remarkable. For example, he wrote a critical review of the western anthropologists in his 84 pages article *Races of India* published as early as 1935 in the prestigious *Journal of the Department of Letters of the University of Calcutta.* In this article, Datta had elaborately shown how the 'diverse reports', 'opposing opinions', and 'new nomenclatures' used by different authors as regards the nature of human populations in India only 'confused the students and frightened the layman'. It is interesting to note that Datta concluded the paper by saying that different 'biotypes' did exist in India (he did not use the term 'race' here) and mentioned that a thorough scientific investigation was needed to link the affinities of the Indian populations with the outside world (Datta, 1935b).

I will end my discussion with Bhupendranath Datta's book on Swami Vivekananda. He wrote two books on his elder brother, one in English (Datta, 1954) and the other in Bengali. The Bengali book Swami Vivekananda published in 1961 is more elaborate. This is a unique, rare, and pioneering culture-personality study. In this detailed anthropo-sociological research Bhupendranath placed Vivekananda in the socio-historical context of the nineteenth century. The essence of Bhupendranath's interpretation of Vivekananda was that the latter was not satisfied only with programmes of public welfare. According to Bhupendranath Datta, Swami Vivekananda wanted a complete transformation of the prevailing exploitative social system. At the beginning of his book, Bhupendranath's words may shock the so-called Marxists. Let me freely translate them into English as follows:

> Marxists may be surprised to know that Swamiji had ideas similar to Marx much earlier. They would be more surprised that Swamiji had openly and frankly admitted himself as 'Socialist' and here lay the inner message of

Swamiji to the youth of India. Many will also be astonished by reading that Swamiji not only used Marx's statement 'Poor are becoming poorer, and the rich are becoming richer', he predicted too that the 'culture of the have nots' will be the culture of the Indian people in future New India (Datta, 1961).

Conclusion

A dedicated revolutionary and scholar anthropologist like Bhupendranath Datta is still a missing hero in the history of Indian anthropology and sociology (Guha 2016, 2018, 2019a and 2019b). An attempt should be made to take initiative to republish the works of Bhupendranath Datta. Sooner the better.

Acknowledgements

First, I express my sincerest thanks to Professor Tirthankar Daspurkayastha for encouraging me to write an article in the *Bulletin of the Ramkrishna Mission Institute of Culture*, Kolkata. This is the slightly elaborated version of the aforesaid article. I am indebted to the Indian Council of Social Science Research (ICSSR) for supporting me with the financial grants for Senior Fellow to research the nationalist trends in Indian anthropology, out of which this paper came out. I am also grateful to the Institute of Development Studies Kolkata (IDSK) for providing me academic and infrastructural facilities.

Notes and References

Bose, NK. 1965. 'Class and caste'. *The Economic Weekly*.17, 35: 1337-1340.

Dasgupta, S. 2018. *Agnipurush Bhupendranath Datta*. Radical Impression, Kolkata.

Datta, BN. 1935a. 'Ethnological notes on some of the castes of West Bengal'. *Man in India*.15, 4:196-224.

Datta, BN 1935b. 'Races of India (A critique of reports of Indian Anthropology)'. *Journal of the Department of Letters*, Calcutta University, 26:1-84.

Datta, B. 1949. *Bharater Ditiya Swadhinatar Sangram*. This book was first published in 1926 and its 2nd edition was published in 1930 and the then British government banned and confiscated the book. After the Independence of India, the book was again published and translated into Marathi and Hindi. Now the book has been republished by the Radical Impression of Kolkata in 2017. It contains a rich history of the freedom struggle in Bengal.

Datta, BN 1961. *Swami Vivekananda* (in Bengali). Nababharat Publishers, Kolkata.

Datta, BN. 1942. 'Origin and development of Indian social polity'. *Man in India*. 22:12-63.

Datta, BN. 1950. *Dialectics of Hindu ritualism* (Part I). Gupta Press, Calcutta.

Datta, BN. 1954. *Swami Vivekananda: Patriot-Prophet*. (Second revised edition published in 1993). Nababharat Publishers, Calcutta.

Datta, BN. 1957. *Hindu law of inheritance (An Anthropological Study)*. Nababharat Publishers, Calcutta.

Datta, BN. and PC Mahalanobis 1938. 'A note on the foot and stature correlation of certain Bengal castes and tribes'. *Sankhyâ: The Indian Journal of Statistics* (1933-1960).3,3: 245-248.

Guha, A. 2016. 'Indian anthropology and its critics'. *Frontier*. 49, 8.August 28-September 3.

Guha, A.2018. 'Abahelito nrittatik Bhupendranath Datta'. *Arek rakam*. (Bengali Periodical).18:13-16.

Guha, A. 2019a. 'Neglected anthropologist'. *The Statesman*. 10.01.2019 (p.6) & 11.01.2019 (p.6).

Guha, A. 2019b. 'Colonial, Hindu and Nationalist Anthropology in India' *Sociological Bulletin* 68, 2: 154–168.

Guha, A. 2019c. 'Bhupendranath Datta: An unnoticed Indian anthropologist'. *Bulletin of the Ramkrishna Mission Institute of Culture*. LXX, 12: 20-23.

Mukhopadhyay, R. 2019. 'Dr. Bhupendranath Datta: remembering a great scholar in Indian anthropology and sociology'. *Journal of the Indian Anthropological Society*. 54: 65-73. In this article, the author did not discuss Bhupendranath Datta's contribution to Physical Anthropology and he also did not throw any light on Datta's contribution towards the understanding of Swami Vivekananda's thoughts and personality.

Ray, SK. 1974. *Bibliographies of Eminent Indian Anthropologists* (with life-sketches) Anthropological Survey of India. Govt. of India and Indian Museum, Calcutta.

Samsad Bangali Charitabhidhan (Bengali). 2010. (Revised 5th edition). Sahitya Samsad, Kolkata.

https://www.marxists.org/archive/lenin/works/1921/aug/26c.htm accessed through Google on 06.02.2021.

4

Tarak Chandra Das

Abhijit Guha

Introduction

Tarak Chandra Das (1898-1964) belonged to the pioneer generation of Indian anthropology during its 'constructive' (1920-1949) and 'analytical' (1950 onwards) periods (Vidyarthi, 1978). During Das's time, the first Department of Anthropology in India was established in 1920 at the University of Calcutta and Indian anthropology also moved from the ethnographic study of the tribes to the sociological study of caste and the Indian villages. Das came to anthropology with his Masters's degree in Ancient Indian History and Culture and remained engaged in research and teaching in social anthropology for the rest of his life up to 1964 without doing his Ph.D. and retired as a Reader at Calcutta University (Ray, 1974). Apart from being a meticulous teacher in the field of anthropology, his notable contributions in the subject spanned over the colonial and post-colonial periods in India. Das started his ethnographic and arm-chair anthropological research (Guha, 2018) in the early 1920s on diffusion and assimilation of cultural traits in the style of Boasian American cultural anthropology, and then he gradually moved into micro-level intensive fieldwork-based studies on individual tribes of eastern and northeastern India by following the methods and theories of the British structural-functional school. According to my evaluation, his contribution to Indian anthropology took its unique shape in the forties, and during World War II and the Indian

Independence, when he became committed more towards the application of anthropology in the investigation of social problems and changes caused by the Great Bengal Famine, the Second World War and various legislations which were being drafted by the policy-makers of the new nation (Guha, 2016). Finally, Das continued his applied anthropological endeavours by devoting the rest of his academic career to framing policies for the development of the tribal populations based on his ethnographic knowledge gained through meticulous fieldwork done over nearly four decades during the colonial and post-colonial periods in India.

Research interests of T.C. Das

One comprehensive available account of the list of publications of T.C. Das including a short life-sketch was prepared not by an anthropologist or a sociologist but by the Reference Librarian in the Central Library of the Anthropological Survey of India. Ray (1974), in his invaluable book *Bibliographies of Eminent Indian Anthropologists (with Life-Sketches)* published by the Anthropological Survey of India in July 1974. The volume contains the list of publications and short life-sketches of 12 eminent Indian anthropologists including Tarak Chandra Das (Ray, 1974: 56-60). It begins with L.K. Ananthakrishna Iyer (1861-1937) and S.S. Sarkar (1908-1969) is the last anthropologist covering a span of more than one hundred years if we take the year of birth of Iyer and the year of death of Sarkar at the two ends of the continuum.

Das conducted extensive fieldwork in Chotanagpur in the then Bihar and Assam. He also conducted field works to assess the impact of industrialisation in Birlapur in West Bengal, wrote thought-provoking articles containing anthropological and sociological analyses on Bengal Dowry Restriction Bill of 1940 and Hindu Code Bill in the years 1940 and 1944 along with articles on the practical suggestions for the improvement of museums in India and an empirical article on the fish-gorge in Bengal in the prestigious journals like *Modern Review*, *Calcutta Review,* and *Ethnos*. He was very much interested in the application of Anthropology and had a great reputation as a teacher and trainer in field methods.

A bibliographical record of T.C. Das shows that he had altogether 40 publications that are almost one in every year of his academic career. He published 31 full-length articles, 2 books, 6 abstracts, two jointly authored books, and one joint article (Ray, 1974: 56-60). The national and international journals in which he published were prestigious and they included *Man*, *Anthropos*, *Ethnos*, *Man in India*, *Calcutta Review*, *Modern Review*, *Sociological Bulletin*, *Journal of Social Research*, *Journal of the Department of Letters,* and *Anthropological Papers* of the University of Calcutta. Apart from kinship and social organisation, his areas of research interest display remarkable diversity which ranged between sun-worship (Das,1924), fish in Bengali culture (Das, 1931-32), the disposal of dead among the tribals (Das, 1940a), improvement of museums (Das, 1943), scheme for tribal welfare (Das, 1960a), the impact of industrialisation on the peasantry (Das,1960b) to an anthropological analysis of Bengal dowry restriction bill (Das,1941a).

The range of his academic interest was very broad and he was immensely moved and concerned with the social impacts of the Second World War, Bengal famine, industrialisation, and also socialism in the USSR. He viewed his anthropological subjects in the global and the national contexts of development and nation-building from an applied anthropological perspective. From 1922 to 1940, that is about 18 years of his active academic life Das did not venture to write any significant article on the application of social anthropology for the welfare and improvement of the communities and cultures he had studied. His main research interest during this period was to record and study the different aspects of culture and social organisation of the tribal and non-tribal communities of the eastern and north-eastern parts of India. In this period he conducted fieldwork and published on the Ho, Bhumij, Kharia, Chiru, Bathuri, and Purum Kuki. His paper in prestigious international journals of Anthropology like *Anthropos*, *Man,* and *Ethnos* (Das, 1940b) had been published during this period.

Contributions of T.C. Das

The year 1941 can be regarded as a major turning point in the academic career of T. C. Das. In 1941, he delivered the presidential address of the Indian Science Congress. The lecture was a 28-page full-length paper entitled 'Cultural Anthropology in the Service of the Individual and the Nation' (Das, 1941b). In this lecture, Das's major objective was to convince his readers about the immense potential of social-cultural anthropology as applied science for the overall development of the Indian population. In the five subsections of the lecture, Das dealt with the application of anthropology in almost all the important sectors of a modern nation, viz. trade, industry, agriculture, legislation, education, social service, and administration. With the help of concrete empirical findings either from his own field experiences or from the ethnographic accounts of world-renowned social anthropologists (e.g. Lucy Mair, Felix Keesing, Issac Schepera, H.I. Hogbin, B. Malinowski) Das justified the inclusion of anthropologists in policy-making bodies and application of anthropological knowledge in every sphere of nation-building (Das, 1941: 1-29). To substantiate his arguments, Das had used rather unconventional sources of data, like Mahatma Gandhi's 1937 article published in *Harijan* about the adverse effects of the methods adopted by the Christian missionaries to convert the economically poorer classes of the Hindu population in different parts of India (*ibid*: 17-23).

One of the most vital sections in the Presidential Address of Das was on the role of anthropologists in building up a proper type of educational system suitable for the real needs of a particular community in the Indian context. Das probably was the first Indian anthropologist to advocate the indispensable role of social-cultural anthropology in nation-building by combining micro-level field observations within a macro framework which is still lacking among the majority of Indian anthropologists. We have a lot to learn from Das even today (Guha, 2012: 40-46).

Despite the institutional amnesia and obliviousness of the individual scholars about the social responsibility and commitment of T.C. Das to human welfare, he is still remembered for his ethnography on the Purum Kukis of Northeast India. His brilliant monograph *The Purums: An Old Kuki tribe of Manipur* published in 1945 by the Calcutta University became one of the major sources of the database in the acrimonious debate on descent versus alliance theories on kinship in Anglo-American Anthropology which involved mavericks like Claude Levi-Strauss, George Homans, David Schneider, Rodney Needham, Floyd Lounsbury, and others. Das's book on the Purums, however, both for the Western anthropologists and their Indian counterparts, remained a subject of purely academic interest. For T.C. Das, the case was different. Let me justify my hypothesis with some concrete data.

I would begin my discussion with L.P. Vidyarthi's reading of the Purum monograph since he is the lone anthropologist who emphasised the applied dimension of Das'work on the tribe. Vidyarthi in the first volume of his book *Rise of Anthropology in India* described in detail the findings of Das in the different chapters of the monograph with much admiration for its meticulousness and penetrating analyses. In the final part of his description, Vidyarthi discussed the suggestions put forward by Das for the betterment of the Purums (Vidyarthi, 1978:77-81). For Vidyarthi, with the publication of the Purum book T.C. Das 'set an example of a systematic presentation of ethnographic data' (*ibid*, 1978:80). He concluded the discussion on Das's monograph with the following comment:

> His monograph, though not well known to Indian scholars, remains a piece of meticulous fieldwork and penetrative analysis. It will continue to serve as a model for ethnographic research in anthropology (*ibid*, 1978: 81).

I would now look more closely into the concluding chapter of T.C. Das's book on the Purum Kuki.

In the first part of his concluding chapter, Das emphasised the dynamic nature of Purum society which had changed through historical times, and also on the different aspects of Purum culture under various kinds of external influences.

Secondly, Das was keenly interested to understand the nature of the 'productive system' (he did not use the Marxian term *means of production* but it was clear that by the term 'productive system' he did not only refer to technology and material culture) in a dynamic rather than in a functional framework.

Thirdly, without borrowing terms from the Western Marxist scholars mechanically Das made a very sincere empirical attempt to record the processes by which the new productive system, characterised by the plough and plains-land cultivation had begun to influence the different sectors of the Purum society, viz., inheritance, marriage, and religion. Apart from looking into the internal socio-cultural changes brought about by the adoption of the plough cultivation among the Purums, Das was also aware of the wider politico-economic forces which were at work in the region where this small tribe inhabited. He stated at the beginning of section I of his concluding chapter.

> Though foreign merchandise has come to Purum home, it is still immune from the money-lenders of the plains. This is partly due to difficulties of transport and partly to the judicious laws of land tenure of the State as well as the nature of the land-economy of the people. Investment is risky where there is no permanently cultivated land with a marketable value. Nobody would invest money against *jhum* fields and the Purums have nothing else from which the loan can be realised. The recent introduction of permanently cultivated fields will sooner or later change the situation and if the State also relinquishes the stringency of the land-laws the Purums will fall easy prey to the land-grabbers who are sure to flock to their home (Das, 1945:273).

Like his Presidential Address delivered in the Section of Anthropology in the Indian Science Congress in 1941, another very significant work of Das remained unnoticed by the scholars on Indian Anthropology. This work of Das was published in the prestigious international journal *Anthropos* as early as 1937 under the title 'Some notes on the economic and agricultural life of a little known tribe on the eastern frontier of India' (Das, 1937:440-449).

In this paper, Das dealt with the relationship between the variation in the technology of agricultural practices with the natural environment and the socioeconomic consequences of this variation within the same tribe. The name of the tribe is Chiru, who like the Purums belonged to the old Kuki group of tribes of northeast India. A careful reading of the paper reveals that the economic life of the Chirus which Das constructed is not a simple description of the methods of shifting hill cultivation and the associated religious rituals and rites. Neither it is an ethnographic report for the search of borrowed cultural traits from the neighbouring tribes and Hinduised populations nor was it an attempt to put the Chirus in the classical scheme of social evolution. The ethnography of Das, on the other hand, is a penetrating analysis of the various socio-cultural dimensions of shifting hill cultivation in an environmental framework and the slow changes that had been taking place at the time of observation.

Of all the contributions of T.C. Das, *Bengal Famine* stands as the most important one. The subtitle of the book *Bengal Famine* is phrased in the following words: 'As revealed in a Survey of the Destitute in Calcutta' (Das,1949). The book is indeed the result of a survey undertaken by a team of anthropologists from 1943-44 in Calcutta city and also in the villages of the ten districts of undivided Bengal. The idea of surveying with a team of trained anthropologists was first conceived by T.C. Das in July-August of 1943 when hundreds of hungry destitute entered the city of Calcutta in search of food. Das proposed the survey to his colleagues and prepared a detailed questionnaire and a team was formed with eleven trained anthropologists including the teachers and research students of the Department of Anthropology of Calcutta University. The data thus collected were analyzed and a preliminary report was written and a major part of the report was submitted to the Famine Inquiry Commission (constituted by the colonial government) in 1944 in the form of a memorandum. The report was later written in the form of a book by T.C. Das in July 1948 and was published in 1949 by the Calcutta University. *Bengal Famine*, therefore, is a unique example of teamwork under the leadership of T.C. Das by a dedicated group of university-based anthropologists who were driven more by a kind of social and moral commitment than by pure academic quest. This, of course, does not mean that the survey was conducted loosely, that methodological rigors were sacrificed to conduct a rapid and quick appraisal of the situation. The team had no national or international funding agency behind them; no political agenda was lying before them. The Calcutta University sanctioned a sum of Rs. 500 only to extend the survey in the rural areas of the 10 districts of erstwhile undivided Bengal. The two chapters on methodology, which are the best portions of the book, reveal its strength. Chapter XI of the book entitled 'Causes of the Famine of 1943' is another treasure-house of the book which places *Bengal Famine* far above the category of a run-of-the-mill 'sample survey'.

The field-based study of the Bengal famine of 1943 was conducted by T.C. Das is not a typical anthropological study of a tribe or a village inhabited by several castes. It is unique in many respects. Let me enumerate the facts.

First, this is the only study done by a team of trained anthropologists under the leadership of T.C. Das on the Bengal Famine. Second, the book which was written by Das has not received any attention from the successive generation of anthropologists and sociologists in India. Third, in this study, Das and his co-fieldworkers employed traditional anthropological methods (e.g. genealogy, case history, participant observation) for the collection of data not from a specific tribe or caste in a rural setting, but a scattered and heterogeneous group of human beings displaced from the different districts of undivided Bengal affected by the acute food shortage. Fourth, the fieldwork and the survey on the famine-affected population were carried out mainly in the city of Calcutta. Fifth, the report and the recommendations based on the anthropological study of the famine in Bengal were taken into consideration by the policymakers and administrators at the highest level of governance. Lastly, the explanation provided by Das on the causes of Bengal famine surpassed the prevalent anthropological interpretations of social events— evolutionary, diffusionist, and structure-functional.

Taken together, the above facts have made Bengal Famine an unorthodox and pioneering anthropological study even by modern standards (Guha, 2010 and 2019).

Another important fact about the book is the style of its presentation. Unlike the usual state of affairs in which the ethnographer has to describe the material culture and social organisation of tribal and caste villages, Das was tackling a much more complex situation in writing about the Bengal Famine. So, he had to adopt an innovative style of presentation.

Finally, we must mention that Das was much ahead of his time in posing the question of ethics in this pioneering anthropological work. Without avoiding the ethical problems, Das raised the questions at the very beginning of the book. In chapter II under the subtitle 'Origin of the Idea' Das wrote:

> In July and August 1943, when the streets of Calcutta were thronged with the destitute the writer conceived the plan of making a sample

> survey of these unfortunate people. To ply those persons who had been moving from door to door for a handful of food with questions of socio-economic interest may appear unkind (Das, 1949: 11).

The anthropological Odyssey of T.C. Das like many of his contemporaries began with observations on tribal social structure, economic organisation, material culture, and religion, but he gradually focused his findings towards application and policy-oriented arguments in a macro framework. Das was not only a meticulous ethnographer but during the middle part of his journey, he also moved out of tribes and ventured into the territories which did not come under the tradition of anthropology developed in India under the western influence. The study of the Great Bengal Famine is the finest example of this genre.

Conclusion

T.C. Das began his journey in Anthropology with folk elements in the marriage customs of high caste Hindus in Bengal (Das, 1922:67-84) and sun-worship among some aboriginal tribes (Das, 1924:87-94). A little later he took up ethnographic studies of three tribes in eastern India, viz. Ho (Chatterjee and Das, 1927), Bhumij (Das, 1931a), and Kherias (Das, 1931b) in the typical British anthropological tradition before moving into northeast Indian tribes on which he wrote his famous Purum monograph. Das's journey took a sharp turn towards the applied and policy dimensions of anthropology during 1940-49 and it was this period when he grappled with bigger macro issues like the role of anthropology in nation-building, Bengal famine, dowry restriction, and Hindu code bills as well as the building of new kinds of museums in independent India. His famous Purum study also comes under this period, although both Indian and foreign anthropologists missed the applied side of the Purum ethnography.

Acknowledgements

I acknowledge my, students, colleagues, and friends in India and abroad for providing me with several articles and books of Tarak Chandra Das without which this article could not have been written. Finally, I am grateful to my wife and sons for inspiring me to continue my research on T.C. Das.

Notes and References

Chatterjee, A, and Das TC, 1927. *The Hos of Seraikella*. The University of Calcutta, Calcutta.

Das, TC. 1922. 'High-caste Hindu marriage of Bengal with special reference to its folk elements'. *Journal of the Department of Letters*. 8:67-84.

Das, TC. 1924. 'Sun-worship amongst the aboriginal tribes of eastern India'. *Journal of the Dept. of letters.* The University of Calcutta. 11, 87-94.

Das, TC. 1931a. *The Bhumijas of Seraikella*. The University of Calcutta, Calcutta.

Das, TC. 1931b. *The Wild Kharias of Dhalbhum*. The University of Calcutta, Calcutta.

Das, TC. 1931-32. 'The cultural significance of fish in Bengal'. *Man in India*. 11, 3 & 4: 275-303.

Das, TC. 1931-32. 'The cultural significance of fish in Bengal'. *Man in India.* 12: 2 & 3: 96-113.

Das, TC.1937. 'Some notes on the economic and agricultural life of a little-known tribe on the eastern frontier of India'. *Anthropos* 32: 440-449.

Das, TC. 1940a. 'Disposal by exposure among the Bathuris of Mayurbhanj State'.*Man*, 39: 3-7.

Das, TC. 1940b. 'Notes on a type of fish-gorge from Bengal'. *Ethnos*. 3 - 4:131-147.

Das, TC.1941a. 'The Bengal Dowry Restriction Bill, 1940'. *Modern Review*. 70, 6: 588-594.

Das, TC.1941b. 'Cultural anthropology in the service of the individual and the nation'. pp.1-29. Presidential Address delivered in the Section of Anthropology in the Twenty-eighth Indian Science Congress. Benaras.

Das, TC. 1943. 'Practical steps towards the improvement of museums in India'. *The Calcutta. Review*. Nov. 97-100. In this article, Das developed the idea of building 'Economic Museums' in which anthropologists and other scientists would work for the economic development of the people.

Das, TC. 1945. *The Purums: An Old Kuki Tribe of Manipur*. Calcutta University, Calcutta.

Das, TC. 1949. *Bengal Famine (1943): as revealed in a survey of the destitute of Calcutta*. Calcutta University, Calcutta.

Das, TC. 1960a. 'A scheme for tribal welfare'. *Journal of Social Research* 3,2: 93-112.

Das, TC. 1960b. 'Method and approach in a survey on the impact of factory-employment on the life of the workers'. *Sociological Bulletin*. 9:1, 46-59.

Guha, A. 2010. 'Bengal famine' and a forgotten author. *Frontier*, (Autumn Number) 43, 12-15:90-94.

Guha, A. 2012. 'Tarak Chandra Das: a forgotten anthropologist'. *Science and Culture*. 78,1-2:40-46.

Guha, A.2016. *Tarak Chandra Das: An Unsung Hero of Indian Anthropology*. 2016. (Foreword by Hari Mohan Mathur). [ISBN: 978-93-858830-1-9]. Studera Press, Delhi.

Guha, A. 2017. 'Chirus, Purums, and how social changes in northeast India provided new windows for TC. Das' *Journal of the Indian Anthropological Society*. 52:116-126.

Guha, A. 2018. 'T.C. Das sitting in the arm-chair: the other side of the fieldworker anthropologist'. *South Asian Anthropologist*. 18, 1: 109-114.

Guha, A. 2019. 'A forgotten book by a marginalised anthropologist'. *Social Change*. 49, 3: 493–506.

Ray, SK. 1974. *Bibliographies of Eminent Indian Anthropologists* (with life-sketches) Anthropological Survey of India, Govt. of India, Indian Museum, Calcutta.

Vidyarthi, LP. 1978. *Rise of Anthropology in India: A Social Science Orientation*, Vols. I & II. Concept Publishing Company. New Delhi.

https://doi.org/10.1177/0049085719863892 (First published online on September 27, 2019).

5

N.K. Bose's Approach to Culture and Civilisation: A Review

Rajat Kanti Das

The 'cultural unity of India', despite its contradictions and differential representations, happens to be the main plank for Nirmal Kumar Bose to prove that the civilisation in India derived its strength from such a manifestation displaying its capacity to absorb and integrate all into one. Incidentally, Bose has taken pains to establish 'an integrated picture of Hindu society' overshadowing caste and creedal distinctions. For the differences that exist in real-life situations between high and low castes, tribes, and other disadvantaged groups, Bose had his explanation. In specific situations, he would see the process of tribal absorption into the Hindu society as almost a natural outcome, as something which was bound to happen. In this connection, he wrote (1975: 115),

> *There was no doubt that the brahminical-governed society was economically better off than the society of the Kols and the Juangs. Mainly because of the assurance that they would not need to alter their customs radically, we see the Juangs, Oraons, and other communities gradually abandoning their independence and moving towards brahminical society.*

In today's context, the arguments might appear almost one-sided, if not totally out of place. Moreover, there are some loose knots to be tightened and some questions may automatically come up for serious scrutiny. Under whose assurance tribal communities like the Juang, Oraon abandoned their independent status and moved towards brahminical society? Was it because of the state initiative or was it because of the verbal assurance given by the representatives of high caste or middle-class Hindu society who were believed to have the authority to speak on behalf of the society as a whole? If it was a deal, how the deal was made or if it was a question of winning the trust of tribes and other disadvantaged groups, who would be responsible or accountable in case the trust was broken? During Bose's time, there was hardly any opportunity to raise these questions because to Bose absorption seemed to be the natural process under the circumstances. But now the questions have assumed much significance to the people whose reference was given in the context of the total process of absorption. While speaking about the 'cultural unity of India', he has singled out pilgrim centers for special reference. The pilgrim centers are not simply places where different groups of people gather only to collect material objects or indulge in some playful activities but to acquire 'religious merit through ablutions, sacrificial offerings, gifts, and the performance of other religious rites under the direction of Brahmin priests'. A kind of cultural unity could emerge through the journeys of a countless number of pilgrims across time and place. The epics telling stories from the ancient texts contribute further to strengthen that unity as they could easily touch the sensibilities of people. Their efficacy could be gauged from the fact that even in today's power game political strategists make use of them to work upon people's minds. *Sadhus* and *sannyasis* have taken a special place in Bose's mode of interpretation, as he observes,

> *The 'sadhus' and 'sannyasis', in moving from pilgrimage to pilgrimage, from village to village, and across the different kingdoms, have contributed something to the establishment of the cultural unity of India.*

They might have, but today, with the loss of their ascetic value and rise of political culture, they are no longer in a position to command unconditional support and respect from all. Bose could trace the development of *sannyasis* from the days of *Buddhadeva* and *Shankaracharya. True sannyasis* were those who as ascetics could renounce the world. The renunciation of all connections with the past was possible only after one would go for adopting *sannyasa*. At present, they merely stand as a symbol of Hindu religious culture, considered to be an essential component of Hindu society. Whether they are still an essential component is a question to be seriously considered.

Bose directed our attention to the rise of 'the monopolistic guild organisation', a sort of class division within the entire framework of the caste system, which had led to 'two very important results' as given below:

> *One was that poor tribal people easily come within the fold of the more successful productive organisation of the Hindus, and the second was that they did not rise in revolt even when they were relegated to a lowly position within Hindu society.*

Here the tribals were shed in poor light – that the production system they were engaged in had little sustaining capacity and their voice was almost muted or they were not in a position to raise their voice against discriminations they had been subjected to. This may not be the story of all tribes, given the range of variation between them. Not to speak of a tribe like Santal who had all the knowledge of settled agriculture, to think of Juang as a community living at the mercy of the surrounding Hindus and that too without any protest or dissension seems to be a little harsh on their identity-conscious, sensitive mind. Probably one has to accept that economic dependence reduces the chance of self-assertion by such a group of people striking a discordant note. Self-sufficiency which used to be associated with tribal existence in its ideal form may be a myth today, but to subscribe wholeheartedly to the view that all tribes at some stage had to face some sort of economic compulsion to join the Hindu rank as something inevitable or a natural form of transformation may not be very easy. We may never know whether Nirmal Kumar Bose was too committed to the unity of India to see tribes firmly entrenched in their specific context far too long. He believed that they were as much a part of the historical process of transformation as the non-tribals were. It speaks of the strength of the Hindu society in terms of its overwhelming capacity to absorb others who were outside or at the periphery of Hindu civilisation. Tribes might have faced some economic compulsion to come in direct contact with the Hindus, but once they did so the overriding influence of Hindu culture created a lasting impression on them. As Andre Beatille (1975) in his 'Preface' to the revised edition of *"The Structure of Hindu Society"* observes,

> *It was the historical imagination that led Bose to examine and re-examine the relations between tribal and non-tribal populations from a larger social and cultural perspective.*

Beatille further remarks in his 'Introduction' of the same book:

> *The hill tribes have lived for centuries under the shadow of Hindu Civilisation even though they had been left to themselves.*

If it was the 'historical imagination' of Nirmal Kumar Bose to find some closeness in the relationship between tribal and non-tribal populations at the social and cultural level, how could he synchronize imagined history with social and cultural reality? It may not escape the attention of a serious reader that Beatille has spoken of 'Hindu Civilisation' and not 'Indian Civilisation'. Bose himself speaks freely about 'Indian culture', 'Indian social institution', and of course, 'Hindu society', but he is somewhat cautious about making any direct reference to 'Indian Civilisation'. In the Indian context, he seems to have equated civilisation with culture. And he writes (1929),

> *...Indian culture – despite its many internal weaknesses – has been able to remain alive in the shelter of Indian social institutions, and unlike many historically famous civilisations, it has not altogether lost the possibility of a revival and a new awakening.*

Two points need to be emphasised. Firstly, Indian culture has many internal weaknesses, and secondly, it could remain alive and functional only in the shelter of Indian social institutions. One, however, keeps wondering as to how the Indian culture with its weaknesses could be a source of inspiration for others to come within its fold. It may be argued that Bose's indirect reference to Indian civilisation only implies 'Hindu Civilisation', but he has not made any clear-cut attempt to equate the two. He has probably realised that the Indian civilisation is not made exclusively of Hindu culture or cultures affiliated to it. Again, while searching for the inner dynamism and vibrant spirit of a long historical tradition, that is, India, it may be safer to speak in terms of culture and society because Indian civilisation gives an impression of heterogeneous formations loosely attached to it. From the social point of view, 'Hindu society has been built up over the ages by the integration of various communities.' Now, what was the role of caste as an integrating principle? Probably, Bose was in favour of seeing caste functioning like a caste community with a specific occupation of its own. For the same reason, he has laid stress on the varna system, which was occupation-based. Hindu society, to him, operated like a brahminical society and when a particular caste adopted a particular occupation, it was left to 'the regulators of brahminical society' to determine whether such a group should have ' a hereditary right over that occupation.' A type of value judgment came into play. His conclusions in this respect are, however, somewhat pedagogical (1975:181),

> *If we bring together the scientific insights into the divisions in Hindu society and the rules by which the authors of the Shastras sought to govern it, we will be able to gradually build up in our minds an integrated picture of Hindu society.*

In another context, while referring to the process of absorption of a tribe into the Hindu society or creating a new occupational group within it, he has used the term *jati* as a coordinated group. We may be a little surprised at how quickly and easily such a group could give up their autonomous position and become absorbed into the Hindu society. The Hindus, according to Bose, 'exercised a policy of *laissez-faire* concerning the social and religious practices of tribal peoples.' In other words, it means even when they came within the fold of Hinduism, they could retain their 'cultural autonomy' which could keep them satisfied and help them come to terms with their subjugated status. Can 'economic freedom' be completely foregone by the tribes simply because their 'original social and religious culture' was left to themselves? Were they not interlinked at some points? Often it is seen that cultural autonomy is used by communities as a ploy to attain some form of economic freedom or self-sufficiency.

Though a type of rigidity marks caste-like formations, there is discernible flexibility in dealing with groups lying outside the caste structure. Together with a diversity of cultural expressions, each with a recognizable form of its own, a situation like this could be ideally suited for a civilisation to grow from here. But to think only in terms of a predictable course of caste-oriented transformations of tribes and tribe-like formations may be a little difficult to accept because it creates an impression that such formations could be easily brought within the fold of caste-ridden Hindu society without any protest or resentment from their side. Surajit Sinha (1982), on the other hand, thinks that tribes should find a place of importance in their rights and things should be looked at from their perspective in matters about the 'Tribe-Caste' interactive process. His position is that acceptance of Hindu social-cultural features by the tribals does not mean their complete absorption into the Hindu society. There could be several examples other than Sinha's characterisation of the Bhumij social movement (1959), in which he not only recognised Bhumij's adoption of cultural traits of higher caste Hindus but also brought into focus a counter-movement launched by the younger section of the Bhumij tribe. Their aim was mainly to organise a secular movement along with other tribes of the region to install a wider regional solidarity structure on their terms. We are all aware of the fact that at present some of these movements have tried to follow an ideological course and even taken recourse to militancy to achieve results in their favour. Not that they were successful in their attempts so far in terms of what they wanted to achieve, but at least they could dispel the notion that they were all along on the receiving side and were willing partners to the initiatives taken by the larger Hindu society to integrate them. In recent times, the interaction between Hindu caste groups and tribes suggests a process of syncretism being adopted in the sphere of socio-religious activities. A section of the Lodhas of Paschim Medinipur may stand as an example. In specific cases, though small in number, The Lodhas now control agriculture production to an extent that they could employ people from other communities including Santals to work in their fields as agricultural labourers. A rare phenomenon as displayed by the dominating position of those Lodhas in the economic field also gets reflected in their desire to exercise ritual control going beyond the limits of their community. In one case, which I had referred to in a Seminar organised by the Department of Anthropology of Vidyasagar University in 2017, a Lodha priest was inducted along with Brahmin priests to perform the worship of the Mother Goddess in a Hindu temple located in an area where the Lodha control over economic resources like the land was no less than the caste Hindus. What is particularly significant in this case was the acceptance of a Lodha as a priest by the Hindus even though he was not very proficient in performing all the activities associated with the brahminical mode of worship. As he did not know Sanskrit, the Brahmin priest had to come to his aid, particularly in uttering *mantras* or hymns. The common explanation could be that it was a gesture on the part of the Hindus to bring the tribals within their fold. But it also speaks of the increasing presence of tribals, in this case, Lodhas, in a multiethnic situation where they were not only present in a substantial number but could demonstrate their increasing economic hold over livelihood activities, which though not enough was comparable to the Hindus. Where the tribals are in a position to compete with the non-tribals in the economic field of activities, often surpassing them, the process of transformation takes a bottom-up direction. To reach the top by those lying at the bottom, an impossible proposition even some time back, is now open to negotiation in a specific situation. For Nirmal Kumar Bose it was probably not possible to foresee a situation when alignment would get the better of absorption and when a newly acquired social mobility would take a tribal belonging to the erstwhile PTG to the top of the ladder in caste-based Hindu society, even if in a symbolical way. Moreover, at the village level caste-wise representation today follows a more or less homogeneous pattern with one caste dominating the scene except for some Brahmin families providing the ritual link and keeping their specialised ritual character unchanged. For a reformer, the installation of a makeshift Lodha priest is suggestive of an act of defiance against absolute ritual control exercised by the Brahmins. The Lodha example may also indicate the possibility of delinking ritual from the social to come to negotiating terms with a group that can no longer be segregated. In other words, it may imply that in a special situation where tribe and caste Hindu are almost on level terms in the economic field the concept of Hindu civilisation, sharply divided into lower and upper reaches of it, undergoes some readjustment. The interactive process has now assumed multiple dimensions and takes specific forms depending on the contact situation. It also displays a level of fluidity, but up to a point is productive enough for the interacting groups. From a different perspective, when ritual as a structural principle shows some flexibility in accommodating a person representing a community of lower social standing, it does not automatically follow that it is a step towards attaining a semblance of social parity between communities of differential order. After all, the core of society has a rigidity of its own, be it tribal or non-tribal in origin. The point of consideration is whether ritual and religion have started showing a different trend and no longer remain within the core of the social structure. At this stage, we take it as an isolated case where local interests seem to get preference even at the cost of breaking the normative principles.

It, however, cannot be denied that the conceptual framework developed by Nirmal Kumar Bose on culture and civilisation in the Indian context has been used exhaustively in the field of social science. At the societal level, the interactions and intersections between the upper and lower reaches of the society and the dynamics of these have been delved upon by Bose. In the context of civilisation, his rendition of the concept of culture and its wider implications bears much significance. He has endeavoured to unfold the uniqueness of the multiple blocks that complemented one another to constitute the civilisation. The book, *The Structure of Hindu Society,* can be regarded as the hallmark of civilisational studies from the Indian perspective focusing on the processes of accommodation and assimilation that continued for ages. In Bose's scheme, the main point of consideration was integration between the higher and lower reaches of civilisation involving different cultures. Integration has been made possible through culture contact, in which the simple culture complements the more complex one. A simple culture to Bose is characterised by a lack of social differentiation, low technological development, and hence, a low level of economic production. This in a way suggests that people of simple culture, tribe, in particular, would be dependent on higher cultures. It seems almost natural for what was initially a compulsion ultimately got transformed into complementarity in relations. Bose observed that not only in marriage but the Hindu influence has also penetrated deep into the tribal religious customs and normative behaviours. Now when the tribal society itself has acquired some of the complexities of the caste-based Hindu society, will the equation still work? Questions have also been raised on the appropriateness of the example of Juang of Orissa as a case in hand. Some of the Juang practices and customary behaviours under reference hardly justify the conclusion that they were manifestations of a latent yearning or craving for such economic security as was enjoyed by the caste Hindus. When they followed the Hindu mode of religious worship, to think that they could get the inner meaning of it, as laid down in the *Puranas,* may appear to be overstretching our range of observation. If they did it mechanically, their level of integration could be questioned. The economic motive could have brought the Juangs closer to their Hindu neighbours making them ever dependent on them, but to think that it had completely changed their life world or prompted them to reorient it in line with the Hindu way of representation maybe a little too ambitious a proposition to make. If anything, it tries to establish the overwhelming power of the Hindu method of absorption and as a justification for Hindu caste groups breaking tribal boundaries. It may fit in Bose's model of demonstrating how the lower and upper reaches of the society constantly interacted among themselves to build up the outer kernel of the living whole represented by the civilisation itself. Here the society covers the absorbed or assimilated ones, which were initially outside the fold of Hindu society. Although Bose was quick to note the tribe's retention of their own culture and living pattern, he did not think these to be invincible or an obstacle against acceptance and acquisition of Hindu ideals and *Vedic* norms and customs. The members of the Juang tribe were living just outside the pale of Hinduism, but they were not directly affected by it until they started finding some affinity with the brahminical life world. This realisation was not because of simple curiosity, but because of prolonged interaction with the Hindu neighbours prompted partly by the economic insecurity faced by them as a result of the loss of traditional occupations like hunting, collecting, and *jhum* cultivation on the slopes of the Malyagiri, which was prohibited by the state. The economic assurance, the exact nature of which was never known, created such a strong force of attraction for the tribals that soon it became an obsession with them to be accommodated within the caste fold. Not that they had lost their cultural autonomy by becoming associated with the Hindu society, but they did bear in unmistakable terms Hindu cultural traits and ideas making deep inroads into their traditional culture. The lone Lodha example of Paschim Medinipur may not quite fit into the scheme except that the impact of Hindu society remains, even though its representation varies from society to society. Side by side, it is also indicative of a process of reorientation of the Hindu line of approach towards the tribals as co-sharers of economic resources. How far the representatives of the Hindu society are prepared to accommodate others belonging to the non-Hindu category depends on the situation both are locked in. The emergence of political leadership from the community level may, however, jeopardize the institutional framework binding the society. Admittedly, any form of centralised control at the level of Hindu society, in general, is difficult to maintain, unless there is strong backing from the state in power, and no state is supposed to uphold the democratic principle as its ideal will be expected to that.

For the civilisation to grow in India, castes no doubt played important functional roles. Bose could visualise that the system of caste was efficacious enough to bring together diverse groups and in the process integrate the various reaches of civilisation. But then if the caste system was only a mechanism for blending and creating equipoise between the opposing cultures, it would not have a lasting impact because the meaning and character of culture would change with time. The caste system as a component of culture could be handed down over the generations, but, as Bose cautiously noted, its continuity depended on its utility. What does utility imply here? Does it also suggest that it is of little importance in creating and maintaining a balance between the various reaches of the civilisation once it starts losing its utility? The present situation bears testimony to that. By stretching the arguments further, we may even say that with castes losing their significance and the productive system taking diverse routes, there is a need to look afresh at the total framework of Indian Civilisation. Consequently, the Hindu method of absorption, as propounded by Nirmal Kumar Bose, may call for a fresh look. Bose himself was no less aware of the maladies of Hindu society, particularly in the form of Brahminical society. Its negative impact has not escaped his attention, when he observes (1975:80),

> *Culture...flows from a politically and economically dominant group to a subservient one. In social matters, too, the former occupies a higher status in contrast to the latter. From this, we may venture to suggest with regard to current problems in our national life, that if we wish to set the Juang, the Munda, or the so-called untouchable castes shoulder to shoulder with ourselves in a*

democratically organised society, we should make sure of economic reorganisation first if we won't build the new social order on a permanent basis.

There can't be any second opinion about the appropriateness of what he has said. On the other hand, Bose has appreciated the virtues of the tradition-centric Hindu civilisation, despite its many negativities, as manifested in its resilience and dynamism and he writes (1975: 153-154),

I believe inequality and dehumanisation are related to the 'varna' system but nevertheless, there was a wit underlying the social fabric. It made men realise that they were finally enslaved to the society. This germinated the idea of division of labour by which people professed various vocations to eke out a living in the society. They look after the society by serving in multiple roles and the society likewise cater to their needs.

But with caste-based social fabric losing its relevance and forces of disintegration and decomposition raising their ugly heads, we may try to find some meaning in Bose's concept of culture as a pre-condition to civilisation. By maintaining value-based principles and strictly following the religious strictures as laid down in the *Shastras*, culture and a combination of it could have contributed to the growth of civilisation in India. Civilisation, according to N.K. Bose, was carried forward through cultures, overtly or covertly performing one *Dharma* or the other in the form of *Artha, Kama,* and *Moksha*, which, though different in their outward manifestation, display a basic unity. Going still further, one may be able to understand the way each of the *dharmas* acts. It acts in phases, namely, *Vastu* or material object, *Kriya* or habitual action, *Samhati* or social grouping, and *Tattva* or knowledge. Again, it is necessary to clearly distinguish between two kinds of *Tattvas* – one which is based on *Vichara* (critical analysis) and the other in which *Viswasa* or faith is the chief element. But in the end, Bose proves himself to be a believer in the integrated structure of Hindu society, as he contends (1975:95),

If we bring together the scientific insights into the divisions in Hindu society and the rules by which the authors of the Shastras

> *sought to govern it, we will be able to gradually build up in our minds an integrated picture of Hindu society.*

In today's context, an integrated picture of Hindu society based essentially on cultural unity developed around the scientific analysis of its divisions may not have the opportunity to re-establish itself. Moreover, when the purpose of critical scientific arguments is reduced to establishing the basic unity lying between cultures of differential order, its scope becomes somewhat limited. More so, when the gap between science and its application areas is widening due particularly to irrationality in action and senseless tempering with values getting the better of reason and a sense of purpose in life. The profoundness and farsighted judgment of the ancient texts which used to go with the functioning of Hindu society has nothing but reference value in contemporary thinking and as such, these are hardly binding. At the practical level, probably the political demagogues make use of them in their way to score a point. Loss of values and its impact on society are the concern of social science in general and social-cultural anthropology is not outside it. N.K. Bose's conceptualisation of culture and civilisation may be an attractive proposition, but when faced with the prospect of its application in the contemporary situation, one cannot but question its relevance. Still, there are people, who, because they find meaning in his scheme, continue to look for supporting evidence deep down from the vast yet varied expanse of civilisation that flourished in India. Bose's realisation may be more meaningful at this stage as he says (1975:189),

> *The days when the ancient 'Varna' system was devised will never come back. Even if they do come back there will be not much advantage, for the number of men has increased; at least in India the amount of land per man has diminished enormously. Even so, if we can discover in the institutions of those times some principles, some designs which may be applied to the present, and we do not use it in spite of its applicability, this will be only an expression of our folly.*

Could be it is our failure to find 'some principles, some design' behind the institutions of the past having utility in the present? When Nirmal Kumar Bose makes a strong plea to us to 'penetrate the smoke that was there in the traditional society in India and use the burning flame beneath it for the happiness of mankind today', it carries a message worth pursuing. Still, we may not be convinced and keep on wondering what purpose it would ultimately serve. But then the happiness of mankind lies in seeking knowledge and deriving knowledge about culture and civilisation in the context of India is an ongoing process, which is yet to see its end. No blind faith, no deep-seated conviction, but a free scientific mind may take us to a position from where we could assess its real value. That will probably be a fitting tribute to Nirmal Kumar Bose at a time when we are celebrating hundred years of teaching anthropology in India.

References

Bose, Nirmal Kumar. 1929. *Cultural Anthropology.* Indian Publishing Co., Calcutta.

Bose, Nirmal Kumar. 1967. *Culture and Society in India.* Asia Publishing House, Calcutta.

Bose, Nirmal Kumar. 1971. *Tribal Life in India.* National Book Trust, New Delhi.

Bose, Nirmal Kumar. 1975. *The Structure of Hindu Society.* Orient Longman, New Delhi.

Sinha, Surajit. 1959. 'Bhumij – Kshatriya Social Movement in South Manbhum'. *Bulletin of the Department of Anthropology,* Government of India, Calcutta. 8, 2: 9-32.

Sinha, Surajit. 1982. *Tribes and Indian Civilisation: Transformation Processes in Modern India.* N.K. Bose Memorial Foundation, Varanasi.

6

Architects of Anthropology in India: A Passage Through Verrier Elwin

Junali Kropi

'The essence and art of anthropology is love. Without it, nothing is fertile; nothing is true'. – **Elwin**

Introduction

Harry Verrier Holman Elwin was a novelist, pamphleteer, poet, anthropologist and auto-biographer, and author. Elwin listed the places where he had been resident since 1927: as a Christian for the congress with *Christa Seva Sangha* in Poona; in 1929-1930 as Gandhian in Sabarmati Ashram, Ahmadabad, Bombay Presidency: as a social worker with Shamrao and the *Gond Seva Mandal* in Mandla; as a roving ethnographer on his own in Bastar and Orissa; as a research administrator with the Anthropological Survey of India in Banaras and Calcutta; as an advisor to the government in Shillong, Meghalaya.

He was a British-born anthropologist, who began his career in India as a Christian Missionary. He first abandoned the clergy to work with Mohandas Gandhi and the Indian National Congress, then converted to Hinduism in 1935 after staying in a Gandhian ashram, and split with the nationalists over what he felt the overhasty process of transformation and assimilation for the tribals. Verrier Elwin is best known for his early work with the Baigas and Gonds of Orissa and Madhya Pradesh in central India, and he married a member of one of the communities he studied. He later also worked on the tribals of several Northeast Indian states, especially the North-East Frontier Agency (NEFA), and settled in Shillong, the hill capital of Meghalaya. He served as the Deputy Director of the Anthropological Survey of India upon its formation in 1945.

Post-independence, he took up Indian citizenship and, in January 1954, became the first foreigner to be accepted as an Indian citizen (Guha, 2016). The Government of India awarded him the third highest civilian honour of the Padma Bhushan in 1961 (*Ministry of Home Affairs, 2015*). His autobiography '*The Tribal World of Verrier Elwin,*' (Elwin, 1964), won him the 1965 Sahitya Akademi Award in English Language, given by the Sahitya Akademi, India's National Academy of Letters (Sahitya Akademy Awards, 2010). Prime Minister Jawaharlal Nehru appointed him as an adviser on tribal affairs for north-eastern India. Later, he was an Anthropological Adviser to the Government of NEFA (now Arunachal Pradesh; British Broadcasting Corporation, 2006).

Early life

Harry Verrier Holman Elwin was born on 29th August 1902 in Dover, the son of Edmund Henry Elwin, Bishop of Sierra Leone. Verrier's father, Edmund Henry Elwin, was born in1871, the fifth son in a family of twelve. Minnie Elwin (Verrier Elwin's mother) was a renowned beauty as being described by one of her son's friends as the most powerful woman he had ever meet. The Elwin family consists of Verrier, his sister Eldyth (a year and half years younger), and their brother Basil who was four years still younger. In November 1909, Bishop Edmund Henry Elwin died in Freetown.

Education

Verrier Elwin joined Dean Close School in September 1915. The school was run more or less as a family enterprise. Two classes ahead of Verrier Elwin were Stephan Neill regards as the School star student. In school, Verrier shadowed Neill's honour for winning like the elder boy, three prestigious prizes for history, literature, and scripture. In summer 1921, Mrs. Minnie Elwin acquired a new and semi-permanent home. She bought a two-storied house on Warnborough road in North Oxford just beyond the perimeter of what counts as University territory with Verrier admission to Merton College.

He was educated at Merton College, Oxford, in 1924 (Laven,1964). Verrier Elwin graduated with a first-class, one of only three such in Merton that year. The college gifted him one hundred pounds to support his next degree, which is a family tradition that was to be in theology. He received his degrees of BA First Class in English Language and Literature, MA, and D.Sc from Merton College.

In 1926, he was awarded a first in his Theology final. A fellowship in an Oxford College was there for taking. Still, his family pressed him to join the Church of England when he was offered the Vice-Principal job at his father's old seminary, Wycliffe Hall, intense pressure on him to accept it. He also remained the President of Oxford Inter-Collegiate Christian Union (OICCU) in 1925. He had a brilliant career at Oxford, where he took a Double First in English and Theology, before being ordained a priest in the Church of England. In August 1926, Verrier as a handed a conference at Swanwick of the student Christian movement meet JC Winslow, who had gone out to India in1905 as a missionary of the society for propagating the gospel (SPG). Disgusted by the barrier between British and Indian Christian and deeply impressed by Mahatma Gandhi's movement of national renewal, Winslow decided to leave the SPG and strike out on his own.

Career

In 1926, Elwin was appointed as a Vice-Principal of Wycliffe Hall, Oxford, and in the following year, he became a lecturer at Merton College, Oxford. On 18th October 1927, five Englishmen bound for India, a dismissal service was held at St Matthew's in Westminster, attended by family and friends, and presides over by the legendary bishop of cloth of Gold, to give his advice, his blessing, and right speech. They traveled through Paris-Rome, Vatican and St Peter's, Assisi, Naples, and arrived at Colombo on 5th November. On the 10th of November, they departed for South India.

Elwin came to India as a missionary in 1927, to join a small liberal *ashram*, the *Christa Seva Sangh* of Poona, which hoped to 'indigenize' Christianity. Over the years, he came under the influence of the philosophies of Mahatma Gandhi, and the national movement. He quickly threw in his lot of interest with the Congress winning Gandhi's affection and becoming a camp follower and occasional cheerleader to the popular movement against British ruler. Seeking fuller immersion in the toil, the sufferings, the poverty of India, he resolved to make his home among the Gonds. To acquaint people abroad with the struggle in India, he wrote: *'The Dawn of Indian Freedom'* (1930) and *'The Truth about India'* (1932).

He first joined the Christian Service Society in Pune. In 1926, Winslow founded the *Christa Seva Sangh* (CSS), which drew inspiration from the traditional *ashram* ideal of Hindus and its more recent reinterpretation by Gandhi, whose ashram at Sabarmati was at once a center of the religious life and service to the poor. Winslow had placed Verrier in charge of the library whose growing collection was targeted by the resident rat. During the hot weather of the monsoon, he suffered a violent attack of dysentery and was admitted to the Sassoon hospital. The doctor advised him to go home to Oxford for a year.

In October 1928, he returned to his mother's home in Oxford. In six months, Verrier produces a book title – *' The Cloud of Unknowing'* which interprets the *Sastras* or holy books in the vernacular language. The book was read and admired by Indian Christians searching themselves for convergence between a foreign faith and spiritual tradition native to Indian soil. By March 1929, he returned to India and on 29th September accompanied by Leonard Schiff bound for the CSS. By mutual consent, Verrier and the CSS decided to part in November 1931, leaving him five months to search for a home and prepare to live in it. A.V. Thakkar founded the Bhil Seva Mandal at Dahod, the first tribal welfare organisation and staff run by Indians. Verrier spent almost a month at Sabarmati, staying with Gandhi in his hut accompanying on his morning walk less willingly submitting to the extraordinarily harsh regiment of a seventeen hour day taken up with prayer, study, spinning, cooking, washing, language class, and more prayer. Verrier left Sabarmati undecided as to his plan was something different. On returning to Poona, Verrier fell ill; the fever brought on one thing by concentrating and self-thought. He spends a week in the hospital. He took a symbolic manner of his departure from Sabarmati.

Jamnalal Bajaj suggested him to work with the Gond tribe for the upliftment of the tribe. In August 1931, Mahatma Gandhi sailed for London and the Round Table Conference to discuss India's freedom movement.

Shamrao Hivale met Mahatma Gandhi and advised him to join his party and return with them to India. Verrier was most pleased to know that Shamrao was coming home, that with him would be Indian bridge to the poor. In the first week of November 1936, Verrier took a train from Bombay to the little market town of Betul, up on Satpura plateau. The first time he visited central India, now the states of Madhya Pradesh, Chhattisgarh, and parts of eastern Maharashtra, was with an Indian from Pune, Shamrao Hivale. Betul, Chindwara, or Mandla, the final decision would have to await his friend's return. For the first time, he visited a remote village in the forests of Mandla district. He and Hivale were to spend some twenty years in Central India, living with and fighting for the rights of tribes. Their studies are on the tribes are some of the earliest anthropological studies in the country. The district of Mandla, in whose northern corner lay the village of Karanjia, was called by a British civilian who had once served there 'Ultima Thule of civilisation, the dreaded home of the tiger, the Gond, and the devil'. Verrier wrote the manuscript '*Truth about India*' in his first week in the village. He and Shamrao Hivale construct their *ashram* Tikeri Tola.

Fighting with his bishop, writing on St Francis, Verrier made little progress for the ashram. Meanwhile, Mrs. Elwin, who had not seen her son in three years, asked him to come home for the summer. His passport was due to expire in July. Reassured by the official he left for London. He faced many problems regarding his passport in London. On 29th July 1932, Verrier was informed he would be issued a fresh passport, but it would be stamped invalid for India. He would go anywhere in the world or the British empire except India. Verrier spread his bets, had also approached Lady Graham (her husband Sir Lancelot Graham was the governor of Sind) with repeated the offer of an undertaking for his work in Karanjia but if he made to remain in England, he would force into all sorts of political activities.

On 23rd August, Home Secretary M.G. Hallet wrote to the Viceroy advising him not to allow Verrier to come back. However, on the evidence put on his table recommendation by Sir Lancelot Graham and carrying copies of his wife's correspondence with Verrier has changed his thoughts and finally approved by the India office asked Verrier

1. Confined himself entirely to missionary work among Gonds;
2. take no part in civil disobedience or any other political movement;
3. refrain as far as possible from associating with any person engaged in political agitation; and
4. refrain from writing articled against the government.

Elwins contribution to anthropological studies in India

On 4th October 1932, Verrier signed the clause and issued a passport. Soon after Father Elwin back in India scream a front-page story in the Bombay Chronicle on 4th November 1932. He was criticized by one bishop of Nagpur as they were doing the work of the devil. Similarly, one bishop of Bombay called their outlook satanic simply because he lived with poor Indians and had begun to see the world through their eyes. However, Verrier's wishes to change or uplift the tribal was initiated by Panda Baba, a Gond magician who was his native informant and his first truly, tribal friend. Verrier counted nineteen elopements in one year in their village alone. Gond divorce was so wonderfully simple; the two parties appeared before their elders, broke a pot, and then a piece of straw in half, and were freed of one another. '*Leaves from the Jungle*' is the most readable of all Verrier works on the illustration of 'rollicking anthropology', which celebrates the irreverent and irresistible joy of the Gonds and their chronicler.

In 1938, the *Gond Seva Mandal* changed its name to *Bhumijan Seva Mandal*. In June, they moved from Sarwachappar to Patangarh, a village nine miles to the north, situated on a promontory just of the Amarkantak Dindori road. The *Bhumijan Seva Mandal* changes its name twice after independence. In 1949, it became The Tribal Art and Research Unit (TARU) and then a year later, The Tribal Welfare, Art and Research Unit (TWARU).

While still in Sarwachappar, Verrier found time to finish two novels '*Phulmat of the Hills*' in 1937. '*The Baiga*' was published in September 1939 published by John Murray days before the outbreak of war in Europe. Elwin's antagonist seized on a proposal made in the closing pages of 'The Baiga' where he argued for creating a national park. Here the tribe would have the freedom to hunt, fish, and practice *bewar,* and non-aboriginal would prohibited entry.

While living in Karanjia, he had woken each morning to the sound of bellows from a furnace run by the Agaria tribe of iron smelters. In Bihar, he had been taken to the territory of the *Asur*, metals workers who lived high up on the Chota Nagpur plateau and who were distantly connected to the Agaria of Mandla (Elwin,1942). '*The Agaria*' was the first of Elwin's books to be published by the India branch of Oxford University Press.

Verrier Elwin lived with the primitive he loved, he defended them. There is a poignant and heroic logic that distinguished Elwin's brand of activist anthropology from academic anthropology.

Verrier married Kosi on 4th April 1940: a decade later, the union ended in divorce. Kosi's family was poor, but devilish dignified given their lineage. In autumn 1940, Verrier and Kosi moved to their new home in Bastar. Verrier Elwin's research in Bastar first focused on one tribe and one institution, the *Ghotul* (dormitory) of the Muria *'The Muria and their Ghotul'*. In 1940, he was appointed Honourary Ethnographer to Bastar State and in 1944, an Honourary Anthropologist to the Government of Orissa.

'*Maria Murder and Suicide*' completed in 1943, sought to understand the origin of violence and set it in control. He worked with a sample of 100 murders and fifty suicide cases. In January 1944, he delivered the Presidential address to the Anthropology Section of the Indian Science Congress speaking on *'Truth in Anthropology*'. In May 1944, Elwin was awarded a doctor of science degree from Oxford University. He had submitted The Baiga and a few essays instead of a dissertation, asking Merton to forward and follow up the case.

In the late summer of 1944, Oxford University Press issued two books by Verrier Elwin. '*Folk-Tales of Mahakosal*' presented 150 folk tales collected from all over the central province, stories labouriously transcribe in those pre-tape recorder days by Verrier, Shamrao, and especially their two assistant Gulabs and Sunderlal. Folk song of the Maikal Hills drew even more directly on home turf in worse from the poetry of Gond and their neighbour.

In 1946, the Anthropological Survey of India (earlier it was part of the Zoological Survey of India) was set up, and its first Director B.S. Guha invited Elwin to join as Deputy Director. Elwin responded favourably, and for a year he lived in Banaras, the then headquarters of the survey, before shifting to Calcutta where he stayed for another year. But he soon grew restless and decided to break free. Although he was later offered the post of director, he declined. Elwin left the survey in April 1949. From 1946-49, he served as Deputy Director of the Department of Anthropology, Government of India.

In 1950, it appeared Elwin's study of the Bondo, the tiny tribe living in the uplands of the Koraput district in Orissa. Elwin's study of the Soara – '*The Religion of an Indian Tribe*', is the most detailed account of an Indian tribal religion that ever flowed from an anthropologist pen. In 1952, while on tour from Bombay to Delhi, Verrier had hoped to meet Nehru but the great man was on tour. He left a letter for him to express his wish to study the beautiful objects of Assam records to unite a sequential of his Tribal art of middle India. On 20th September 1953, Lila and Verrier were married before a Magistrate in Jabalpur.

Elwins contribution to Northeastern India

In June 1947, he was first invited to visit Assam by his friend W.G. Archer who was a high ranking army officer. Elwin and Shamrao were received at Na-Kachari railway station from where they embarked on a four-day journey to Mokokchung on foot. The first tribe he meets was Tagin, he moved on to the Konyaks and their neighbour the Phoms, had been head-hunters and headhunting had been recently forbidden by the government. Verrier was the first outsider to move into this village without an escort to stay in the village of Shiangha Chongnyu Morung (dormitory) where 400 skulls were displayed.

Elwin's second visit to Assam was in 1952 was invited by the former Governor of Assam, Joyramdas Daulat Ram, to prepare a report about the tribes of this region. Accordingly, Elwin visited tribal villages in Dimapur, Kohima, and Imphal, and returned to Shillong. In his report submitted to the Governor, Elwin wrote: 'I may kindly be considered as an individual for whom it would be a matter of great pleasure if I could be of some use for the tribals of this region' (Elwin, 1961).

In December 1953, Elwin received an invitation from T.N. Kaul, the then joint secretary in the ministry of external affairs, to reach Delhi to help the administration select officers for the proposed cadre for NEFA. This cadre was named Indian Frontier Administrative Service (IFAS), and Elwin joined the selection committee. He was later informed that the prime minister wanted to join the NEFA administration to advise it on a tribal question. Finally, in December 1953, Verrier Elwin reached Shillong as assumed responsibilities as an anthropological consultant on 1st January 1954. After a year, he was made advisor for tribal affairs, the post he held till the end.

During this period, the nature of his research changed. He began touring the 33,000 square miles of mountainous territory to survey the situation, collect ethnographic data, write reports on the general condition of the tribes, and make suggestions to the administration. He was also asked to assist the research department of NEFA that had different sections- cultural, philological, and historical. He became involved in the process of establishment of the Tribal Research Institute for Assam. During this period, he was appointed Honourary advisor for tribal affairs for both Manipur and Tripura.

In 1956, Elwin visited the great monastery at Tawang, the epicenter of NEFA Buddhism (narrow street and great library). The Khempu or Abbot, Gelong Kesang Phuntsot of Tawang present a token (a brass figure of the Buddha) found to be always in his pocket, at home, or on tour from that day onwards. After visited Tawang, he came to pin his faith in some form of liberal Buddhism (Zama, 2004). In 1957, Elwin stayed with the Khamptis, the temple at Chowkham. Tawang pilgrimage was one of the most memorable adventures NEFA has offered.

Elwin often spoke of making the whole of NEFA a work of art. In 1956, he suggested the creation of a Tagore Memorial fellowship for the study of Dance and Music and the promotion of these in areas where they are absent and a Gandhi Memorial Fellowship for where the study and guided spread of indigenous tradition of weaving. In 1959, Elwin chaired a national committee to study the progress of development in selected tribal areas. By the time Elwin was almost over with the final report of the committee in April 1960, he was a member of the scheduled areas and scheduled tribes commission headed by U.N. Dhebar.

The final report of this commission received substantial inputs from Elwin. This report candidly admitted that the Fifth Schedule was a complete failure. The land was still alienated on a staggering scale that millions of tribesmen were in the clutches of money lenders.

Elwin's 'philosophy' was aptly summarised by himself. To him, the five most important needs in the context of schemes of development of agriculture, communications, medical facilities, education were:

1. That their land should be guaranteed to them and that any further alienation of it to outsiders should be stopped;
2. that their rights in the forest should be respected and that the forest authorities should take an entirely new attitude towards them;
3. the problem of indebtedness should be solved without delay;
4. that the problem of industrialisation of tribal areas must be regarded much more seriously; and
5. the long isolation of the tribes should come to an end. (Elwin,1957)

Following his appointment as the Adviser to the Governor on Tribal Affairs criticism was leveled against his approaches and activities concerning the tribals.

In the emergence of a new 'anti-Elwin' wave, a large number of intellectuals, socially conscious citizens, and politicians played the most significant role. Elwin's NEFA policy met its harshest test in October 1962 when a storm broke over the blue hills of NEFA (The Assam Tribune, 2002). The Chinese forces overwhelmed the Indian defence in parts of Kameng, Siang, and Lohit. Tawang, Se La, Bomdila, Wallong fell to the Chinese succession. Elwin later recounted that 'in Shillong there was panic and several people sent their families away, but I took the line that we all belonged to the tribal people and Assam. Since the whole population couldn't be evacuated, we should remain where we are' (Elwin, 1970). Elwin was proved right for the ceasefire followed, and the Chinese withdrew unconditionally.

The initiative of Elwin, in the Third Five-Year Plan, made the Government of India sanction a whopping amount of 30 crores for new tribal blocks. However, the 1962 Chinese invasion drew fresh criticism of Nehru-Elwin's NEFA policy. The opposition parties accused of isolating the territory from the rest of India to deadly effect. Cornered, Nehru's government was desperate. The opposition politicians in Delhi pushed for settling 100,000 farmers from Punjab in NEFA for the assimilation of tribals and to dissuade the Chinese from coming again.

Meanwhile, Elwin, despite his ill health, went to attend a meeting of the Frontier Services Selection Board on 20th February 1964 as he always liked to help pick the best young officers for NEFA. On the 21st, Verrier visited the home ministry. His young colleague, Rashid Yusuf Ali now worked there; when Verrier walked into his office, he had on his desk a fresh proposal to send sturdy 100,000 Punjabi farmers to settle in NEFA, which was proposed by the rightwing opposition leader (Razzeko, 2018).

Elwin objected tooth and nail to this proposal profusely the whole day. He was back in the home ministry the next morning, the 22nd; Elwin, in any case, wanted the intruders out. That evening (22nd February 1964, Delhi) he complained of heartache, and within two hours, he was dead at the age of 62.

As William Paton had predicted many years earlier, Verrier Elwin lulled himself in India with overwork. On the 23rd Nehru was the first to offer a wreath. The next day the body was flown to Shillong. On the afternoon of 24th February 1964, Elwin was cremated, amidst the chanting of Buddhist hymns. As per the will of Elwin, his ashes were immersed in the Siang River (Guha, 2016).

To conclude, when one considers his manifold duties and interests, his list of publications is of impressive size. It would be of great use to have a complete bibliography of his writings, including articles and reviews. His scientific research brought him many honours.

He was awarded:

- the Welcome Medal in 1942 and the Rivers Medal in 1948 by the Royal Anthropological Institute.
- The Roy Gold Medal in 1945 and the Annandale Gold Medal in 1951 by the Asiatic Society of Bengal.
- The Society Medal in 1947 and the Campbell Medal in 1960 by the Bombay Asiatic Society; and the Dadabhai Naoroji Prize in 1961.
- He was a Fellow of the Royal Anthropological Institute.
- Fellow and Council Member of the Royal Asiatic Society of Bengal.
- Fellow and Council Member of the National Institute of Science of India.
- Hon. Member of the Ecole Francaise d'extreme-Orient, and
- Member of the International Society for Folk-Narrative Research.

Biswajeet Bora, who hails from Assam, has made a documentary film in English on Elwin. The title of the film is '*Angel of the Aboriginals: Dr. Verrier Elwin*' (Ali, 2010). This film recounts the works and life of Elwin. Elwin has once expressed that in India, he found sorrow and joy, disappointment and fulfillment but above all, an answer to the prayer: 'From the unreal, lead one to real.' For Elwin, anthropology was his love, and fieldwork was his life (Datta, 2002). Elwin considered the application of anthropology as the significant influencing aspect in the field of tribal welfare. He relentlessly worked for making them known to the leaders of the country and for making them known as worthy of respect and special welfare attention. Both as a prolific writer on tribal affairs and as a member of high-level Government committees he helped in moulding Government policies into a far more useful instrument for tribal welfare (Bera, 2008).

He synthesised both humanistic and Social Science approaches in drawing his conclusions about the tribal life of India. Elwin was not only a prolific anthropological writer of his time but also ' *a missionary with an anthropological mission*' (Bera, 2002).

References

Ali, ANM. Irshad 2011. 'Dr. Verrier Elwin and Assam'. *The North-Eastern Hill University Journal*, 9, 21:5-24.

British Broadcasting Corporation. 2006. News British scholar's Indian widow in penury. 4th May.

Bera, GK., 2002. 'Verrier Elwin: An anthropologist with romanticism'. *The Oriental Anthropologist.* 2,1:81-96.

Bera, GK., 2008. *Passage Through Aboriginal India: Anthropological Profile of Verrier Elwin.* The Oriental Institute of Cultural and Social Research, Allahabad.

Datta, P., 2002. 'Destiny Calls'. *The Telegraph* (North East), 7th September.

Elwin, Verrier, 1961. *Nagaland.* NEFA Administration, Shillong.

Elwin, Verrier, 1957. *A Philosophy for NEFA.* North-East Frontier Agency, Shillong.

Elwin, Verrier, 1964. *The Tribal World of Verrier Elwin: An Autobiography.* Oxford University Press, New Delhi.

Elwin, Verrier, 1970. *A New Book of Tribal Fiction.* North-East Frontier Agency, Shillong.

Elwin, Verrier, 1942. *The Agaria.* Oxford University Press, London.

Elwin, Verrier,1958. *Myths of the North-East Frontier of India.* North-East Frontier Agency, Shillong.

Guha, R., 2016. *Savaging the Civilised: Verrier Elwin, His Tribal, and India.* Penguin Random House, India.

Levens, RGC, 1964. *Merton College Register 1900-1964.* Basil Blackwell, Oxford.

Ministry of Home Affairs. Government of India. 2015. Padma Awards (PDF). *Archived from* the original. Retrieved 9th March 2020.

Razzeko, D., 2018. *'Verrier Elwin: the Architect of NEFA and Defender of Indian tribal people'. The Arunachal Times. 30th August.* Retrieved 6th March 2020.

Sahitya Akademi Award. 2010. Sahitya Academy Awards 1955–2007. Archived from the original official listing on 11th June. Retrieved 9th March 2020.

The Assam Tribune. 2002. 'The Untrained Anthropologist' (editorial). Monday, 8th April, Guwahati.

Zama, M.2004. *The Prose of Our Times.* Orient Longman Private Limited, Kolkata.

7

Professor P. C. Biswas: An Architect of Indian Anthropology

P. K. Chattopadhyay

Anthropology, the study of man, though very ancient, developed as an independent academic discipline in India with the introduction of the subject in Calcutta University in 1921, the faculty consisting of such eminent teachers as Panchanan Mitra, Anantha Krishna Iyer, S.C. Mitra, and Ramaprosad Chanda. When one looks back over the list of a galaxy of Indian Anthropologists one of the many names that stand out as an Architect of Anthropology in its development is Professor Prafulla Chandra Biswas, widely known as Dr. P. C. Biswas.

Born in 1903 in Calcutta he had his School, College, and University education in Calcutta. Dr. Biswas obtained his Master's Degree in Anthropology from the University of Calcutta in 1931 and went to Germany as a Humboldt Fellow to work with Professor Eugene Fisher at Berlin University. He received his Ph.D. degree for his thesis entitled *Uber Hand Und Fingerleisten Von Indern*, the first Indian to get the Ph.D. Degree in Dermatoglyphics. On his return, he joined the Department of Anthropology, Calcutta University as a member of the Faculty. When Sir Maurice Linford Gwyer, the Vice-Chancellor of the University of Delhi, was looking for someone to take charge of the newly created Department of Anthropology he requested Dr. B.S. Guha, the Doyne of Indian Anthropology who was working as the

Director of the Anthropological Survey of India to suggest a suitable name to take charge of the newly created Department. At the instance of Dr. Guha, Dr. Biswas moved to Delhi on his appointment as the Reader and Head of Anthropology Department in 1947 becoming a Professor in 1958.

A man of few words Professor Biswas was a man of great vision and conviction lying slowly and gradually the road map for the development of the subject. On the one hand, he developed a strong curriculum/syllabus for teaching (theory and practicals) he spent a lot of his efforts in popularising the subject through talks in various forums such as the All India Radio and other agencies. He was greatly helped and assisted by his colleagues Drs. Mrs. H. Raj, Mrs. F. Mukherjee, A.K. Mitra (a great Physical Anthropologist who obtained his D.Sc. Degree from Munich University, Germany) and a number of his former students who joined the Department as members of the faculty such as Drs. I.P. Singh, J.D. Mehra, S.C. Tiwari, and A. Sharma to name a few in updating the syllabus, and building the Department into an Institute of world repute.

The teaching curriculum was so devised that every aspect of the subject - social, cultural, and physical anthropology was adequately covered in the First Year of the Master's Programme to give the students a broad overview of the subject with the option to choose for specialisation either in Social, Physical or Prehistoric Archaeology in the Final Year. He felt that to develop a strong base there is the need to have an undergraduate course in Anthropology which ultimately led to the starting of the B.Sc. Honours Course in Anthropology in 1962. He was also instrumental in starting the One Year Post-Graduate Certificate Course in Forensic Science in 1968 an evening course catering mostly to the needs of Police, Customs, Intelligence Bureau, the Central Bureau of Investigation, Chemical Examiner's and Forensic Science Laboratories, Revenue and Narcotics Bureau, etc.

Dr. Biswas recognised the importance and significance of Field Work/Field Studies whereby Field Trips to various locations were organised under the supervision of two or more teachers to guide the students.

Professor Biswas encouraged staff and students to participate in seminars and discussions periodically organised from time to time. Visiting scientists coming to or passing through Delhi were invited to deliver lectures and interact with the students to update their knowledge and develop their communication skills. Galaxy of scientists such as R. R. Gates, J.B.S. Haldane, J.M. Tanner, Hans Gruneberg (U.K.), Arno G. Motulsky, Frederik S. Hulse, H.L. Shapiro, Henry Field, D. Mandelbaum (U.S.A.), Emil Breitinger (Austria), F.Vogel, S. Schliarmaccher (Germany), and several others from other parts of the world visited the Department. I must say that I have benefitted immensely from these lectures especially the ones from R.R. Gates and J.B.S. Haldane.

As a teacher, Professor Biswas's mastery can be gauged from the fact that whatever he taught in a very simple language illustrated with examples/anecdotes lucidly are still remembered and talked of by his students even today.

Professor Biswas paid special attention to build a good Library, properly equipped Laboratories, and a well organised Museum in the Department. He could persuade and impress upon friends and well-wishers not only from India but also from other countries as well to donate stone tools and several objects to enrich the Museum. A special word must be mentioned here that the first Prime Minister of Independent India Pandit Jawaharlal Nehru was a great Patron of the Department and donated several objects for the Museum. Exhibits for the Museum were also collected from various places by the teachers and students during the several Field Trips organised by the Department.

As mentioned earlier he excelled as a researcher especially in the area of Dermatoglyphics. His paper Ethno-Geographic Variation in Dermatoglyphics is a landmark in the subject. Such was his influence that almost every student of Physical Anthropology had a paper in Dermatoglyphics, and on occasions even by students of social anthropology notable among them is that of Dr. J.D. Mehra. Professor Biswas can also be regarded as a pioneer in Medical Anthropology in India - his paper on the distribution of cultural traits related to beliefs and practices about disease and cure published in the 25th Issue of the Journal of the Department of Letters, Calcutta University bears testimony to this. His work also included papers on population genetics, eugenics, growth studies, and several monographs including the one on Santhals of Santhal Pargana, Juvenile Delinquency, Ex-Criminal Tribes of Delhi, etc.

Professor Biswas was very highly revered and respected as an anthropologist not only in India but also in other countries of the world. He was a Senior Vice-President of the International Union of Anthropological and Ethnological Sciences and several other organisations. He was the President of the Anthropology Section of the Indian Science Congress, President of the Indian Anthropological Association and organised the Summer School in Anthropology at Dalhousie, Himachal Pradesh in 1964, the International Symposium on Dermatoglyphics in the Department in 1966 and had several Research Projects sponsored by the Indian Council for Medical Research, Council for Scientific and Industrial Research, Planning Commission of the Govt. of India, Bhartiya Adimjati Sewak Sangh, etc. He played a stellar role in the inclusion of Anthropology as a subject in the UPSC for Competitive Examinations for Administrative Services.

Professor P. C. Biswas in a nutshell can be described as one of the architects of anthropology in India. Starting from a very humble beginning with himself and a clerk and two chairs and a table, at the time of his retirement, the Department had thirteen teachers, well-equipped laboratories (including a Photographic Laboratory), seminar and classrooms, a proper and separate sitting room for every teacher, a place for the Assistants, etc. with scope for future expansion. The visionary teacher breathed his last in 1984. He, however, will always be remembered by the generation of students studying anthropology at Delhi University. The Department of Anthropology of Delhi University which he so painstakingly built up, as long as it exists, will always remain as a monument to his glory.

Acknowledgements

I have to thank Dr. P. C. Joshi, Professor of Anthropology and Vice-Chancellor, University of Delhi; Dr. P. Dash Sharma, formerly Professor of Anthropology, Ranchi University, Bihar (presently

Jharkhand); Dr. Shashi Bhatia, Lecturer, Department of Anthropology, Lucknow University and Dr. Naba Kumar Duary, Anthropologist, Anthropological Survey of India, Kolkata for kindly sending me some materials on Professor P. C. Biswas; but for their help and support it would not have been possible to prepare the paper.

Few Important Research Publications

Biswas, PC. 1936. *Uber Hand und Fingerleisten von Indern*, Druck E Klett., Stuttgart.

Biswas PC. 1956. *Santals of the Santal Parganas*, Bharatiya Adimjati Sewak Sangh, Delhi.

Biswas, PC 1960. *The Ex Criminal Tribes of Delhi State*, Hindustan Publishing House, Delhi.

Biswas, PC. 1964. *Present State of the Problem of Correlation between Racial and Caste Differentiation in India*, Nauka Publishing House, Moscow.

Biswas, PC and Singh, IP. 1966. *Aspects of Indian Anthropology*, Proceedings of the Summer School in Anthropology, Dalhousie, Department of Anthropology, University of Delhi, Delhi.

Biswas, PC and Bhattacharjee, DK. 1966. 'Deviation quotient of digital triradii: a new dimension in the metric variability of palmar dermatoglyphics'. *Zeitschrift fur Morphologie Und Anthropologie,* Bd 57, H 2, pp. 199-206.

Biswas, PC 1967. *Socio-economic Survey of Budhpur, A Delhi Village* (Monograph Series), Volume 1, Part VI, Office of the Registrar General, India. Ministry of Home Affairs, New Delhi.

8

Professor D.N. Majumdar's Indelible Contributions to Anthropology

Geetika Ranjan

The year 2020 marks the glorious completion of hundred years of teaching of Anthropology in India and such an important landmark calls for celebration, and what better way would there be to celebrate this than to deliberate upon the contributions of the founding fathers, the pioneers, the stalwarts in the field of Anthropology. How they, through their utmost dedication for the subject of Anthropology and their passion to emboss its huge significance in understanding the life of the humans, tirelessly persevered teaching and research of Anthropology in India.

Professor Dhirendranath Majumdar was one such stalwart. When I thought of writing about Professor D.N. Majumdar, I, quite naturally traversed back in time when I had just passed the 12th standard and taken admission in the BA course at the University of Lucknow in 1991. I had offered Anthropology as one of the subjects, apart from History and English Literature. I clearly remember my first day at the university when I walked into the Department of Anthropology and into the Head of the Department's room to fulfill some admission related requirement. It was there that I first saw a huge portrait of Prof. D.N. Majumdar.

As I started learning Anthropology, at Lucknow University, I became aware of the academic stature, the colossal contribution of Professor Majumdar, and his magnetic personality from the lively talks of Prof. Gopala Sarana, my teacher and one of the most illustrious students of Professor Majumdar. It was through Professor Gopala Sarana that we, his students, became so familiar with Professor Majumdar's name that we felt as if we knew him directly and extremely well. The pride and joy with which Professor Gopala Sarana spoke about Professor Majumdar citing several anecdotes, rubbed on us as well who even before reading about the works of Professor Majumdar and getting to know him through his works, felt a strong connection with him and took pride in being in the same space where he taught Anthropology.

Sources of information

Apart from reading the rich collection of books and articles written by Professor Majumdar I had the opportunity of knowing about him from his associates and students. Their writings on Majumdar (Madan and Sarana, 1962; Mathur, 1987; Saksena, 2015; Madan, 1961) are rich explorations of his works and personality. My conversations with some of his direct students like Professor Gopala Sarana and H.S. Saksena further enlightened me about Professor Majumdar.

Professor Majumdar's writings reflect his deep-rooted concern for the marginalised. The sheer diversity of his areas of interests which cut across all the three major branches of Anthropology, as well as his infectious enthusiasm in bringing new areas within the ambit of Anthropological research, make Majumdar a leading figure in the growth and development of Anthropology in India.

The early years

Majumdar was born in 1903 in Patna. A meritorious student, he got his graduation and post-graduation degrees from the University of Calcutta. At this time he came under the influence of Sarat Chandra Roy, recognised as the Father of Indian Anthropology, who instilled in Majumdar the relevance of ethnographic research. Majumdar writes, "It was in January 1924, I accompanied Mr. Sarat Chandra Roy, editor,

Man in India, Ranchi, on an ethnographic tour into the Kolhan Government Estate. I received my first lessons in field investigation from him. Since then Mr. Roy has given me all the necessary help in my work. My debt to him is too deep to be expressed in words" (Majumdar: 1937; acknowledgement). Majumdar carried out long and intensive fieldwork among the Ho of Kolhan (in present-day Jharkhand). He was a recipient of a prestigious scholarship, the Prem Chand Roy Chand scholarship most coveted award for the meritorious students of Calcutta University pursuing higher studies. The other illustrious recipients of this scholarship were Sir Ashutosh Mookerjee, Jadunath Sarkar, Meghnad Saha, and others.

A promising young man, Majumdar's destiny took him to Lucknow which became his *karma bhumi,* and where he tirelessly laboured to take the teaching and research in Anthropology to astounding heights.

It was in 1921 that the combined department of Sociology and Economics was started at Lucknow University under Radhakamal Mukherjee. Mukherjee appointed Majumdar as a lecturer in Comparative Economics in this department. Lucknow University grew to be recognised as a center of academic excellence with intellectuals like Radhakamal Mookerjee, D.P. Mukherjee, and D.N. Majumdar.

A breakthrough came in Majumdar's life in 1933 when through sheer dint of his merit, he got the Honour of working towards his doctoral degree on the Ho tribe at Cambridge. He received a doctorate from the University of Cambridge in 1935. Thereafter he returned to Lucknow University and continued to strive for the cause of Anthropology. 1951 is a landmark year in the history of Anthropology in India when an independent department of Anthropology was opened at Lucknow University (the third in India) and D. N. Majumdar was appointed as its Head. He toiled hard to establish the Department of Anthropology at Lucknow University, as a highly reputed center of learning Anthropology. Furer-Haimendorf called the department of Anthropology at Lucknow university the most active department in South Asia (Furer-Haimendorf, 1960). Devoting his entire energy to teaching and training his students, Professor Majumdar breathed his last in 1960 while still in service.

D.N. Majumdar: The anthropologist

Professor Majumdar's love for Anthropology made him, what can be safely said, an Anthropologist or a General Anthropologist. We are living in an age when those pursuing Anthropology are broadly categorised as either Cultural Anthropologists or Physical Anthropologists. The label, General Anthropologist for anyone invites some smirks as it is sometimes erroneously and parochially construed that it applies to one who is a jack of all branches of Anthropology but master of none. While on one hand, Majumdar's expertise and scholarship in understanding the socio-cultural scenario amongst the tribes, castes, and city life are well reflected in his writings, his deep interest and inclination towards Physical Anthropology are well seen in his works as well. While at Cambridge pursuing his research on the Ho, he studied cultural anthropology with T.C. Hodson and physical anthropology with G.M. Morant. His works show a major influence of B. Malinowski. Parallelly he learned Physical Anthropology religiously from Morant and Gates and studied serology with Gates.

Professor Majumdar kept emerging as a rising sun in the field of Anthropology and his expertise was sought for crucial endeavours. In 1941, the Census Commissioner Mr. M.W. Yeats sought his services to carry out an anthropometric and serological survey of the then United Provinces. He conducted anthropometric measurements and did blood testing on a large population. The data collected by him was analyzed by two renowned statisticians, Professor P.C. Mahalanobis and Dr. C.R. Rao. He carried out a similar exercise on invitation in Bengal and then in Gujarat, Kathiawar, and Cutch. The proceedings of the second Indian Statistical Conference, Lahore,1939 deal with a detailed discussion on the application of statistical methods in anthropometry by D.N. Majumdar, P.C. Mahalanobis, and K.P. Chattopadhyay (1939).

Professor Majumdar's sincere efforts in driving home to all the significance of Physical Anthropology's application won him several laurels. He was Honoured with the Gujarat Research Society's medal in 1950, for his outstanding contribution to physical anthropological studies in India. (Madan 1961: American Anthropologist https://anthrosource.onlinelibrary.wiley.com/doi/pdf/10.1525/aa.1961.63.2.02a00080) vol 63.

Prof. Majumdar's array of published works form a very rich collection of books and articles. His much-celebrated book, *Races, and Cultures of India* published in 1944 is remarkable on many counts. In this exhaustive volume, Majumdar brings under one canopy the multidimensional facets of human existence and their correlations. The wide range of topics covered meticulously in this work range from a discussion on races in prehistoric India, habitat, economic grading, caste origins and caste incompetence, youth organisation, family and marriage, polyandry to primitive religion. He brings together in this book the details about the races and cultures of India in a seamless way. If on one hand his sincerity as a fieldworker is well brought out in a comprehensive ethnographic account of the Khasa of Jaunsar Bawar, his deep interest in studies related to blood finds an interesting chapter on *The Blood Map of India*. In this book he tries to bring together under one umbrella three pertinent areas of research within Anthropology – Indian prehistory and a discussion on the racial groups in India; ethnological and ethnographical concepts and data; and the third one - tribes and castes in India and their situation in the process of directed culture change. The study of culture change was one of the most focal areas of Majumdar's interest. A significant aspect of this book is that it is written in such a way to appeal to a diverse range of readers – the students of Anthropology, social activists, politicians, and others who hold curiosity about getting to know India better. His empathy towards the problems of the tribes and castes in India finds a passionate vociferous call for the same. He states, "planned rehabilitation must take into account the hopes and aspirations of the people, misconceived though they may be. The two axioms of cultural rehabilitation should be: (1) we cannot be civilised unless every one of us is civilised, and (2) every people, however primitive or civilised, has a right to its way of life, and to the development of its traditional culture. To reconcile these two requires a complete grasp of the details and a sympathetic understanding of the realities of tribal aims and aspirations" (Majumdar, 1951: 812).

Majumdar was a man driven. Driven in his ceaseless effort to teach and take his love for Anthropology to his students; driven in encouraging intensive research to understand the tribes and castes in India and their problems, and driven to understand practically every area of human living. He founded the Ethnographic and Folk-Culture Society in 1945, a premier organisation devoted to research. The building of this organisation popularly referred to as EFCS continues to be a center for serious reading. A rich collection of valuable books and journals adorn its rich library, drawing not only students and professors of Anthropology but even those from other walks of life such as the bureaucrats, social workers, and anybody interested in knowing about human beings and their lives. Started in 1945, EFCS has grown to become an organisation having a large number of members spread all over the world. In 1947, Majumdar started a journal of international repute, *The Eastern Anthropologist,* a peer-reviewed journal. Majumdar was its editor till his death in 1960.

Majumdar: The fieldworker

Majumdar firmly believed that in the pursuit of understanding humans and their cultures, thorough ethnographic research is an absolute must. The plethora of his works is primarily ethnographic writings based on his study amongst the Ho of Kolhan, the Khasa (Jaunsar Bawar), the Korwa, the Tharu, the Bhil, and the Gond. Anthropology has carved a niche for itself on account of its characteristic bent on long term intense fieldwork. In unearthing the unseen and nuanced realities of the lives of a people and bringing out their way of life holistically, there is no substitute for detailed fieldwork. Majumdar practiced this with utmost sincerity and encouraged his students to follow suit. He carried out long term fieldwork lasting several years. His fieldwork among the Khasa was completed in about 5 years and he stayed there for 22 summers in total (Maumdar, 1962: ix).

Majumdar studied culture as a whole and not in a piecemeal way. The entire way of life of a people came under the purview of his meticulous fieldwork. He was deeply concerned with understanding the problems of a people and understood these best against the backdrop of their entire culture. Problems do not exist as independent, isolated realities. They need to be understood in their cultural context. There should be a concerted effort to understand a culture holistically. This was a message which Majumdar sent out through his various publications. Cultural contact and the resultant culture change were prime areas of his inquiry.

When one goes through his publications, one cannot miss his empathy and concern towards the trials and tribulations of vulnerable people. Furthermore, as a responsible Anthropologist, he extends valuable suggestions to overcome those. Inspired by B. Malinowski, Majumdar firmly believed in the importance of the functional approach in understanding cultures. According to him, the functional approach is the best way to collect and interpret data related to human living and human behaviour. "The emphasis on the functional study has been on 'culture' rather than on cultures. From this point of view the functional approach is surely significant" (Majumdar1950)

His seminal work on the marginalised Ho tribals, *A Tribe in Transition* (1937) is recognised as one of the earliest works on the impact of the non-tribal world on the tribal one. How a community struggles to come to terms with the fast-changing scenario of its own life as a result of industrialisation and acculturation, is well brought out in this work. Malinowski's influence is visible in the methodological approach which he adopts to look at cultures. Hutton writes that in *A Tribe in Transition*, Majumdar "states as his methodological ideal synthesis of Malinowski's approach in 'The Argonauts' with that of Ruth Benedict in 'Patterns of Culture" (Hutton, 1938). Hutton further states that "the book is an important contribution to Indian ethnography, particularly in its estimate of the impact of Hinduism on the culture of the Hos, and marks a rather new departure in Indian ethnographical literature" (*ibid*).

His work *Fortunes of Primitive Tribes (1944)*, is an interesting collection of ethnographic accounts on the tribes of Uttar Pradesh – the Korwa, Khasa, and Tharu. The chapter on the criminal tribes brings forth Majumdar's exhaustive research on these tribes and his style of writing manifests his sensitive and human side particularly when he treats the term 'criminal' shorn of all stigma. A rather eye-catching feature of the book, *Fortunes of Primitive Tribes,* is the picture of a tribesman with a rather pensive, worried look. Majumdar captions this picture as "The Frowns of Tribal Fortune", instantly drawing the attention of the reader to the paradoxical coexistence of 'frown' and 'fortune'.

Majumdar while discussing the change in tribal cultures enumerates the processes which lead to the transformation and modification of tribal cultures. These processes are – simple adoption, acculturation, social commensalism, or plural association (Majumdar, 1947).

His long-standing research among the Ho takes the form of another publication *The Affairs of a Tribe* (1950), wherein he delves into the adverse effect of the impact of rampant industrialisation on the tribes.

Majumdar's deep concern " for the weak tribals was reflected in the approach of MARC which he put forth. MARC, standing for Man, Area, Resource, Cooperation. Culture change can be discussed over the base of culture and hence it is the base that becomes important. Majumdar writes about the base of the culture which for him is the result of the interaction between four factors - Man, Area, Resources and Cooperation (MARC), which he wrote of in order of importance (Ranjan, 2016:56).

Apart from the study on the tribes and castes, Majumdar significantly contributed towards the study of villages in India particularly in the context of cultural change. . The period after India's independence saw a major focus on the study of village India by some anthropologists like the American anthropologists' Morris Opler, David Mandelbaum, Mc Kim Marriott, Oscar Lewis, and Indian anthropologists like S.C. Dube, M.N. Srinivas, and D.N. Majumdar. Majumdar's book *Caste and Communication in an Indian Village* (1958) brings out the dynamics of inter-caste relations in the village Mohana near Lucknow. The juxtaposition of leadership, factional politics, and economy along with the analysis of caste mobility has been comprehensively discussed by Majumdar in this book. What is very interesting and pertinent here is that he understands and explains all of these as he sees the Indian village as a way of life. One of the unique features of this book is that it brings out the situation of the women in this village. Majumdar informs that, in terms of liberty and women's empowerment, a clear difference could be seen between the situations of the low caste women and the high caste women. The lower caste women were found to be more independent and empowered than the upper caste ones. The former was found to challenge the rules of patriarchy more than the latter. Majumdar write's, "...Chamar women work as wage labourers quite often, but they seldom give their earnings to their husbands. This is contrary to the accepted custom and cannons of social behaviour. Chamar women go against the accepted domestic rules in another way too, for they sometimes eat their food before their husbands have eaten theirs, whereas among other castes women generally partake of their food only after the husbands have finished their meal (Majumdar, 1958:205).

This book was the result of the Cornell-Lucknow project.

Another major contribution of Majumdar towards a holistic understating of village India is in the form of another book – *Chhor Ka Ek Gaon* (1960). In this work, Majumdar writes about his research on a village, Chittora in Mirzapur district, Uttar Pradesh in 1955. This was carried out under the aegis of the Cornell-Lucknow research project. The study of a village such as Chittora by Majumdar carries major significance because it looks into the coexistence and correlations between the tribes and the non-tribes living in the same village. Pivotal aspects of this work are that it throws light on how tribal people get Hinduised as a result of their living together with the Hindu caste groups; how the village is going about its business and daily living in the absence of a dominant caste, which happens to be more of a norm than an exception as understood from most of the studies on the villages. Such an authentic and meticulous description of life in a village in India goes a long way in enriching the growing compendium of village studies in Anthropology. The book plays an instrumental role in being the torchbearer of sorts for future village studies that were carried out. The book is originally written in English under the title " A Village on the Fringe" and it was translated into Hindi under the title of *Chor ka Ek Gaon* (1960). The translation of the book into Hindi deserves applause as it has been done aptly. The translated version of the book is also a significant contribution as it increases the reach of the book. This book was the outcome of the Cornell-Lucknow research project.

Not many are aware that Majumdar's perennial quest to give a conspicuous shape to the pertinence of Anthropology in addressing practically every sphere of human life found yet another breakthrough of the sort when he contributed towards the emergence of medical anthropology in India. This fact has been lucidly articulated by eminent anthropologist, Professor P. C. Joshi (2016). Professor Joshi writes that the early 1930s saw the publication of two significant papers, one by Prof. D.N. Majumdar, and the other by Professor P.C. Biswas which, in a way set the ball rolling for the researchers in line with the development of medical anthropology in India. Professor Joshi credits Majumdar for addressing the mainstream concern of medical anthropology for the first time. Majumdar's article, titled *Disease, Death, and Divination in Certain Primitive Societies in India* (1933), brings forth the comparative ethnographic details of various tribes like Veddhas, Polias, Munda-Dravidian tribes, Hos, Korwa, Majhwars, Cheros, Panikas, Kharwars, Oraons, Bengalese, Rawaltas and Tharus. "Majumdar was a very keen observer of the ethnographic details and therefore one could see him explaining the variations in the beliefs and practices concerning death customs, witchcraft and treatment methods across the length and breadth of the country. D. N. Majumdar's descriptions amply reflect his mastery over myriad customs of the 'savages', most of which were known to him through personal experience but for other, he relied on the writing of doyens such as S. C. Roy." (Joshi, 2016:4). Professor Joshi highlights that in this article Professor Majumdar not only discussed the beliefs and practices related to death and disease among these communities and explained how they differed from each other, he further went ahead to give the disease causation theory among the 'primitive societies' wherein he classifies disease causation into two categories - internal and external, "the former subscribing to now widely known supernatural or personalistic (see Foster, 1976, p. 775) while the latter to natural or naturalistic cause" (Joshi, 2016:4).

As I went through the exhaustive writings of Majumdar, I realised that Majumdar was completely confident and wholly committed to putting anthropological approach and knowledge to good use in understanding the life of a people and sharing his vision and suggestions as a responsible researcher and academician. It is in this vein that he carried out a survey of the city of Kanpur, in Uttar Pradesh. Kanpur is an industrial city bringing in a large number of labourers towards the industrial enterprises thriving in it. Majumdar writes, "Our towns and cities are growing, our vigilance must not vane, sociologists must line up for social research and help the administration in its assigned task of building an urban population, socially aware and mentally conditioned for the city life" (Majumdar *et. al,* 1960).

Through his in-depth understanding of people which he gained through serious ethnographic research, Majumdar made valuable suggestions in the direction of national development. He firmly believed that anthropological research with its exclusive bent on exploring reality at the grass-roots level through intensive long-term fieldwork is fully equipped to contribute towards national development. He was a member of the Research Programmes Committee of the National Planning Commission, and in that capacity, he pointed out that by being trained in carrying out an intensive study of people and their cultures, the anthropologists and sociologists could significantly contribute towards administration. They are equipped to soundly understand the problems of the marginalised people. Further, they can correctly assess the various government plans, programmes, and schemes catered towards the welfare of the people at the grass-roots level such as at the village level. Majumdar firmly believed that Anthropology in India should develop in the context of the reality of Indian society and culture. The anthropologists in India must "separate the native warp from the foreign woof" (1939:1-2).

"In his various works (1937, 1947, 1950), Majumdar highlighted that development of a people is quite an uphill task. There is a gnawing gap between the documentation of the ideals underpinning development and their replication into reality, as the contact of weaker people with caste Hindus has drained them economically and psychologically. Majumdar urged for initiation of planned cultural contacts with the tribals through the assistance of anthropologists" (Ranjan, 2011:54). According to Madan "anthropology could offer useful knowledge and usable advice to the policymaker, the administrator and the social worker... The changed situation in the early 1950s offered new challenges and he (Majumdar) responded to them swiftly and energetically' (Madan, 1994:29). For Majumdar, extreme cultural relativism had no meaning and he did not hesitate in identifying cultures as 'dominant' and 'decadent' (1994:219). He did so to press upon the urgency to deal with the obstacles in the path of development.

Majumdar as a teacher

I think the most important factor which makes a subject immensely popular in a University is the persona of the teacher teaching that subject. Professor Majumdar was an extremely devoted teacher. His personal touch with his students and his parent-like concern for them went on to make him and the Department of Anthropology, one of the favourites at the University of Lucknow. His sincerity towards his students was well reciprocated by their loyalty towards him. He wrote in his book *The Matrix of Indian Culture* (1947), that he dedicates the book to his "pupils of the M.A. final class in anthropology, whose love and loyalty I sincerely reciprocate". In my conversations with Professor Majumdar's students, like Professor Gopala Sarana and Shri H.S. Saksena, I learned about his love for his students and his passion to make them understand the very essence of Anthropology and while doing so, driving home to them the very essence of holistic living. Whenever my teacher, Professor Gopala Sarana spoke to us about his teacher Professor Majumdar, his expression would be infused with much warmth, respect, and adulation for his 'master' on whose 'feet he sat and learnt about Anthropology'.

Conclusion

Professor Dhirendra Nath Majumdar combined in himself the best attributes of a teacher, a researcher, a pioneer who steered the way for the development of Anthropology in India through his untiring efforts. He left behind a priceless treasure in the form of his writings and, his students who took the baton forward in their march towards taking Anthropology in India to greater heights. His charismatic personality found many supporters who strove with him alongside. I am reminded of these lines written by the famous poet Majrooh Sultanpuri,

> *Main akela hi chala tha janib-e-manzil magar*
> *Log saath aate gaye aur karwaan banta gaya*
> (I started alone towards my goal.
> People kept joining me and the caravan kept forming)

References

Foster, George M. 1976. 'Disease etiologies in non-western medical systems'. *American Anthropologist*. 78:773-782.

Furer- Haimendorf, C von. 1960. 'Obituary of D.N. Majumdar'. *Man*, LX (212).

Hutton, JH. 1938. Supplement to Nature. March 12.

Joshi, PC. 2016. 'Emergence of medical anthropology in India'. *The Eastern Anthropologist*, 69:1.

Madan, TN.1994. *Pathways – Approaches to the Study of Society in India,* OUP, New Delhi.

Madan, TN.1961. *American Anthropologist.* https://anthrosource.onlinelibrary.wiley.com/doi/pdf/10.1525/aa.1961.63.2.02a00080

Madan, TN., and Sarana Gopala 1962. *Indian Anthropology: Essays in Memory of D.N. Majumdar*. Asia Publishing House, New Delhi.

Majumdar, DN. 1937. *A Tribe in Transition: A Study in Culture Pattern*. Calcutta and Longmans Green & Co, London.

Majumdar, DN. 1939. *Tribal Cultures and Acculturation*. Indian Science Congress Association, Calcutta.

Majumdar, DN. 1944. *Fortunes of Primitive Tribes*. Universal Publishers Ltd, Lucknow.

Majumdar, DN. 1944. *Races and Cultures of India*. Kitabistan, Allahabad.

Majumdar, DN. 1947. *The Matrix of Indian Cultur*e. Universal Publishers Ltd, Lucknow.

Majumdar, DN. 1950. *The Affairs of a Tribe: A Study in Tribal Dynamics*. Universal Publishers Ltd, Lucknow.

Majumdar, DN. 1951. 'Tribal rehabilitation in India'. *International Social Science Bulletin*. 3,4:802-814.

Majumdar, DN. 1958. *Caste and Communication in an Indian Village*. Asia Publishing House, Bombay.

Majumdar, DN. 1960. *Social Contours of an Industrial City*. Asia Publishing House, Bombay.

Majumdar, DN. 1960.*Chhor Ka Ek Gaon*. (Hindi), Asia Publishing House, Bombay.

Majumdar, DN. 1962. *Himalayan Polyandry.* Asia Publishing House, Bombay.

Majumdar, DN., Mahalanobis PC., and Chattopadhyay KP. 1939. 'Discussion on the Application of Statistical Methods in Anthropolometry'. *The Proceedings of the Second Indian Statistical Conference, Lahore*. Statistical Publishing Society, Calcutta.

Mathur, KS.1987. *Anthropological Perspectives: Essays in the Memory of Prof. D.N.Majumda*r. Ethnographic and Folk Culture Society, Lucknow.

Ranjan, Geetika. 2011. 'Ethnography for development'. *The North-Eastern Hill University Journal,* Vol. IX, No. 2.

Ranjan, Geetika. 2016. *Approaches to the Study of Indian Culture and Society*. Pragun Publications, New Delhi.

Saksena, HS. 2017. *Tribal Studies and Beyond: Contributions of D.N.Majumdar to Indian Anthropology*. Rawat Publications, New Delhi.

9

Contributions of Irawati Karve Towards the Growth of Anthropological Studies in India

Arindita Goswami

> *" I travelled from place to place never knowing where my next step was to be nor where my next meal was to come from....Rest pauses between work, meal times, and travel in buses full of people, and in third class railway compartments filled with men and women.... ".*
>
> ***Professor Irawati Karve** (1953: 18)*

Professor Irawati Karve is credited to be the first woman anthropologist in India during the phase when anthropology and sociology were still in the nascent stage of being established as university disciplines. Her keen interest in the different branches of anthropology viz. physical anthropology, social anthropology, prehistory, and folklore made her stand as an all-around anthropologist. Channa (2010: 260) brings to fore the comment of Hutton in a preface to the second edition of her pivotal work *Kinship Organisation in India* (1965) which attests to the fact that even in world anthropology at the middle of the twentieth-century women scholars formed a minority. To quote Hutton (1965, viii), 'It is probably symptomatic of a new India, unknown to my generation, that this contribution has been made by one of the sex... at any rate, it is one which anyone of either sex might feel proud to have accomplished'.

A glimpse into the early life of Irawati Karve

Born in a Chitpavan Brahmin family of Maharashtra in 1905, she was christened 'Irawati' after the Irrawaddy river in Burma (present-day Myanmar) where her father, an engineer, Ganesh Hari Karmarkar worked in the Burma Cotton Company. Barely when Professor Irawati was seven years of age, she was admitted to the Huzur Paga boarding school for girls in Pune where she had the turning point of her life. She was adopted by R.P. Paranjapye, Principal of Fergusson College who was the father of her classmate Shakuntala Paranjapye. It was in her new family that she got introduced to an intellectual atmosphere with a wide range of books including judge Balakram who first bestowed her with the flavour of anthropology.

Professor Karve did her graduation in Philosophy from Fergusson College, Pune in the year 1926. She then obtained the Dakshina Fellowship and joined the Bombay University under the guidance of Professor G.S. Ghurye, Dean of the Department of Sociology. Her post-graduate thesis was completed in two parts, one dealing with the Parashurama myth and the other with the Chitpavan Brahmins enabling her to obtain her M.A. degree in 1928. Meanwhile, she married the chemist Dinkar Dhondo Karve, the second son of the great social reformer of Maharashtra – Dhondo Keshav Karve, better known as Maharshi Karve who was an initiator of widow remarriage and women's education in the state as well as the founder of the famous SNDT (Shreemati Nathibai Damodar Thackersey) Women's University in Mumbai. Despite facing strong opposition from her father-in-law who himself was an advocate of women empowerment, Irawati Karve was left alone for Germany in 1928 for pursuing her Ph.D. at the University of Berlin. Sundar (2007: 370) remarks that it was the rock support of Irawati's husband Dinakar Karve who himself had done his Ph.D. in organic chemistry from Germany that provided her the necessary impetus to go ahead at the age of 23, returning two years later after completing her doctoral research. Soon after coming back to India she joined the SNDT Women's University and worked as the Registrar from 1931 - 1936 and was also engaged in some post-graduate teaching in the city. In 1939, she joined the Deccan College Post-Graduate and Research Institute in Pune (as the Reader in Sociology), headed the Department of Sociology and Anthropology, and continued teaching there till the end of her career with her death in 1970. She also made a significant contribution by setting up the Department of Anthropology at the University of Pune in 1963. Professor Karve presided over the Anthropology Section of the Indian Science Congress held in New Delhi in 1947 which was a great honour for Indian anthropologists during that period. As Sachichidananda (1971: 554) mentions from 1951 - 1952 Irawati Karve remained at the School of Oriental and African Studies at the University of London as a visiting lecturer which was a feather added to her hat of numerous academic achievements. Further, before her return to India, she had the honour to deliver lectures at several centers of learning in the U.S.A. In 1955, she attended the Pan-African Congress as a delegate of the Government of India. She was invited along with her husband as distinguished scholars at Berkeley, the University of California from 1959 - 1960. In the South Asia Colloquium at Berkeley, she gave a series of talks on the Indian Caste System which formed a major area of her research work.

Professor Karve was a prolific and acclaimed scientific writer with an equal hold in Marathi and English where her versatile topics ranged from caste systems, family relationships to religion, mythology, folklore, and kinship. In 1968, Karve's well-acclaimed book *Yuganta: The End of an Epoch* (1967) won the Sahitya Academy Award where she treated the epic of Mahabharata as a critical historical document and the usually venerated godly characters are subjected to a rational inquiry thereby challenging the familiar and formulating new interpretations of this ancient epic. Further, her monumental work *Kinship Organisation in India* (1953, 1st edition) based on extensive fieldwork across the country had earned her an international repute which discusses the different kinship systems prevalent in the north, south, central, and eastern regions of India as well as the point of similarities between them. In recognition of her outstanding inputs in the field of research, the Museum of Anthropology within the Department of Anthropology in the Savitribai Phule Pune University (SPPU) established in 1978 was renamed as the Irawati Karve Museum of Anthropology on December 15, 1993.

Academic contributions of Irawati Karve in anthropology

The illustrious career of Professor Irawati Karve spanned from the time of colonial rule to the post-independent phase of India which was characterised by a distinctive interpretation of the diverse Indian society. Sundar (2007: 373) mentions the major intellectual influences on Karve which, in the later years got expression through her elaborate works. The first and foremost was that of her M.A. supervisor Professor G.S.Ghurye who followed an Indological tradition which was also very much endorsed by Karve. Secondly, there was an ethnological tradition visible through the extensive surveys of castes and tribes within India which as Vincent (1990: 83) points out later came to be known as diffusionism. Thirdly, Karve's subscription to a German Physical Anthropological tradition during her Ph.D. in Germany furnished a genetic explanation for the existence of diverse groups and it played a significant role in shaping her research work in the field of Physical Anthropology. Lastly, her dedication and sheer interest in fieldwork helped her in adding up to new areas of research including socio-economic surveys as well as palaeo-anthropological studies through archaeological explorations with Professor H.D. Sankalia.

Sundar (2007:389) refers to a comprehensive bibliography of the entire works of Irawati Karve prepared by K.C. Malhotra in 1970 - 1971, just after her demise which includes a list of 102 articles and books in English, 8 books in Marathi, several unpublished papers, and several ongoing projects (Malhotra, 1973). One of the leadoff in anthropological research in India, Irawati Karve conducted her research on an all-encompassing range of subject matter including mapping kinship and caste utilising anthropometric and linguistic surveys, contemporary surveys of the status of women using census data, urbanisation, weekly markets, dam-displaced people, pastoralists, family, folklore, myth, culture, villages, and townships in India and so on. Malhotra (1971:26) provided an ordering of the contributions of Karve: palaeo-anthropology, Indological studies, physical anthropological investigations, cultural anthropological investigations and building up of a cadre of trained personnel while Sundar (2007:389) places the anthropological production of Karve under four heads viz; (i) physical anthropology and archaeology consisting of anthropometric and blood group investigations and excavation of stone-age skeletons, (ii) cultural anthropology emphasising on kinship, caste, folksongs, epics, oral traditions, (iii) socio-economic surveys – weekly markets, dam-displaced people, urbanisations, pastoralists, spatial organisation and (iv) contemporary social comment – women, language and race. Karve tried to understand cultural variation in the Indian society with the help of intensive surveys that she conducted on different groups found in and within particular regions and these were broadly based on anthropometric and blood group studies (a genetic approach based on her German training) combined with explanations and discussions from the Indological perspectives. The contributions of Irawati Karve in the different areas of anthropology are briefly discussed in the following sections:

Irawati Karve as a physical anthropologist and archaeologist

Irawati Karve's exposure to the fields of race, human anatomy, and genetics during her Ph.D. experience under Eugene Fischer at the Kaiser Wilhelm Institute of Anthropology, Human Heredity, and Eugenics in Germany was an instrumental factor in shaping her research work in physical anthropology. Her Ph.D. topic was *The Normal Asymmetry of the Human Skull* for which she examined the skulls of different racial groups and her study concluded that there were no racial differences observed in the asymmetries found between the left and right side of the body (Karve, 1937: 68-69). The outcome of her study was significant to physical anthropologists as their conclusions about racial differences depended on physical measurements, and, if there were major differences, it would be required to take the measurements on different sides of the body. Anthropometric study to determine racial composition of India was already in vogue from the last part of the 19th century popularised by the British administrators but Karve viewed that instead of random measuring of Indians there should be a mapping of social and biological variations concentrating on different linguistics regions and all the endogamous groups were to be considered in place of a few groups. Malhotra (1971:29) mentions systematic surveys carried out by Karve using her statistical expertise in Maharashtra, Mysore, Orissa, Andhra Pradesh, and Tamil Nadu and for her Maharashtrian data, she applied the highly sophisticated statistical tool of Mahalanobis's D^2 statistics in collaboration with Dr. V.M. Dandekar. Under her able guidance, K. C. Malhotra compared the physical measurements and heritable traits (gene frequency analysis or genetic data like blood group, colour vision, hand-clasping, hypertrichosis, etc.) of eight Brahmin castes (Karve and Malhotra, 1968) while another student R.K. Gulati studied nine potter castes (1969) and the expansion of these type of investigations on genetic heterogeneity of various endogamous groups of castes or sub-castes in India by Karve and her colleagues continued that primarily points towards Karve's devotion to the task of social and biological mapping of the variations in the society. Through such studies, Karve advocated that caste in India should be used as a unit of study and research tool for socio-biological investigation, and as Malhotra (1971: 30) opines this very concept revolutionised Indian Anthropology.

Irawati Karve's knack for prehistory is revealed through the joint exploration in 1944 that she undertook with her colleague Professor H.D. Sankalia from the Deccan Institute in the prehistoric mound at Langhnaj in Gujarat which resulted in the finding of as many as thirteen skeletons along with microliths and animal remains and this endeavour of Karve drew a wide range of admiration from the international circle as well.

Irawati Karve as a social/ cultural anthropologist

Irawati Karve's noteworthy contributions in the field of Indian social/ cultural anthropology mainly include her in-depth analysis of the configuration of linguistic regions, the institution of caste and the family organisation which she believed was a prerequisite for understanding any cultural phenomenon in Indian society (Karve, 1993:50). It was her Indological expertise with good hold in Pali and Sanskrit coupled with physical anthropological knowledge that enabled her to conduct meaningful research in the above-mentioned areas of Indian society by adopting an integrated approach. Karve's classic work *Kinship Organisation in India* (1953) is regarded as a basic source book and guide for researches in the domain of kinship. As mentioned by Malhotra (1971: 33) and Sundar (2007: 394) the book is based on extensive data collected on kinship terms and usages and family organisation from both ancient Indian literature like Rigveda and Atharvaveda and the Mahabharata (1943) as well as empirical data from a wide range of areas including Maharashtra, Gujarat, Kathiawad, Karnataka, Orissa, Bihar, Kerala, Tamil Nadu, and Uttar Pradesh. It is worth mentioning here that data from all these sources were published as research articles before the publication of Karve's major work in 1953. In this book, Karve mapped the kinship patterns on to linguistic zones and highlighted the four different zones within which she again pointed to the variations between castes and sub-castes as – (1) Indo-European or Sanskritic organisation in the northern zone; (2) Dravidian kinship in the southern zone; (3) a central zone of mixed patterns (for instance found in Maharashtra); and (4) Mundari kinship systems in the east. This macro-study based on a considerable amount of material on kinship terms and behaviour pattern, marriage regulations among castes along with certain features of the joint family brought to fore the fact that though kinship system follows approximately the linguistic pattern there are variations in particular aspects as she mentioned that though the Maharashtrian region belongs to the area of Sanskritic languages its kinship organisation has a striking similarity to that of its neighbouring Dravidian south region. Similarly, she found that the literature of the Dravidian speaking people of Karnataka and Andhra is saturated with Sanskrit words and epics having the use of certain northern kinship terms. Further, she observed that the tribal groups of Oraons and Gonds inhabiting within the northern linguistic area have almost 50 percent of words borrowed from Sanskritic languages in their kinship vocabularies.

Karve also elaborately dealt with the concept of caste in her book *Hindu Society - An Interpretation* (Karve, 1968/[1961]), while as Sundar (2007:398) observes several articles dealing with the explanation of caste from culture (Karve, 1955, 1958b, 1958c, 1958d, 1959) and anthropometric (1933a, 1933b, 1941, 1948, 1954) viewpoints preceded this book where data on kinship terminology and usages were collected from a variety of caste groups like from Maharashtra, Karnataka, Orissa and so on. By using anthropometric data along with the cultural ones Karve in her seminal paper in *Current Anthropology* along with K.C. Malhotra (1968) and Channa (2010:275) observes that Karve viewed the various castes are as a result of the amalgamation and the system as such shows no racial difference between one caste and another, least of all between the Brahmins and others. For her caste is an endogamous group inhabiting a particular area, having one or more traditional occupations, and ranked in a certain order in the social stratification. She argued that for sociological and anthropometric purposes the sub-castes or smallest social units must be investigated separately (for example, the Chitpavans of Maharashtra) and treated as caste while the overall broad category like the Maharashtrian Brahman should be treated as 'caste cluster'. She believed that such separate studies for the numerous endogamous units or sub-groups could shed light on the historical processes of migration and socio-cultural assimilation that have been taking place for a long time in Indian society. Karve views caste to be even more fundamental than religion (Karve, 1941). Karve also contributed to the study of the joint family system in India and tried to see the variations in the structure, differences in rural-urban setting, the impact of industrialisation, etc. For instance, her student Ranadive (1960) was assigned to study the family pattern in rural and urban Maharashtra, and based upon empirical, statistical, and genealogical observations it was found joint family was more in a rural area compared to an urban area. Her analysis of vast data on families in terms of types and structure led her to put forward the fact that 'jointness of family are in many respects not separate social events, but maybe represented as alternating stages of the same family' (Karve, 1967: 42).

Irawati Karve's academic output also encompassed the diverse forms of socio-economic surveys that she carried out which at present, would include applied anthropological significance. She worked among the Bhils residing in Western Khandesh (1958a) which was her first survey work. She put forward her arguments in several academic writings (1957a, 1969) based on her studies among the tribals of Maharashtra that no outside cultural code should be imposed on them in the name of assimilation and advancement though she advocated their education, initially in their mother tongue and then through regional language which can assist them to participate in regional activities and discourses. Karve with her colleague Damle authored the book *Group Relations in a Village Community* (1963) based on the study of three villages in Maharashtra which revealed the fact that kinship, caste, and locality are the determinants of inter-personal and inter-group relationships. In another brilliant work *Social Dynamics of a Growing Town* (Karve and Ranadive, 1965) a small sugar town Phaltan in the Satara district of Maharashtra, and its relation to the hinterlands was studied. The study showed that small towns in India acted as an intermediary and channel of communication between a village and a big city having both rural and urban characteristics. They suggested that such small towns should be uplifted with proper social planning to cater to the needs of both the ruralites and urbanites that would contribute to the real progress of the rural areas.

Karve's interest in the religious life of the Hindus reflected in the work of her Ph.D. students Dingre (1968) who by a thorough study of the famous Pandharpur temple in Maharashtra dedicated to Lord Vitthoba (incarnation of Lord Vishnu) found structural similarities in the principles underlying the Hindu caste system and the religious life. Karve and Acharya (1970) in their study *The Role of Weekly Markets in the Tribal, Rural and Urban Setting* carried out in Baglan Taluka of Nasik observed that even in typical rural and tribal setting weekly markets provided an excellent communication center for the surrounding villages bringing together people and traders from different regions who apart from exchanging or buying commodities participate in annual fairs, folk drama and the like which was a new kind of study focusing on the implications of the social relations. Karve with such studies of the influence of spatial organisations on social relations which were gaining ground in academia displayed her ability as well as interest in the diverse areas of anthropology and sociology.

Karve's work with her daughter Jai Nimbkar *A Survey of the People Displaced Through the Koyna Dam* (1969) is a model in its way for studies on dam-displaced people which discusses the issues about the sudden submerging of their habitation and adjustment problems faced by the displaced lot in terms of loss of ancestral land, friends, marriage connections, etc. The authors voice their concerns and try to draw the attention of the government for proper foresight and approach to tackle such matters. Karve in collaboration with Malhotra (Malhotra, 1971: 36) initiated an investigation among the nomadic groups of Dhangars (shepherd) the food producers, and Nandiwalle – partly beggars and entertainers which were continued by him after the death of Karve that took the shape of human ecological studies.

Professor Karve's ability as an able fieldworker undertaking strenuous field journeys at a time when in Indian society was quite unusual for a woman especially a married one deserves strong appreciation. In this regard, Sankalia (1978: 57, 111 - 112) mentioned instances of their joint expeditions that involved rigorous walking along the Mula - Mutha river in Pune to find stone age tools and their sleeping in a truck during a certain field task due to non-availability of rooms. The first chapter of her monumental work *Kinship Organisation in India* (1953) reflects on her fieldwork methods the research for which extended to other parts as well apart from Maharashtra from 1938 - 1939 onwards. In her words:

> I moved from region to region taking measurements, blood samples, and collecting information about kinship practices and terminology. The contacts were established through friends, students, and Government officials. Supposing I had an acquaintance in Dharwar (in Karnataka), I would make that my first station and then get introduced to the friends or relations of these acquaintances who, in turn, would take me to their homes and villages and so I traveled from place to place never knowing where my next step was to be nor where my next meal was to come from....Rest pauses between work, meal times, travel in buses full of people, and in third class railway compartments filled with men and women gave me the opportunities I sought for collecting kinship material. A small beginning would suffice to set the ball rolling and each would come out with his or her stories. I had naturally to tell also all about myself, my husband and children and the parents-in-law and others would tell about their kin. At such times it was not always, however, possible or advisable to take notes. Kinship terms and situations involving personal narratives or family usages, scraps of song, and proverbs were, however, taken down. The working day meant over twelve hours of work. When there was not material for measurement the time was spent canvassing contacts and there were never enough funds or time to do this type of work for more than two months a year. After coming back to Poona the data would be looked into and verified linguistically by referring to some good dictionaries and then a study of some literature would be undertaken to find out how far the literature reflected the kinship attitudes. These studies were very rewarding. They revealed the intimate connection

between literature and society, especially the kinship organisation, and helped to interpret certain facts which had seemed obscure to me. Such studies also gave a feeling of sureness while dealing with people (Karve, 1953: 18).

Conclusion

Professor Irawati Karve was the pioneer anthropologist in India to have applied an integrative approach combining her knowledge from physical anthropology, socio-cultural anthropology, archaeology, history, and Indology to study the organisation of the Indian society holistically. Her study enabled us to understand the diversity in Indian society in terms of the physical characteristics of populations as well as the complex variety of behaviour patterns and customs prevalent among them. The subjects on which she undertook study were quite advanced and ahead of her time. She rested her main theoretical assertion on the need to comprehend society or culture as far as possible by reviewing the development and transformation through historical times. Her versatility as an anthropologist involving anthropometry, serology, archaeology, or the collection of kinship terms and usages for studying the diverse Indian population through dedicated fieldwork has remained a model for us even after many decades. Further, it is noteworthy that the name of Irawati Karve has been considered along with ten other eminent women scientists of India from different fields like botany, chemistry, meteorology, biomedical research, etc. by the Ministry of Science and Technology, Government of India on the occasion of the National Science Day, February 28, 2020 for establishing chairs in their names at institutes across the country (India Today, February 29, 2020) which indeed speak volumes of her insightful contribution in the area of her research and study.

References

Channa, Subhadra Mitra, 2010. 'Irawati Karve and the production of an Indian Anthropology'. In HS. Saxena, Vinay Kumar Srivastava, Nadeem Hasnain and Sameera Maiti (Eds): *Anthropology in India*, pp. 258-277, Serials Publications, New Delhi.

Dingre, GV. 1968. *A Study of a Temple Town and its Priesthood*. Unpublished Ph.D. Thesis. Poona University.

Gulati, RK. 1969. *An Analysis of the Inter-Group Differences in an Artisan Caste of Maharashtra.* Unpublished Ph.D. Thesis. Poona University.

Hutton, JH. 1965. 'Foreward'. *Kinship Organisation in India* (2nd revised edition) by Irawati Karve. Asia Publishing House, Bombay.

India Today https://www.indiatoday.in/india/story/11-chairs-names-women-scientists-established-institutes-across-country-smriti-irani-1651017-2020-02-29. Assessed on March 2, 2020, 8.30 pm.

Karve, I. and Acharya Hemlata 1970. *The Role of Weekly Markets in the Tribal, Rural, and Urban Settings*. Deccan College Building Centenary and Silver Jubilee Series No. 70, Poona.

Karve, I., and Ranadive JS. 1965. *The Social Dynamics of a Growing Town and its Surrounding Area*. Deccan College Postgraduate and Research Institute, Poona.

Karve, I. and Nimbkar Jai. 1969. *A Survey of the People Displaced Through the Koyna Dam*. Deccan College Building Centenary and Silver Jubilee Series, No. 61.

Karve, I., and Malhotra KC. 1968. 'A biological comparison of eight endogamous groups of the same rank'. *Current Anthropology* 9, 2 - 3: 109-24.

Karve, I., and Damle YB. 1963. *Group Relations in Village Community*. Deccan College Monograph Series No. 24.

Karve, I. 1933a. 'The ethnic affinities of the Chitpavans (Part I)'. *The Journal of the University of Bombay* 1, 4: 383-400.

Karve, I. 1933b. 'The ethnic affinities of the Chitpavans (Part II)'. *The Journal of the University of Bombay* 2, 1: 132-58.

Karve, I. 1958a. *The Bhils of West Khandesh*. The Anthropological Society of Bombay, Bombay.

Karve, I. 1958b. 'What is caste? (I): Caste as extended kin'. *The Economic Weekly.* 10,4-6:125-38.

Karve, I. 1958c. 'What is caste? (II): Caste and occupation'. *The Economic Weekly.*10,12:401-7.

Karve, I. 1958d. 'What is caste? (III): Caste as a status group'. *The Economic Weekly.*10,26-8:881-8.

Karve, I. 1959. 'What is caste? (IV): Caste society and Vedantic thought'. *The Economic Weekly.*11,4-6:149-63.

Karve, I. 1968/[1961]. *Hindu Society - An interpretation* (2nd edition). Poona: Deshmukh Prakashan.

Karve, I. 1969. 'The tribals of Maharashtra'. *Urgent Research in Social Anthropology*, Transactions of the Indian Institute of Advanced Study, Simla. 10: 1-7.

Karve, I. 1993. 'The kinship map of India'. In Patricia Uberoi (Ed): *Family, Kinship and Marriage in India*, pp. 50-73, Oxford University Press, New Delhi.

Karve, I.1967. 'Analysis of jointness and non-jointness of family'. *The Anthropologist*. 14,1:41-5.

Karve, I. 1961. *Hindu Society: An Interpretation* (2nd edition). Deshmukh Prakashan, Poona.

Karve, I. 1941. 'Anthropometric investigation of the Madhyandin Brahmins of the Maratha country'. *Bulletin of the Deccan College Research Institute* 1, 1: 79-95.

Karve, I. 1948. *Anthropometric Measurements of the Marathas*. Deccan College, Monograph Series No. 2:1-71.

Karve, I. 1953. *Kinship Organisation in India*. Deccan College Monograph Series, No. 11, Poona.

Karve, I. 1954. 'Anthropometric measurements in Karnataka and Orissa and a comparison of these two regions with Maharashtra'. *Journal of the Anthropological Society of Bombay* 8, 1: 45-75.

Karve, I. 1955. 'Caste in modern times and some measures to combat its evils'. *Report of the Seminar on Casteism and Removal of Untouchability*, Indian Conference of Social Work, Bombay: 1-4.

Karve, I. 1957. 'Social education of the scheduled tribes'. *Vanyajati*. 5, 4: 164-9.

Karve, I.1937. 'Normal asymmetry of the human body'. *The Journal of the University of Bombay*, 6(1): 66-74.

Malhotra, KC.. 1973. 'Bibliography of Professor Irawati Karve's works'. *Bulletin of the Deccan College Research Institute* 31-32, 1-2: i-viii.

Malhotra, KC. 1971. 'Anthropological studies at the Deccan College'. *Bulletin of the Deccan College Post-Graduate and Research Institute and Souvenir*, Deccan College, Pune. 30: 26-40.

Ranadive, JS. 1960. *Family in Urban and Rural Areas*. Unpublished Ph.D. Thesis. Poona University.

Sachchidananda. 1971. 'Sketch of Irawati Karve (1905-1970): Life and Work'. *Anthropos,* 66: 554-558.

Sankalia, HD. 1978. *Born for Archaeology*. B.R. Publishing Corporation, New Delhi.

Sundar, Nandini, 2007. 'In the cause of Anthropology: The life and work of Irawati Karve'. In Patricia Uberoi, Nandini Sundar and Satish Deshpande (Eds): *Anthropology in the East: Founders of Indian Sociology and Anthropology:* pp. 360-416, Permanent Black, New Delhi.

Vincent, Joan, 1990. *Anthropology and Politics: Visions, Traditions, and Trends*. The University of Arizona Press, Tucson.

10

Hashmukh Dhirajlal Sankalia

Sukanya Sharma

Indeed, with his death, an entire era has come to an and - an era of total dedication to the cause of the discipline; of careful planning and accomplishment of research projects; of prompt publication of results of fieldwork; of the initiation of several new branches of archaeology; and of ceaseless efforts to spread the knowledge of the past to the society at large (Paddayya 1989). Sankalia inculcated these values in the minds of his students which resulted in the sustenance and sparkling growth of the Department of Archaeology at Deccan College which continues to occupy a leading role in Indian archaeology decades after Sankalia's retirement. The growth and development of Deccan College, which at one point in time was synonymous with the name of Prof. H D Sankalia will be the main focus of this chapter.

Sankalia joined Deccan College in 1939 as Professor of Proto-Indian and Ancient Indian History and remained in it till his retirement in 1973. In the same year, the Bombay Government upgraded the college to a postgraduate and research institute for imparting postgraduate education and undertaking research in linguistics, archaeology, and anthropology. Dedicated services and path-breaking research schemes planned and accomplished by workers like S. M. Katre (Linguistics and Sanskrit), Sankalia himself, and the late Iravati Karve (Anthropology and Sociology) and their associates, the Institute was catapulted into fame within a short time and carved for itself a prominent place among the foremost institutions of higher learning and research in and outside the country.

Soon after he joined Deccan College Sankalia realised that the archaeologist's job of reconstructing past human lifeways must be aided by various biological and earth sciences, and began to take immediate steps in this direction. The Department of Archaeology at Deccan College is one of those few archaeological institutions in the world which have a full complement of scientific and technical laboratories (geology and geomorphology, palaeobotany, archaeozoology, palaeontology, physical anthropology, archaeochemistry, photography and drawing sections, and now even computer archaeology). Realising also early in his career that India is one country in the world where the past lives into the present, Sankalia made provision for using the extant tribal and peasant ways of life as an interpretative means for clothing the dumb archaeological remains in flesh and blood. He thereby pioneered a branch of archaeology in India called ethnoarchaeology.

Sankalia played a pivotal role in the development of pre- and protohistoric studies in the country and himself attached the greatest importance to his contribution to these two branches. His excavations at Langhnaj and other sites in Gujarat (from 1941 to 1963) were the first of their kind in the country aimed to reconstruct the Mesolithic phase (its stratigraphical position, material culture, and food economy, and the racial features of its authors). His classic river valley studies at Nevasa on the river Pravara in Maharashtra (1955) established the relative chronological contexts of Stone Age cultures (Lower Palaeolithic to Mesolithic) based on alluvial stratigraphy and, additionally, brought to light the Middle Palaeolithic culture for the first time in India. Subsequently, his colleagues and students recognised a similar succession of Stone Age cultures in many parts of central, western, and south India. Step by step he created teaching posts in different branches of archaeology and technical posts for drawing, survey, photography, and modeling. Sankalia fully recognised the need for expertise in the physical and biological sciences to study varied archaeological materials and to provide comprehensive training for young archaeologists. To this end, he created teaching and research posts in archaeological chemistry, geology, geomorphology, palaeontology, and palaeobotany, and arranged the construction of laboratory facilities in these fields. He also built a fine museum in the department, mainly to display finds from the excavations and explorations conducted by him, his colleagues, and his students. The University Grants Commission accorded it first the status of the Department of Special Assistance and later of the Center of Advanced Study. No other archaeological center in South Asia today can boast of having staff or facilities to equal those of Deccan College, or of enjoying such a high reputation. That Sankalia's colleagues and students have maintained the dynamism he encouraged and the high standard of research he set is a tribute to the spirit of research Sankalia was able to inculcate among them.

Dr. Sankalia's involvement in archaeology and Deccan College was proverbial. His lifelong dedication to archaeology was crowned by the discovery of Stone Age tools in the compound of his residence. Sir Mortimer Wheeler testified: 'As one who has known him well since his student days forty years ago in England, I am glad to have the opportunity of adding my testimony. He was and remains the student par excellence. Alongside the legendary fame of the Poona Horse he has added that of his Deccan College Research Institute which has long redounded to the reputation of Poona in a more academic world!' (Antiquity, XLVII, 1973, p. 87).

Soon after joining Deccan College, Sankalia began to work in prehistoric archaeology. Although he worked in every sub-discipline of archaeology, he devoted the largest part of his time and energy to prehistory, which he called his life's work. In 1941, he organised an expedition to Gujarat and discovered many new palaeolithic and mesolithic sites, the most important being the Mesolithic site of Langhnaj in Mehsana district. He carried out excavations at this site and discovered the first physical remains of Stone Age man here. The results of this work were published in 1946 under the title 'Investigations into the Prehistoric Archaeology of Gujarat'. The consolidated results of these excavations were published in three volumes in 1965, under the title Excavations at Langhnaj 1944-1963. During his thirty-five years at Deccan College, Sankalia conducted excavations and explorations in almost all parts of India, from Gujarat to Assam and from Kashmir to Kerala, uncovering evidence of several Stone Age cultures. He published the results of these explorations and excavations in numerous articles. Alongside his work in prehistory, Sankalia turned his attention to proto-history as well. In the 1940s little was known of India's history between the Stone Age and historical times, except for the Indus Civilisation whose known remains were then confined to northwest India (now Pakistan). In the early 1950s, Sankalia excavated the site of Jorwe in the Ahmednagar district of Maharashtra, where he discovered a Chalcolithic culture. This excavation provided the first evidence of a settled farming people in Maharashtra and opened a new chapter in the archaeology of India. Over the next two decades, Sankalia carried out excavations at several Chalcolithic and Neolithic sites-Nevasa and Inamgaon in Maharashtra, Maheshwar, and Navdatoli in Madhya Pradesh, Ahar in Rajasthan, and Tekkalakota and Sangankallu in Karnataka. These excavations threw a floodlight on the culture and society of the pioneering agricultural settlers in western India.

Sankalia's work also encouraged other archaeologists to explore and excavate similar sites in different parts of the country. Due to these pioneering efforts today we have a fairly clear picture of the continuous human occupation of different regions of western India from Rajasthan to Karnataka. Sankalia promptly published the results of his excavations in the form of papers in Indian and foreign journals and has comprehensive reports. Besides conducting original research and writing up the results, Sankalia also wrote several syntheses on Indian prehistory and protohistory in the form of articles and books, which he revised periodically to bring them up-to-date. Among his major publications of this kind are *Prehistory and Proto-history of India and Pakistan* (1962, 1974), *Indian Archaeology Today* (1962, 1979), and *Prehistory of India* (1977). His 'Prehistory of India and Pakistan' remains the most masterly and exhaustive survey of the subject. Although Sankalia's major research interest throughout his career remained prehistory and proto-history, he found time to pursue other lines of research as well. For example, he excavated the historical sites of Kolhapur, Nasik, Nevasa, Dwarka, and Tripuri. He also retained his early interest in the traditional historical archaeology - the study of art, iconography, architecture, numismatics, epigraphy, and palaeography and wrote many papers on such subjects. One of his main interests was the reconstruction of historical geography and cultural ethnography from the data available in inscriptions. He applied this methodology to the inscriptions from Gujarat and reported his conclusions in the Thakker Vassonji Madhavji Lectures which he delivered at the University of Bombay in 1944. The lectures were later published as a book. Yet another important field of Sankalia's research was a critical study of the Ramayana in the light of the internal evidence of the epic and available archaeological data. He concluded that the story could not have been composed before the early centuries of the Christian era and that Ravana's Lanka could not have been the present-day island of Sri Lanka. Rather, the Lanka of the Ramayana was located somewhere in the area defined by the borders of Madhya Pradesh, Andhra, and Orissa. He elaborates his ideas on the historicity of the Ramayana in several papers and two books, *'Ramayana: Myth or Reality?'* (1973) and *'Ramayana in a Historical Perspective'* (1982). These unconventional views made him the target of severe criticism from orthodox Hindus, but he held his position steadfastly.

Sankalia trained several generations of students, and Indian archaeology as it is today was largely shaped by him. Sharing his knowledge with students and others was a passion for Sankalia, and he was able to inculcate in his students a spirit of inquiry, a love of knowledge, and a sense of commitment and dedication. Sankalia did not treat archaeological knowledge as the cloistered preserve of the professional elite. He strongly believed that since the archaeological activity was carried out with public money, the people had a right to the knowledge gained from this research. To this end he wrote copiously in newspapers and popular magazines and published several booklets in simple language in English, Hindi, Marathi, and Gujarati, explaining his research findings. He also organised exhibitions at his excavation sites so that the local people could learn the history of their region. He was strongly critical of archaeologists who did not care to share their findings with the public. With his popular writings, Sankalia became a household name all over India, to such an extent that in the popular mind he came to be identified with archaeology. This is a rare achievement in academics and it can be equated with Newton and the Theory of Gravity or Einstein and the Theory of Relativity.

Deccan College remains his lasting contribution. He was a visionary who planned for the future of the institution block by the block during the 35 years of his service. As a student of St Xavier's College, Mumbai received his early training under Father Heras whose encouragement and guidance he always acknowledged as the reason behind his success. Sankalia today is remembered as an exceptionally simple, unassuming, and honest human being. In Deccan College, people still remember him as somebody who was easily accessible to everyone, irrespective of status, in his office, or at home. It seems he took a keen personal interest in the welfare of his students and the employees of the college. During his daily morning walks around campus, people would approach him with their problems; he would listen to their story and then direct the appropriate official to attend to the matter promptly. He had great respect for the dignity of labour and did not consider any type of work inferior to any other. He strongly disapproved of waste and was scrupulous about the thrifty and proper use of both public and private funds. His increasing fame and status did not in the least affect Sankalia's intrinsic humility and simplicity. For example, he avoided being nominated to serve on government committees, since he considered them a distraction from his research.

Brief history of Deccan College

It was established on 6 October 1821 as Hindoo College and it is one of the oldest institutions of modern learning in India. The foundation stone of the present main building of the college was laid on 15 October 1864.

The college started functioning on the new campus on 23 March 1868. At this stage, it was renamed Deccan College in recognition of the enrollment of students from the entire Deccan region. William Wordsworth (grandson of the poet William Wordsworth) and E.A. Wodehouse (brother of P.G. Wodehouse) were principals of the college during 1862-74 and 1934-39 respectively.

Deccan College temporarily shut down its teaching activities in 1934 due to a lack of funding. It was reopened by the order of the Bombay High Court on 17 August 1939 as a post-graduate and research institute for promoting higher learning and research in Indology and Social Sciences. The re-opened institute originally had four teaching and research departments: Archaeology, Linguistics, History, and Sociology-Anthropology.

It was incorporated by the Poona University (now Sabitribai Phule University) in 1948, becoming one of its recognised research institutions. At present, it is a Deemed University with three departments Archaeology, Linguistics, and Sanskrit and Lexicography.

Major books and excavation reports of H. D. Sankalia

1. 1934 The University of Nalanda. Madras. (Revised edition, 1973).
2. 1941 The Archaeology of Gujarat, including Kathiawar. Bombay.
3. 1946 Historical Geography and Cultural Ethnography of Gujarat. Poona.
4. 1946 Investigations into the Prehistoric Archaeology of Gujarat. Baroda.
5. 1952 Excavation at Brahmapuri (Kolhapur) 1945- 46. Poona. Jointly with others.
6. 1952 The Godavari Palaeolithic Industry. Poona.
7. 1955 Report on the Excavations at Nasik and Jorwe 1950-51. Poona. Jointly with others.
8. 1958 Excavations at Maheshwar and Navdatoli. Poona. Jointly with others. 1960 From History to Prehistory at Nevasa. Poona. Jointly with others.
9. 1962 Indian Archaeology Today. Bombay.
10. 1963 Prehistory and Protohistory of India and Pakistan. Bombay. Revised Edition, 1974. Poona.
11. 1965 Excavations at Langhnaj: 1944- 63: Part I Archaeology. Poona.
12. 1965 Introduction to Archaeology. Poona.
13. 1965 Stone Age Tools: Their Techniques and Probable Functions. Poona. Reprinted, 1982.
14. 1969 Excavations at Ahar (Tambavati). Poona. Jointly with others.

15. 1969 Mesolithic and Pre-Mesolithic Industries from the Excavations at Sanganakallu, Bellary 1965. Poona.
16. 1971 Chalcolithic Navdatoli. Poona and Baroda. Jointly with others.
17. 1973 Ramayana: Myth or Reality. New Delhi.
18. 1977 Prehistory in India. New Delhi.
19. 1977 Mahabharata and Ramayana: Fancy or History. Bombay.
20. 1977 Aspects of Indian History and Archaeology (Collected Essays). Delhi.
21. 1978 Prehistoric Art in India. Bombay.
22. 1982 The Ramayana in Historical Perspective. Delhi.
23. 1987 Prehistoric and Historic Archaeology of Gujarat. Delhi.
24. 1988 Excavations at Inamgaon: Volume I, Parts I, and II. Poona. Jointly with others.

11

Professor (Fr.) Stephen Fuchs: An Ethnologist Par Excellence of the Dalits and Tribals of India

Akhono Sakhrie

Professor (Fr.) Stephen Fuchs, SVD, was born on 30th April 1908 at Bruck an der Mur, a town of Styria, Austria. He did his philosophical studies at Sankt Augustin near Bonn, Germany thereafter he returned to Austria to pursue Theological studies at St. Gabriel Institution. Although initially trained to be a priest, three interconnected events turned the course of his life completely. The first turning point came when he met Prof. Wilhelm Schmidt, SVD, and the founder of *Anthropos* and the Culture Historical School of Ethnology, who introduced him to Anthropology. Eventually, this encounter motivated him to dedicate the rest of his life to scholarly pursuits in Anthropology. Secondly, Fuchs joined SVD (Society of the Divine Word) in 1927 which was a Catholic religious congregation dedicated to the study of cultures of humanity. It was dedicated to training its members to serve people in different cultural settings. In many ways, this proved beneficial to Fuchs in pursuing his interest in Anthropological studies. Thirdly, in 1934, Fuchs reached Indore, a city of Madhya Pradesh, wherein the society of the Divine Word had begun their charity work from 1932 onwards. Here, he spent his first few years learning the local dialects, Hindi and English, which not only built the foundation for his later anthropological works but also developed into a deep attachment with the rich Indian tribal and *Dalit* heritage that would last for more than 60 years. He can be considered as a contemporary of Verrier Elwin as they both brought out their first work in the 1930s. However, the irony remains that Professor Fuchs and his works remain relatively unknown.

Professor Fuchs started his first research work among the Chamar, an untouchable caste of central India. He was attracted by their culture and published his first article in 1937 on their marriage customs and festivals in *Anthropos*. Besides the untouchable castes, he also studied several tribal communities in central India. He also reflected on the observations and notes he had already collected on the customs and beliefs of the Nimar Balahis. He was arrested around 1944 as he was mistaken to be a German spy but in 1945 it was discovered that he was an Austrian and was released. By this time, he had collected rich data from his fieldwork. So, reflecting on his rich research findings from India, during his confinement sparked in him the idea of starting a research institute for culture in India. He taught for a very brief period in various universities, firstly, as Professor of Cultural Anthropology at St. Xavier's college Bombay (1950-54); secondly, on Physical and Cultural Anthropology at various Institutes in India; and thirdly, at the Philippines at San Carlos University, Cebu City as a Visiting Professor of Anthropology and Indian Philosophy. But he soon realised that teaching was not his cup of tea, as it affected his first love – anthropological fieldwork. Eventually, he followed his heart and chose to concentrate only on doing research. This proved a blessing, as he became a remarkable researcher, and ethnographer par excellence especially of the *Dalits* and tribals of India leaving behind a legacy paralleled only by a few. In 1950, he was awarded a doctorate from the University of Vienna, for his study of the Bhumias (a branch of the Baiga tribe). His dissertation was entitled "*Das Schweineopfer der Baiga in seinen kulturhistorischen Beziehungen*" (Pig Sacrifice among the Baiga in its Culture- Historical Context). Around the same time, along with Matthias Hermans, SVD, he opened the Indian branch of Anthropos Institute, Bombay at Bandra (central Bombay) which later was renamed as, 'Institute of Indian Culture' in 1967. This Institute became the starting point for extensive research projects and studies as well as a meeting place and conference center for researchers, scientists, and interested people of various nationalities, religions, races, and castes. A well-stocked library was also established eventually. Later (after about twenty-six years), the Institute was moved (along with its library) to Andheri (North-west Bombay) where Fuchs lived, worked, wrote, and published till his final departure for Austria in 1996. He spent his last days, in an ailing condition with poor health and passed away on 7th January 2000 at St. Gabriel, Mödling, Austria.

Contributions to Indian anthropology

Globally, Professor Fuchs was well known among social scientists as an anthropologist-cum-folklorist-cum-social scientist, the one who dedicated himself to scholarly activities for the cause of Indian people, particularly the *Dalit* and the tribals. He had worked on aspects of archaeological anthropology and physical anthropology too, but his heart was in cultural anthropology, especially about the downtrodden and unrecorded groups in India. He was the first to examine their cultures to understand and record his insights on them for posterity. During his lifetime he made enormous contributions to the study of the cultural wealth of India, undertaking several critically acclaimed research projects which were eventually written into massive volumes.

He not only engaged in research *per se* but he also strived towards a vision for anthropology in India. He delivered lectures at various seminars, conferences, and anthropological meetings to make the Indian students aware of their own cultures and also the culture of the tribals in India. His main aim was to make them responsible and sensitive to the cultural diversity surrounding them. Along with all these, he also maintained his research and writing at an amazing tempo, he contributed to various journals and was on the editorial board of one prominent journal too. He was a source of inspiration to a large number of scholars who researched the marginalised people of India. It will also be worth mentioning here, that during his time of academic exercise in India, a host of celebrated scholars namely, Nirmal Kumar Bose, Verrier Elwin, G.S. Ghurye, T.C. Das, K.P. Chatopadhayay, D.N. Majumdar, Irawati Karve, A.R. Desai, S.C. Sinha, L.P. Vidhayarthi, B.K. Roy Burman, P.K. Bhowmick, S.C. Dube, and others made a substantial contribution to Indian Anthropology placing it on the global arena. Side by side, his involvement with the St. Xavier's College and his establishment of the 'Institute of Indian Culture', further aided in bringing Indian Anthropology to the global standards. In his lifetime, he produced enormous quantities of written material but out of which only 22 books and 150 articles (around 9000 published pages) would be recorded. The rest of his unpublished materials it is said was discarded after he left for Austria which is unfortunate, as some of his important works might have been lost before they could see daylight.

As stated, Professor Fuchs contributed immensely to Indian Anthropology both as a researcher and as a pioneer in the field. However, it would be quite impossible to enumerate all of that in just one article due to paucity of time and space. Therefore, given below are some selected important contributions made by him.

Contribution to *Dalit* studies

His most important contribution was to the study of lower caste beliefs and customs, especially among the Nimar Balahis and Chamar caste groups. In one of his earliest articles, '*Nimar Balahi Code of Caste Laws and Its Enforcement*' (1943) he describes in great detail the maintenance of rules and regulations among the Balahi, which he states is a special task entrusted to the *panchayat* of each community. It served as the biggest motivation for the Balahis to stay on a straight course of life which is however low compared to general moral standards. The downside of this dependence on the *panchayat* results in them was becoming morally loose when they migrate to another place without such a strict body to govern their activities. Interestingly, this *panchayat* is again presided by a higher authority called *Jat-Patels* controlled by the higher castes. Beyond this *Jat-Patels,* no appeals are possible, except to the state authority. Here he not only gave great detail of hitherto unknown aspects of the lower castes groups, but his writings also reflected a soft corner for these oppressed *Dalits* (as well as the tribals). For example, in the end, he poignantly states that 'treated as untouchables and outcasts by the higher castes, exploited by their employers, the Balahis have little means to protect and defend their most elementary rights. Thus, they have a little self-respect, and not much moral strength or ambition...A great part of the Balahis lead morally good lives.'(pg. 104)

His ethnography of the Nimar Bilahis in the book '*The Children of the Hari*' (1950) turned out to be a monumental classic. It was the first ethnographic volume and first comprehensive scientific study of a *Harijan* caste in India. Herein, he also clearly and boldly states that if entire India is to progress, it should stop the maltreatment of the depressed classes who constitute a majority of the Indian population and instead assign to them a proper category. Otherwise, he warns in the long run this might give rise to disruptive and divisive political movements within India or in extreme cases severance of this category of people from the Hindu religion and society.

His other book '*At the Bottom of Indian Society*' (1980) also highlighted unknown aspects of caste in India. Firstly, he provided an alternative explanation for the origin of caste and untouchability in India, dating it back to the pre-Aryan past of the Aryans and Dravidians, and threw light on some rarely mentioned aspects in the literature on caste and untouchability. Thus, putting forth the idea that untouchability originated among the high caste groups and the caste system can be terminated only when these higher caste groups cooperate. Secondly, he gave a detailed overview of different Harijan castes in India. Finally, he offered practical implications for the abolition of untouchability and solving the problem of casteism which had been a perpetual source of tension and conflict in India.

Contribution to Indian tribal life and culture

His other important contribution was to the field of study of tribal communities in central India, especially those considered insignificant by other anthropologists. He carried out fieldwork among tribal groups, such as the Bhils and Bhilalas of Madhya Pradesh; Gonds, Baigas, and Bhumias (a branch of the Baiga) of Eastern Mandla; and Korkus of the Vindhya Hills.

His book, '*The Aboriginal Tribes of India*' (1977) provided a valuable introduction to tribal India and attempts to provide the most suitable perspective with which this growing segment of the Indian population needed to be approached. He also painted a vivid picture of the tribal scene in its cultural spectrum. Towards the end, as a matter-of-factly he advocates making the welfare activities carried out by the government for their upliftment, to be more proactive and participatory which gave his work a very modern contemporary outlook, an aspect Indian Anthropologists are striving to attain even in the present.

In '*The Gonds and Bhumias of Eastern Mandla*' (1968), he tries to demonstrate how the Gonds and the Bhumias are inter-related and inter-depended on each other at different levels. He opines that though they both borrowed many cultural traits from their neighbouring Hindus yet they remain loyal to their own traditional tribal culture and traditions. In this book, he also focuses on the aspects of changes brought among them due to contact with a modern civilisation which has led to the loss of many of their original cultural traits and ensued a constant struggle to fit into the new ideals. However, he ends on an optimistic note that the numerous welfare measures undertaken by the Government will have a positive impact at all levels.

Professor Fuchs also gave detailed information on the Korkus, who are the westernmost branch of the Munda tribes, through his monograph '*The Korkus of the Vindhya Hills*' (1988). It was believed that before this monograph was written anthropologists used to rely on gazetteers or census accounts to get information on the Korkus. But thanks to Fuchs who offered a reliable, exhaustive, holistic, description of the Korku way of life and culture. His description ranged widely from their material culture, kinship and family, village and tribal organisation, rituals, beliefs, magic, folklore, and mythology, which was sufficient to serve as a sort of thesaurus of the Korkus for generations of an anthropologist to come.

Original and path-breaking contributions

Professor Fuchs works were not only those concerning the lower strata of people in India, he also contributed some original works of his own which are given below:

Methodology: He was greatly influenced by his mentor Prof. Wilhelm Schmidt, who was a diffusionist, and as a result, he considered anthropology as a historical science. Accordingly, he believed that the ethnohistorical approach to anthropology remains valid and is indispensable for an understanding of contemporary cultures of any level and complexity. He opines that the development of the human races and cultures bring order and system into the confusing abundance of anthropological data and allows its division into different human strata such as food gatherers, primitive hunters, advanced hunters, primitive cultivators, and nomadic animal breeders. At the same time, he cautions that when anthropology is spoken as a science, one should not make the mistake of demanding from it the precision and method of the natural sciences.

Secondly, he dealt with the origin of human art, incorporating human art, painting and sculpture, poetry, dramatic art, dancing, and music and proposes that since cultural anthropology analyses and studies cultural forms which man produced deliberately and by his ingenuity, in this way also anthropology should be considered as a historical science.

Religion: Besides his general contributions towards understanding tribal beliefs and practices both for the Indian and western audiences, and Vaishnavism, Islam, Zoroastrianism, Jainism, and Buddhism, a few of his unique contributions to the understanding of religion stand out.

In his works, '*Rebellious Prophets: A Study of Messianic Movements in Indian Religions*', '*The Origin of Man and His Culture*' (1983), and '*Messianic Movements in Primitive India*' (1965), etc., Professor Fuchs makes an original contribution by providing information on messianic movements, specifically focusing on the Indian scenario. He states that messianic movements are not indigenous to the Christian religion but is present in the societies where a cultural clash occurred between populations in different stages of cultural development. He goes on to enumerate 14 important features or traits of all messianic movements hitherto not provided by any other. Side by side, he also invites anthropologists to undertake scientific analysis and contemporary interpretation of many simmering movements that will have all-pervading and the highest practical significance. Similarly, in his book, '*The Origin of Man and His Culture*' (1983) and some other articles, his suggestion for understanding the origin of religion is also quite interesting and distinctive and contrary to many other theorists. He states that the study of 'primitive' religions will not provide an accurate picture of the earliest religion; one can only assume the earliest religion from such studies. He also does not quite agree with the evolutionary scheme of the development of religion. Instead, he suggests that studying the religious beliefs and practices of the present-day food gatherers and subsequently food-producers will provide more accurate data about the origin of religion. He elaborately provides data from many such societies in the world to establish his proposition.

Impact of cultural contact: Another noteworthy area of exploration by Fuchs is the observation and analysis of the courses of development of Hindu caste groups, the lower castes and untouchables, and aboriginal or tribal groups, after contact with modern civilisation. Through his works, he shows that the high-caste Hindus are getting more and more unorthodox in their views as well as in their behaviour. On the other hand, the lower castes and the untouchables were becoming more and more orthodox by attempting to imitate the higher caste members. Thus, they seem to move along a path diametrically opposite to that of the higher caste groups. In contrast, he is perplexed with the position of the aboriginal tribes, with some of them try desperately clinging to their traditional ways of living but some of them (similar to the lower castes groups) were trying to get themselves into the Hindu fold and gain equal status with the high-castes in the process rapidly amalgamating their culture with the more dominant culture of Hinduism.

Awards, titles, and honours

This great ethnologist of India received many awards and Honours in recognition of his contributions, both nationally and internationally. They were as follows:

- The University of Mumbai, recognising his enormous contributions to the understanding of Indian culture and society, upgraded his Institute of Indian Culture to a Postgraduate Research Center in Anthropology and Sociology in 1997. Thereafter, it was given the right to admit students for the degrees of MA (by research) and Ph.D. in Sociology and Anthropology.
- On March 26, 1998, he was Honoured by the Austrian Government, *Bundesministerium für Bildung, Wissenschaft*

und Kultur (Federal Ministry of Education, Science, and Culture) and received the Honourary Cross for Science and Art First Class for his scientific work and his fifty-year long dedication to research among the tribes of India.

- He was also awarded the Golden Doctor Diploma award (50 years after his doctorate) on 14th November 1999 particularly for his contributions to the field of Indian Anthropology stating that he had '...gained the highest merit for the ethnology of India' *(qui de ethnologia Indiae optime meritus est).*
- In appreciation of his contribution to Indian Anthropology Professor S.M. Michael, SVD, the director of the Institute of Indian Culture edited two Festschrifts in his Honour,
    1. *Anthropology as a Historical Science: Essays in Honour of Stephen Fuchs* (1984).
    2. *Dalits in Modern India: Visions and Values* (2007).
- *Sanskriti* – North Eastern Institute of Culture and Religion, Guwahati instituted an award in his name and five lectures were delivered by prominent anthropologists from 2008 (his centenary year) till 2009.

Criticisms

Professor Fuchs is generally criticized for being too general in his presentation and which he does not deny. However, he proceeds to justify himself stating the limitation of time and space. For example, in his book, '*The Origin of Man and His Culture*' (1983), in the preface, he explains: "Some critics have complained that the book contains many undue generalisations. But such generalisations are unavoidable in a book of such limited size. A more detailed description of the development of human culture would require many volumes." (p. ix) Another aspect of this generalising is making cultural correlations and clubbing together with some selected societies randomly to formulate a Grand theory. As one of his critic states, "Illustration with a half a dozen examples is not at all a convincing demonstration of a generalisation for scores or hundreds of societies...." (Befu, 1965; 170).

Secondly, the drawback cited in his work is the problem of the reliability of data (Pflug, 2018). Any research to be accepted should undergo the process of reliability. In his case, due to the pioneering nature of most of his work whether his data is reliable or not, there is no way of confirming it. Additionally, he does not analyze his data using a grounded theoretical framework. This too he agrees openly but leaves it for other future scientists to work it out which leads to a sense of awkwardness and incompleteness for someone going through his works. However, keeping in mind the fact that he entered the scene at the pioneering stage of Indian Anthropology and a transitional phase of global anthropology Professor Fuchs undeniably succeeded in giving a fresh perspective and thrust to anthropological studies in India.

List of published works

Books and Articles

1937 'Die Hochzeitsgebräuche der Balahis'. *Anthropos* 32: 885-904.

1937-38 'Het Problem der Kastenlozen', *Voor-Indie. Studien* (Hertogenbusch) (November): 388-394, (January): 20-29.

1939a 'Birth and childhood among the Balahis'. *Primitive Man* 12:71-84.

1939b 'The origin of the idea of God'. *The New Review*, Calcutta (November): 397-409.

1940a 'The cult of the Dhaj Mata'. *The New Review*, Calcutta (October): 341-347.

1940b 'The funeral rites of the Nimar Balahis'. *Primitive Man* 13: 49-79.

1940c 'They make vows!'. *The New Review*, Calcutta (November): 392-398.

1940d 'Tracing monotheism in India'. *The New Review*, Calcutta (August): 120-129.

1941a 'Anthropométrie measurements of Barelas'. *Census of Central India*; Vol. 16: Holkar State, Part 1: pp. 307- 310.

1941b 'Anthropométrie measurements of Bhils'. *Census of Central India*; Vol. 16: Holkar State, Part 1: pp. 301-306.

1941c 'Anthropométrie measurements of Nimar Balahis'. *Census of Central India*; Vol. 16: Holkar State, Part 1: pp. 291-299.

1941d 'Calling the monsoon'. *The New Review*, Calcutta (July): 54-57.

1941e 'Changes in the low castes of Central India'. *The New Review*, Calcutta (November): 370-377.

1941f 'The cult of the earth-mother among the Nimar-Balahis'. *Internationales Archiv für Ethnographie* 40,1 -3: 1-8.

1941g 'Holi'. *The New Review*, Calcutta (March): 208-214.

1941h 'Of princely blood. The sweeper caste of India'. *The Christian Family and Our Missions* (Techny): 373.

1941i 'Priests of the earth-mother. Strange cult of Kali-Mata among the aboriginals of Central Provinces'. *The Bombay Chronicle* (February 23).

1942a 'Clan-god myths and worship among the Nimar Balahis'. In: J. P. Mills et al. (Eds.), *Essays in Anthropology Presented to Rai Bahadur Sarat Chandra Roy*; pp. 194-205. Maxwell, Lucknow.

1942b 'The hand-loom industry in the Khandwa Tahsil, District Nimar, Central Provinces'. *Journal of the K. R. Cama Oriental Institute Bombay* 35: 52-57. *Anthropos* 95.2000 540 Berichte und Kommentare.

1942c 'The marriage rites of the Bhils'. *Man in India* 22: 105-139.

1942d 'The matriarchal elements in the ethnography of the Nimar Balahis'. *New Indian Antiquary* 5,4-5: 1-18.

1942e 'Mysterious islands'. *The New Review*, Calcutta (July): 63-73.

1942f 'Property concepts among the Nimar Balahis'. *Journal of the Bombay Branch of the Royal Asiatic Society* 18: 79-89.

1942g 'Racial problems'. *The New Review*, Calcutta 15, 85 (January): 9-28.

1943a 'Aboriginal education in Central India'. *Princely India* (August 22 and 29, September 5, 12, and 19: 4-5.

1943b 'Aboriginal uplift work in Hyderabad state and elsewhere'. *Princely India*, Khandwa 22, 37 (October 31): 1-2, 22, 38 (November 7): 1-2.

1943c 'Is India a Nation?' (by Mr. Straight Forward) *Princely India*, Khandwa 22, 33 (October 3): 1-2, 22, 34 (October 10): 1-2.

1943d 'The Nimar Balahi code of caste laws and its enforcement'. *Primitive Man* 16: 81-104.

1943e 'Primitive culture'. *The New Review*, Calcutta 18,104 (August): 105-121.

1943f 'The primitive family'. *The New Review*, Calcutta 18,108 (December): 436-448.

1943g 'The scales of Sitala Mata'. *The Christian Family and Our Missions* (Techny): 454.

1943h 'The secret of the Mask'. *The New Review*, Calcutta (February): 146-158.

1943i 'The Vikings of the Pacific'. *The Examiner*, Bombay (May 29): 256-257.

1944 'The Nimar sweepers'. *The New Review*, Calcutta 20,115: 54-69.

1945 'Property among primitive peoples'. *The New Review*, Calcutta 22,127: 5-12.

1945 *The Great Synthesis*. Ranchi: Catholic Press. (The Light of East, 32)

1946-49a 'Changes and developments in the population of the Nimar District in the Central Provinces of India'. *Anthropos* 41-44: 49-68.

1946-49b 'What some tribes and castes of Central India think about God'. *Anthropos* 41-44: 883-887.

1947 *Non-Christian Parallels in the Christian Religion*. Ranchi: Catholic Press.

1950 'A snake ceremonial cure of the Bhumia'. *Primitive Man* 23: 1-13.

1950 *The Children of Hari. A Study of the Nimar Balahis in the Central Provinces of India.*

1951a 'Ancient cultural links between America, Asia, and Oceania'. *The Journal of the Anthropological Society of Bombay* 5, 2: 51-75.

1951b 'Ancient links between Asia and America'. *Bharat Jyoti* (February 4).

1951c 'Anthropology and the Missions'. 197-200.

1951d 'The original wedding ritual of the Bhil'. *Anthropos* 46: 256.

1951f 'Tattooing among the Baiga'. *The Word* 10,8: 229-230.

1952a 'Another version of the Baiga creation myth'. *Anthropos* 47: 607-619.

1952b 'Ansätze zu einer einheimischen christlichen Kunst in Indien'. *Zeitschrift für Missionswissenschaft und Religionswissenschaft* 36: 127-133.

1952c 'The parrot. Indian folk tale retold'. *The Word* 11,5: 161-165.

1952e 'The social organisation of the Gond in Eastern Mandla, Central India'. In: Wilhelm Koppers, Robert Heine Geldern und Josef Haekel (Hrsg.), *Kultur und Sprache;* pp. 204-217. Wien: Verlag Herold. (Wiener Beiträge zur Kulturgeschichte und Linguistik, 9)

1953 *Jïvan Srot* [*Am Quell des Lebens. Eine Erklärung des Taufritus*]. Indore: Satprachar Press.

1953a 'Changes in Soviet marriage and family law'. *Sociological Bulletin* 21: 35-46.

1953b 'The contribution of Anthropology to Indian history'. In: B. G. Gokhale (ed.), *Indica. The Indian Historical Research Institute Silver Jubilee Commemoration Volume*; pp. 154-160. Bombay: St. Xavier's College.

1953c 'From birth control to maternity medal'. *The Bombay Chronicle* (April 5): 12 and 17.

1953d 'Individual and communal property concepts among primitive peoples'. *The Journal of the Anthropological Society of Bombay* ll: 9-28.

1953e 'Joseph Schmidts (t) Vokabular und Grammatik der Murik Sprache in Nordost-Neuguinea'. *Anthropos* 48: 274-277.

1956a 'Anthropological research problems in Central India'. In: Robert Heine Geldern et al. (Eds), *Actes du 4e Session du Congrès International des Sciences Anthropologiques et Ethnologiques*, Vienne, 1-8 September1952; Vol.3: Etimologica: pp. 276-280. Wien: Verlag Adolf Holzhausens.

1956b 'Der Hochgottglaube bei den Primitivstämmen des nordöstlichen Vorderindien'. In: J. Haekel et al. (Hrsg.), *Die Wiener Schule der Völkerkunde*. The Vienna School of Ethnology. Festschrift anläßlich des 25 jährigen Bestandes des Institutes für Völkerkunde der Universität Wien (1929-1954); pp. 281-290. Wien: Verlag Ferdinand Berger.

1956c 'Prehistoric and primitive races in India'. *The Leader* 16 (September): 2. 1956-57.

1956d 'The priests in primitive religion. Mens nostra'. *Annual of Sacred Heart Seminary, Poonamallee* (Madras): 6-7.

1957 *Social Origins*. Bombay: Gyanayatan Publications.

1957a 'The Aborigines of India'. *Apostolic Approach* (Nagpur): 39-42.

1957b 'Anthropological research problems in India'. *International Social Science Bulletin* 9: 341-351.

1958 'Bhagat movements in Chotanagpur'. *Bulletin of the Tribal Research Institute Chhindawara* 2: 84-87.

1959a 'Renaissance in tribal life'. *The Madhya Pradesh Chronicle*, Bhopal (December 13): 3.

1959b The Scheduled Castes of Northern India. *Apostolic Approach* (Nagpur): 26-33.

1959c 'Tribal life in Central India'. *The Asia Bulletin* (Bombay) 7 (December 6): 3.

1951e 'The scavengers of the Nimar District in Madhya Pradesh'. *Journal of the Bombay Branch of the Royal Asiatic Society* 27,1: 86-98.

1960a 'Central tribes'. *Seminar (*Delhi) 14: 35-38.

1960a *The Gond and Bhumia of Eastern Mandla*. Asia Publishing House, London.

1960b *Tales of Gondavana*. Dhawale Popular. Bombay (Nandi Books, 3).

1960b 'The origin of human culture and society'. *Indian Sociologist* 2,3: 6-14.

1961 'Comment on integration of culture. A review of concepts' by E. E. Hoyt. *Current Anthropology* 2: 420. 1962 Korku Magic Rites. Caritas (Alwaye): 43-47.

1963 *The Origin of Man and His Culture*. Asia Publishing House London (2nd Edition, Munshi Monoharlal, 1983).

1963a 'The aboriginal races in North-Eastern Central India'. In: *Festschrift Paul Schebesta Zum* 75. Geburtstag; pp. 349-356. Mödling: St. Gabriel Verlag. (Studia Instituti Anthropos, 18.

1963b 'Messianic and chiliastic movements among Indian'. *Aboriginals. Studia Missionalia* 13: 85-103.

1964a 'Anthropometry of the Gujarat tribes'. In: P. G. Shah (Ed.), *Tribal Life in Gujarat. An Analytical Study of the Cultural Changes with Special Reference to the Dhanka Tribe*; pp. 263-275. Bharatiya Vidya Bhavan, Bombay.

1964b 'Magic healing techniques among the Balahis in Central India'. In: Ari Kiev (ed.), *Magic, Faith, and Healing*. Anthropos 95.2000 Berichte und Kommentare 541 Studies in Primitive Psychiatry Today; London.

1965 *Rebellious Prophets: A Study of Messianic Movements in Indian Religions*. Asia Publishing House, Bombay (Publications of the Indian Branch of the Anthropos Institute, 1).

1965a 'Folktales of the Gond and Baiga in Eastern Mandla'. *Asian Folklore Studies* 24, 2: 53-116.

1965b 'Introduction'. In: Sher Singh "Sher" *The Sansis of Punjab*; pp. ix-xi. Munshiram Manorharlal, Delhi.

1965c 'Die magischen Vorstellungen der Korku'. *Mitteilungen der Anthropologischen Gesellschaft in Wien* 95: 92-100.

1965d 'Messianic movements in primitive India'. *Asian Folklore Studies* 24,1: 11-62.

1966a 'Clan organisation among the Korkus'. *Journal of Asian and African Studies* 1: 213-219.

1966b 'Comment on Une Sous-Caste d'Inde du Sud and Hierarchy and Marriage Alliance in South Indian Kinship' by L. Dumont. *Current Anthropology* 7: 330-331.

1966c 'Messianic movements in Tribal India'. *Journal of the Anthropological Society of Bombay* 12,1: 15-33.

1966-67 'The Dravidian problem'. *Journal of the Asiatic Society of Bombay* 41-42: 153-163.

1967a 'Anthropométrie analysis of the Waghris'. In: P. G. Shah, *Vimukta Jatis. Denotified Communities in Western India;* pp. 124-145. Bombay: Gujarat Research Society.

1967b 'Foreword'. In: E.W. Baptista, *The East Indians. Catholic Community of Bombay, Salsette, and Bassein*; pp. iv-vii. The Bombay East Indian Association, Bombay.

1968 *The Gond and Bhumia of Eastern Mandla*. New Literature Publishing Company, Bombay. [2nd, rev. ed.]

1968a 'The Germans at Rourkela'. *The Journal of the Anthropological Society of Bombay* 13,1: 56-68.

1968b 'Laru Kaj, ein Schweinefest in Zentralindien'. In: *Anthropica. Gedenkschrift zum* 100. Geburtstag von P.W. Schmidt; pp. 126-140. St. Augustin: Verlag des Anthropos-Institute. (Studia Instituti Anthropos, 21)

1968c 'The Ugly Missionary'. *Verbum SVD* 10: 303-306.

1968d 'Die Zukunft der Urstämme Indiens'. *Deutsch Indische Blätter* (Bombay) 10, 3-4: 8.

1969a 'Applied Anthropology in India'. In: M. C. Pradhan et al. (eds.), *Anthropology and Archaeology.* Essays in

Commemoration of Verrier Elwin, 1902-1964; pp. 258 -271. Oxford University Press, Bombay.

1969b 'The High-God belief among the primitive tribes of Northeast India'. In: John V. Ferreira, Stephen Fuchs, and Klaus Klostermaier (eds.), *Essays in Ethnology*; 328-339. New Literature Publishing Company, Bombay.

1969c 'Nomadic tribes in the plains of North India'. *Journal of Gujarat Research Society* 31 (April): 92-101.

1969d 'A Royal "Saviour" of the Bastar tribes'. *The Journal of the Anthropological Society of Bombay* 14,1: 1-15.

1969e 'Urgent anthropological research in Middle India'. *Urgent Research in Social Anthropology* 10: 1-7.

1972 *Sagen und Geschichten aus Indien*. St. Augustin: Steyler Verlag.

1972a 'Anthropométrie analysis of the Korkus and Nahais in the Melghat'. *Man in India* 52: 73-81.

1972b 'Land scarcity and land hunger among some aboriginal tribes of Western Central India'. In: K. Suresh Singh (Ed.), *The Tribal Situation in India*; 367-373. Indian Institute of Advanced Study, Shimla.

1972c 'A new mission method for India'. *Verbum SVD* 13: 225 -235.

1973a 'Mahatma Phule and the "Indianisation" of the Church'. Verbum SVD 14: 237-240.

1973b 'Priests and magicians in aboriginal India'. *Studia Missionaliall*: 201-236.

1973c 'Shamanism among the Korkus of Central India'. Fu Jen Studies (Commemorative Issue): 11-19.

1973d 'Völker und Stämme Indiens'. *Steyler Missionschronik* (St. Augustin): 37-41.

1974 *The Aboriginal Tribes of India*. The Macmillan Company of India, Delhi (2nd edition, 1977).

1975 'Origin of religion'. *Introduction to History of Religion*. Alwaye: Pontifical Institute of Theology and Philosophy. (Pontifical Institute Publications, 19).

1975a 'The concept of sin among the Indian aboriginal tribes'. *Verbum SVD*, 16: 40-58. Anthropos 95.2000

1975b 'The Indian concept of family'. *Home Life* (Bombay): 27, 29.

1975c 'Indian women through the ages'. *Home Life* (Bombay): 11-12.

1975d 'The Korku family'. In: Dhirendra Narain (Ed.), *Explorations in the Family and Other Essays*. Prof. K. M. Kapadia Commemoration Volume; pp. 163-192. Thacker and Co, Bombay.

1976a 'The religio-ethical concepts of the Chamars in Northern India'. *Missiology* 4: 43-52.

1976b 'Strange marriage customs'. *Home Life* (Bombay): 50- 53.

1977a 'Central Indian tribes'. In: Romesh Thapar (Ed.), *Tribe, Caste, and Religion in India;* pp. 47-53. Macmillan of India, Delhi.

1977b 'Comment on the primitive norm and its evolution' by A.I. Pershits. *Current Anthropology* 18: 413-414.

1977c 'Courting'. *Home Life* (Bombay): 16-19.

1977d 'Pre-marriage period'. *Home Life* (Bombay): 18-21.

1977e 'The tribal population of Dadra and Nagar Haveli'. In: *St. Francis Xavier Mission Souvenir*; pp. 29-34. Klianvel.

1978a 'The Baiga understanding of ultimate reality and meaning'. *Ultimate Reality and Meaning* 1: 153-180.

1978b 'The origin of the Mundas'. In: P. Ponette (Ed.), *The Munda World*. Hoffmann Commemoration Volume; pp. 68-80. Catholic Press, Ranchi.

1979 *Anthropology for the Missions*. St. Paul Publications, Allahabad.

1979a 'Messianic movements in India'. In: Akshayakumar R. Desai (Ed.), *Peasant Struggles in India*; pp. 28-46. Oxford University Press, Bombay.

1979b 'Preface'. In: Mahipal Bhuriya, Folk-Songs of the Bhils; pp. iii. Mahipal Publications, Indore.

1979c 'Some facts and figures'. *Christianity in India. A Critical Study*. Vivekananda Kendra Patrika 8, 2: 80- 83.

1980a 'The Christian situation in Varanasi Diocese'. *Indian Missiological Review* 2: 232-240.

1980b 'Euthanasia in India'. *Sevartham* 5: 4-25.

1981 *At the Bottom of Indian Society. The Harijan and Other Low Castes*. Munshiram Manoharlal Publishers, New Delhi.

1981a 'Culture in the service of evangelisation in India'. *Indian Missiological Review* 3: 4-18.

1981b 'Marriage problems of Congo'. *The Journal of Family Welfare* 17 (June): 31-35.

1982a 'Besessenheit und Exorzismus in nichtchristlichen Religionen'. In: *Egon von Petersdorff, Dämonologie;* Bd. 1: 423-424. Stein am Rhein: Christiana-Verlag.

1982b 'The Bhils. People of the bow'. In: *Gods of the Byways*; pp. 33-47. Museum of Modern Art, Oxford.

1982c 'The concept of salvation in tribal religions'. *Indian Missiological Review* 4: 361-372.

1982d 'A different Christmas story'. *Home Life* (Bombay): 6-9.

1985 'Family planning in India'. *Verbum SVD* 26: 389-398.

1986a 'Anthropométrie measurements of Barelas'., *Human Science* 35,4: 348-360.

1986b 'Anthropométrie measurements of Bhils'. *Human Science* 35,3: 251-266.

1986c 'The conversion of the tribes'. *Indian Missiological Review* 8: 102-114.

1987 'Anthropométrie measurements of Nimar Balahis'. *Human Science* 36,1: 92-126.

1988 *The Korkus of the Vindhya Hills*. Inter- India Publications, New Delhi. (Tribal Studies of India Series, T 124)

1988a 'Anthropology in the service of the Indian Missions'. In: Joachim G. Piepke (Ed.), *Anthropology, and Mission*. SVD

International Consultation on Anthropology for Mission (Pune, India, Dec. 29, 1986, to Jan. 4, 1987); Berichte und Kommentare 113-122. Nettetal: Steyler Verlag - Wort (Studia Instituti Missiologici Societatis 41).

1988b 'Inculturation. An Anthropological and Theological Perspective'. In: Lars Thunberg (Ed.), *Dialogue in Action. Essays in Honour of Johannes Aagaard*; pp. 134-151. Prajna Publications, New Delhi.

1990 *Das Leben ist ein Tanz. Lieder der indischen Ureinwoh-ner. Ausgewählt, aus den Stammessprachen übersetzt und eingeleitet von* Stefan Fuchs. Zürich: Benziger Verlag.

1990a 'The importance of Anthropology for evangelisation'. *Indian Missiological Review* 12,1: 5-16.

1990b 'The races of Northeast India'. *Indian Missiological Review* 12,3-4: 160-172.

1993 'The races of Northeast India'. In: S. Karotemprel (ed.), *The Catholic Church in Northeast India,* 1890-1990; pp. 363-377. Shillong: Vendrame Institute.

1992a *The Aboriginal Tribes of India*. New Delhi: Inter-India Publications. (Tribal Studies of India Series, T 152) [3rd, rev. ed.]

1992b *Godmen on the Warpath. A Study of Messianic Movements in India*. Munshiram Manoharlal Publishers, New Delhi.

1995a 'Evangelisation among Dalits'. *Indian Missiological Review* 17,1: 31-37.

1995b 'The fundamentalists'. *Indian Missiological Review* 17, 2: 5-11.

1996 *The Vedic Horse Sacrifice in Its Culture-Historical Relations*. Inter-India Publications, New Delhi.

Articles

India Wien: Verlag Herold. (*Wiener Beiträge zur Kulturgeschichte und Linguistik*, 8.

Coauthored Works

Silva, Séverine, and Stephen Fuchs 1965 'The marriage customs of the Christians in South Canara, India'. *Asian Folklore Studies* 24,2: 1 -52.

Verhoeven, Theodor, and Stephen Fuchs 1959 'A microlithic site at Adamgarh. *Anthropos*, 54: 580-581.

Edited volumes

Ferreira, John V., Stephen Fuchs, and Klaus Klostermaier (Eds.) 1969 *Essays in Ethnology*. New Literature Publishing Company, Bombay.

Festschrift in his honour

Bhuriya, Mahipal, and S.M. Michael (Eds.) 1984. *Anthropology as a Historical Science. Essays in Honour of Stephen Fuchs*. Sat Prakashan Sanchar Kendra, Indore.

Ferreira, John V.1991. Stephen Fuchs, In Christopher Winters (Ed.), *International Dictionary of Anthropologists*; p. 221. Garland Publishing, New York.

D'Silva, Louis, et al. n.d. 'The Christian contribution to tribal uplift and welfare'. In: L. D'Silva et al. (Eds): *Christian Community and the National Mainstream*; pp. 168-178. E. Pinto, Bombay.

References

Befu, Harumi. 1965. 'The origin of man and his culture'. Stephen Fuchs. *American Anthropologist*, 67, 1:170-171.

Fuchs, S. 1943. 'The Nimar Balahi code of caste laws and its enforcement'. *Primitive Man*, 16, 3,4 81. doi: 10.2307/3316280.

Fuchs, S., 1949. 'Changes and developments in the population of the Nimar district in the Central Provinces of India'. *Anthropos*, 1, 3: 49-68. Retrieved March 10, 2020.

Fuchs, S., 1950. *The Children of Hari*. 1st ed. Verlag Herold, Vienna.

Fuchs, S., 1965. 'Messianic movements in primitive India'. *Asian Folklore Studies*, 24,1:11.

Fuchs, S., 1983. *The Origin of Man and His Culture*. 2nd Ed. New Delhi Munshiram Manoharlal Publishers Pvt. Ltd.

Jose, K., & Bera, G. 2013. *Remembering the Rebellious Prophet-*. New Delhi: Abhijeet Publications in collaboration with Sanskriti-NEICR (SVD), Guwahati.

Micheal, S. M., 2000. 'Obituaries Stephen Fuchs SVD (1908-2000) Founder of the Institute of Indian Culture'. *Asian Folklore Studies;* Nagoya, 9, 1: 141-145. Retrieved December 10, 2019, from www.search.proquest.com/openview.

Salmen, Josef and Ernest Brandewie 2000. 'Fr. Stephen Fuchs (1908-2000)'. *Anthropos*, 95,2: 537-542. Retrieved March 10, 2020.

12

Contribution of Christoph von Fürer-Haimendorf Towards Anthropological Studies in India

Juri Borah

Early life and education

C von Fürer-Haimendorf, the future renowned anthropologist was born in Vienna, Austria on 22nd June 1909. He was brought up in a cultured atmosphere. His father held a senior position in the Austrian Civil Service, as the Governor of Sudetenland. However, members of his family had served the Hapsburg Dynasty since the year 1273.

Fürer-Haimendorf started his academic career as a student of anthropology in the Theresianische Akademie of the University of Vienna in 1927. During the 1920s, anthropology in Vienna was under the influence of the 'Kulturkrieslehre' school which was directed by the linguist, Wilheim Schmidt, and the head of the Institute of Ethnology, Professor Koppers. Fürer-Haimendorf was trained in anthropology by Schebesta, Frobenius, and Heine Geldern.

He received a D.Phil in 1931. His doctoral thesis was purely based on book research emphasising the social organisation of the hill tribes of Assam and Northwest Burma. Fürer-Haimendorf received the opportunity for field-work with funding assistance from the Rockefeller Foundation when he worked as a Research Assistant in Vienna between

1931 and 1934. Although he got an opportunity of studying in America, it was declined because of his inclination towards India. Instead, he was at the London School of Economics and attended the famous seminars of Professor Bronislaw Malinowski. In London, he could meet many other future British anthropologists namely, Raymond Firth, Meyer Fortes, and Audrey Richards. After attending the famous seminar of Professor Bronislaw Malinowski Fürer-Haimendorf decided to apply the 'participant-observation' method for research what Malinowski had already developed. It meant joining the tribe to be studied in their work in the fields, their hunting and fishing trips, and taking part in their festivals and feasts (Macfarlane and Turin, 1996).

First fieldwork among the Nagas

Being inspired by one of his mentors, Professor Heine Geldern, who did archaeological research in Southeast Asia, Fürer-Haimendorf chose the Naga Hills of Northeast India as the site for his first field-work. For this purpose, he left London in 1936.

Fürer-Haimendorf's research journey in Naga Hills was for 13 months and with other later visits there perhaps 18 months in all. Of the continuous 13 months he spent in the Naga Hills district, he stayed about 09 months among the Konyak Nagas in the northern parts - an area which at that time was only in parts administered by the British colonial government. For most of the time, he lived in the village of Wakching.

Fürer-Haimendorf's Naga research among the Konyak was the first long-term stay by a trained anthropologist among a single group of the Naga Hills, focussing only on a small number of villages. Before him, mostly the British colonial administrators and military people had been in contact with the various Nagas tribes. But only a few of them had any interest in their culture. John Henry Hutton, former Deputy Commissioner of Assam was one of them. He had written about the Konyak Naga in a short publication that Fürer-Haimendorf had come across while planning his journey for research. While studying for some time in London from autumn 1935 until spring 1936, Fürer-Haimendorf met J.P. Mills, J.H. Hutton's successor who became a close friend of him. He was also interested in the cultural backgrounds of the Nagas and promised Haimendorf to help with his research plans.

Fürer-Haimendorf had arrived in India on 11th May 1936 on-board the 'Victoria', a steamer through which he traveled from Venice in Italy to Bombay. For a few days, he was in Simla (now Shimla) and had short visits to Agra and Calcutta too. After that, he was heading towards 'Manipur Road' station in Assam by train to enter the Naga Hills. All the necessary information regarding the place of destination and official requirements for entering into the Naga Hills was already done by his friend J.P. Mills, the then Deputy Commissioner of the Naga Hills district. Hence, Furer-Haimendorf and his luggage were quickly transported to the district capital Kohima by car and he was put up in the comfortable bungalow of Mills.

On 2nd June 1936, both of them left Kohima for a tour of the area of the Eastern Angami Naga. They were accompanied by a young man named Thevoni, the 'head interpreter' for the region, several porters, servants, and other helpers. The tour was conducted to count the taxable households of the area. Through the tour, Fürer-Haimendorf could learn how to approach the Nagas and how to manage traveling in the Naga Hills. The group was joined by W.J. Smith on the 6th of June, who was soon to take over the administration of the Mokokchung sub-district. After visiting several villages in the southern parts of the district, they finally returned to Kohima on the 13th of June. Haimendorf also visited several Angami villages around Kohima.

On 4th July 1936, both Mills and Fürer-Haimendorf started their journey towards the north of the district to study the Konyak people. On the 9th of July, they reached the Konyak village of Wakching. Mills had again offered his companionship and helped to introduce the Fürer-Haimendorf to the Konyak people. After some days with J.P. Mills among the Konyak, they left for Mokokchung. On the way, several Konyak and Ao villages were visited. After bidding farewell to Mills, Haimendorf walked back to Wakching. Fürer-Haimendorf again visited some of the places when he was coming back to Wakching and thereby collected some stories of Ao mythology. After arriving at Wakching on 25th July 1936, he started to take a deeper look at a multitude of topics he came across. Whatever interesting happened there he tried to document it and questioned people about it. He extensively used photography to document the cultures he experienced and used the field diaries to note it down. During the second half of August 1936, Fürer-Haimendorf conducted several day-visits to the nearby Konyak villages. In the third week of September, he visited the Konyak village of Kongan. After several days of work at Kongan, and a brief visit to a tea estate near the colliery, he returned to Wakching on the 29th of September 1936.

Fürer-Haimendorf had to join a punitive expedition against the Kalyo-Kengyu village of Pangsha with Mills, Major Williams, commander of the military arm of the expedition consisting of 150 Assam Rifles and W.J. Smith, in charge of the 360 coolies. During the time of the expedition, Fürer-Haimendorf used the chance to take a photograph of most of the villages the expedition passed through on its journey. The destination for the expedition was an unadministered tribal area that lay between the Naga Hills and the frontier of Burma where there had been a spate of tribal raids. After around one month from the time of departure (7th November), Furer-Haimendorf went back to Wakching to continue his research among the Konyak. They returned with several dried skulls as trophies for the delighted Nagas. A long series of "head-receiving" dances and rituals were performed when a piece of these skulls reached the village of a coolie and Fürer-Haimendorf had the unique chance to document dances and rituals observed by the villagers. He continued his documentation of the head receiving feasts and general Konyak culture and festivals for the next five months, only interrupted by a short trip to the Abor Hills during the last week of January. In April 1937, he was joined by Hans-Eberhard Kauffmann, who was also doing a study on the Nagas at the same time.

During this first expedition with Mills, Haimendorf realised the importance of linguistic competence for successful ethnography. After only five months among the Nagas, he managed to learn the local lingua franca, Nagamese, or Naga-Pidgin. He became acquainted with some of the local Konyak dialects too.

After the completion of intensive field-work, he left Wakching on 10th June 1937. For a few days he was in Shillong and thereby continued his travels to Europe via Calcutta, Madras, and Trichinopoly, and finally returned by ship to Europe. Before leaving the research area, he finally packed up his gathered objects and sent them off to Europe earlier (von Stockhausen, 2013).

Second field trip and assignments in India

Haimendorf along with his wife were en route to the Naga Hills again for the second period of research in 1939. As the Second World War broke out he was arrested by the authorities for owning a German passport. Both of them were promptly interned as an enemy alien. They were released soon after having various contacts and the active support of the Nizam of Hyderabad. But they found it convenient to confine themselves to Hyderabad state under the jurisdiction of the Nizam. During that time along with his wife, he was able to undertake some of his best field-work among some less known population groups lived therein. They were with the Chenchus, a hunter-gatherer group for nine months. He could understand the point of contrast as well as compared the Chenchu gather-hunters with the splendidly decorated Nagas. During the period 1941-43 years he did further fieldwork amongst the Raj Gonds of Adilabad, the Gadabas and Bondos, the Reddis and other hill tribes of the Deccan, and filming along the way. He made roughly one hour of a film on the Chenchus, and approximately over two hours of other films taken in that period and some in the later 1940s, in the Deccan.

He was offered the post of Special Officer and Assistant Political Officer to the North East Frontier Agency in his fourth year of stay in Hyderabad. Therefore, he could move back to Northeast India again. He was permitted to do field-work among the remote and warlike Apa Tanis of the Arunachal Pradesh area of Assam. His duty was to monitor the security threat posed by the partial occupation of neighbouring Burma by Japan. After engaging in the job he got an opportunity of conducting in-depth field-work for the whole two years, 1944 and 1945. Twenty separate films on the Apa Tanis, comprising some five hours of film (excluding the 25-minute film shown on the BBC assembled from this footage) was made by him. It is some of the very best of Haimendorf's filming in terms of both the quality of the footage and the intimacy and interest of the materials. It can be considered as a unique resource together with Haimendorf's diaries, books, and photographs (Harrison and Macfarlane, 2014).

Fürer-Haimendorf was appointed to the position of Advisor for Tribes and Backward Classes to the Nizam's Government of Hyderabad at the end of the war. It was to deal with the complicated issue of land reform. In the course of his work, intending to preserve and safeguard indigenous cultures and languages he set up various educational and other schemes for tribal peoples. He also received a teaching appointment at Osmania University which he later relinquished (Macfarlane and Turin, 1996).

Professional career

Fürer-Haimendorf accepted the lectureship at the SOAS in 1949. Shortly he was made Reader, and then Chair of Asian Anthropology in the London's School of Oriental and African Studies in 1951. After 25 years of service as a Professor, he retired in the year 1976. He always encouraged his staff and students to conduct field-work as frequently and intensively as possible. He was also appointed as Acting Director for the academic session 1969-70 while the then Director, Professor (Sir) Cyril Philips served as Vice-Chancellor of the University of London (Macfarlane and Turin, 1996).

Third field trip to India

Fürer-Haimendorf was in Nepal for a period of perhaps three or more years in total. In 1953, both Haimendorf and his wife went back to southern India including Kerala, where he did some more filming. During that time the Kingdom of Nepal was officially opened to foreign travelers and Professor Haimendorf took the opportunity to visit the country. During these visits, he was accompanied by one of Nepal's first indigenous anthropologists, Dor Bahadur Bista, as well as his wife Elizabeth (Betty) Fürer-Haimendorf. He became the first foreign anthropologist who was able to research the peoples of Nepal. He was interested to study the Sherpa people of Nepal because of their stark contrast in terms of religion and culture to the populations of tropical India with whom he had been previously occupied. Another reason he was at first drawn to the Sherpas of Eastern Nepal because of their reputation in the scaling of Everest. Until the mid-1960s, Haimendorf concentrated almost exclusively on Nepal and tried to visit various regions of the country. Later on, he also encouraged his students for more detailed study in those areas. He filmed extensively in many regions, including Kathmandu, the Sherpa region, the middle hills around Gorkha and Kaski, Muktinath, Mustang, and Dolpo, Dang in the Southwest, and Humla and Jumla in the extreme Northwest of Nepal (Harrison and Macfarlane, 2014).

Works and achievements

For over forty years Professor Fürer-Haimendorf traveled, filmed, and wrote extensively on the peoples of the Central and Eastern Himalayas and also Central India. He studied the languages and culture of between three and six societies in each area he visited. He had published 3,650 pages of ethnographic notes describing a dozen tribal groups and took more than 10,000 separate photographs, capturing memorably many aspects of tribal culture. He had written ten ethnographic monographs, half a dozen more general books as well as several other volumes of essays and theoretical works based on his field-works. *The Naked Nagas* (1939), *The Chenchus* (1943), *The Reddis of the Bison Hills* (1945), *The Raj Gonds of Adilabad* (1948), *The Sherpas of Nepal* (1964), and The Konyak Nagas (1969) are some of the notable monographs written by Haimendorf. Other familiar published volumes include *Morals and merit* (1967), *Return to the naked Nagas: an anthropologist's view of Nagaland 1936–1970* (1976), and *The tribes of India: struggle for survival* (1982). He was one of the only anthropologists of the great inter-war generation in Britain to realise the importance of visual documentation. He was also one of the most prolific British ethnographic film-makers, starting to film in the 1940s and shooting over 100 hours of 16 mm films. He filmed in black and white as well as also in colour. Some of his familiar contribution towards the film industry includes *The land of the Gurkhas* (1957), *The land of Dolpo* (1962) and *The men who hunted heads* (1970). He made many hundreds of hours of tape recordings to accompany the films which is also an extensive collection of artifacts for the anthropology museums at Vienna, Cambridge, and elsewhere. He built up the largest Department of Anthropology of his time in Britain.

He received numerous academic honours. As well as the Sykes and Roy Medals, he was awarded the RAI Rivers Memorial Medal in 1949. He was the President of the Royal Anthropological Institute from 1975 to 1977. He was the recipient of the award, The King Birendra Prize by the Royal Nepal Academy in 1976 and the Austrian Order of Merit for Art and Science in 1982 (Macfarlane and Turin, 1996).

Personal life

As a person, Fürer-Haimendorf was courteous, genial, charming, and extremely personable, with a wide circle of friends. He won the trust of both Europeans and his many non-European co-workers and colleagues because of his great ability to make friends and to manage human relationships, especially in difficult situations. After anthropology, he inclined to the classical music of his native Austria, which helped to give him solace in old age. He was a committed Catholic who went to Mass every Sunday in London.

Fürer-Haimendorf got married to his colleague Elizabeth (Betty) Barnado in April 1938. They had a son named Nicholas who was born in 1946. He depended very heavily on his wife, who was his co-worker, organiser of his expeditions, inspiration, and herself a notable ethnographer. She died in the year 1987. His autobiography was a tribute to her which was published in the year 1989. After the death of his wife, he suffered a slow and distressing decline. He did not recover from his health problems and passed away on 11th June 1995 in London.

Preservation of Fürer-Haimendorf's collection

The vast amounts of materials gathered by Fürer-Haimendorf throughout his entire life were given to the SOAS Library by his son after his father's death. All the notebooks, diaries as well as identifiable scanned photographs had been digitized and stored in the SOAS library. Nick Haimendorf still owns the copyright of those materials (von Stockhausen, 2013).

Apart from the photographic and written materials, Fürer-Haimendorf also collected a large number of objects for the then called Museum für Völkerkunde in Vienna. His collections from the village Wakching were finally given to the museum in Vienna which included over 800 pieces, 165 of which were stone axes. His collection of Vienna surely ranks among the best collections of Naga artifacts outside Britain, especially because of the great variety of Konyak ceremonial hats. Another smaller collection of objects including copies of photographs during 1936-37 years was given to the collection of the Museum of Archaeology and Anthropology at Cambridge.

Conclusion

Christoph von Fürer-Haimendorf is certainly the best-known scholar who had a profound contribution to the development of the subject of anthropology. He was an all-rounder who got involved in all possible ways throughout the entire academic journey. His tactic of documentation of an event, the habit of writing the field diaries extensively, capturing the photograph for the visual documentation, filming, etc. all is admirable. His photography and written records of various communities will remain the important source of knowledge not only for the current generation but also for the students and scholars with the anthropology background of each forthcoming generation.

References

Harrison, S, and Macfarlane, A. 2014. 'Encounter with visual Anthropology'. Available from: www.alanmacfarlane.com.

Macfarlane, A, and Turin, M 1996. 'Professor Christoph von Fürer-Haimendorf 1909-1995', *Bulletin of the School of Oriental and African Studies,* Vol. LIX, pt. 3, pp. 548-551.

von Stockhausen, A 2013. Christoph von Fürer-Haimendorf and his work among the Nagas, *Archiv fiir Volkerkunde*, 61-62 : 3-30.

13

Architect of Prehistoric Anthropology in India: Dharanidhar Sen and Asok K. Ghosh

Ranjana Ray

The teaching of Prehistoric Anthropology turned hundred years in Kolkata, the erstwhile Calcutta. The University which is celebrating hundred years of teaching Anthropology has retained the older name, Calcutta University. The Asiatic Society of Bengal was the cradle for nurturing the discipline into its growth. Sir Ashutosh Mukhopadhyay, the then Vice-Chancellor of the University of Calcutta, as a member of the Asiatic Society attended all the meetings and discussions of scholars on various aspects of 'Man and Environment'. He felt the need for proper and formal training of future generations in Anthropology. Anthropology first began to be taught as a branch of Ancient Indian History and Culture. Anthropology was established as a separate department of the University for conferring the degree of Masters in the year 1920 (Ray, 1993).

At present, there are four major branches of Anthropology (Ember et al, 2002). They are physical/ biological, social-cultural, prehistoric archaeology, and linguistics. Physical and Social Anthropology initially were considered as two important branches of Anthropology. Prehistoric anthropology and linguistics were included in the branches of physical and social Anthropology.

With time vast amounts of information were accumulated and prehistoric anthropology, initially known as prehistoric archaeology emerged as a separate sub-discipline of Anthropology. Linguistics is very recently separated as another branch of Anthropology. Terminology for the branch of prehistoric archaeology changed through time. Instead of the prehistoric culture forming the main issue of prehistoric archaeology, man the creator of the culture loomed large for a proper understanding of prehistoric culture through time and space. The evolution of mankind and the development of its capacity to adapt to the changing ecosystem became very important in studies of prehistoric archaeology. The fossil pieces of evidence and the subsequent cultural remains resulted in the debate for a rethinking of the terminology. As a result terms like Paeoanthropology emerged. At present terminology for this branch is fixed by the University Grants Commission (UGC) as Archaeological Anthropology. Anthropology as a discipline has developed in India during colonial time and its growth may be considered as part of the Anglo-American legacy (Paddayya, 2013).

Study and research in prehistoric anthropology developed in its full form under the guidance of late Dharanidhar Sen and Asok Kumar Ghosh, Professors of the department, and specialising in prehistoric Anthropology. They may be considered architects of prehistoric Anthropology in India but they did not build the subject from scratch. Credit goes to a British geologist Robert Bruce Foote, who picked up a handaxe from Pallavaram, a site on the bank of River Kortalayar flowing through the erstwhile Madras Province in the year 1863 (Foote, 1866). Foote was much influenced by the development of prehistory in Europe and aimed at finding similar prehistoric remains from India. He is considered as the father of prehistory in India. He pursued the search for prehistoric sites and cultural remains for the next forty years till 1904. He discovered a total of 459 prehistoric sites in India. Out of these 42 were Palaeolithic sites and 252 were of Neolithic culture. Foote sold part of his collection of prehistoric tools to Madras Museum and a part of it was given to the Indian Museum in Kolkata (Sen and Ghosh, 1966).

Prehistory became an important subject of study with the opening of the department of Anthropology at Calcutta University. The foundation for the sub-discipline was laid down by its founder teachers.

Mention may be made of Haran Chandra Chakladar (from 1918), Rama Prasad Chanda (from 1919), and Panchanan Mitra (from 1923), the faculty members, who joined the department on the invitation of Sir Ashutosh Mukherjee from various other disciplines. All of them had left their contributions to the prehistory of India in the form of books and articles. Specialisation in prehistoric archaeology in the department of Anthropology, Calcutta University started in 1957 with Dharanidhar Sen at the helm. The first student to specialise in Prehistory was Asok Kumar Ghosh, an appropriate follower of Dharanidhar Sen. Both of them had established Prehistoric Anthropology in its proper importance in India and abroad.

Professor Dharanidhar Sen

Professor Dharanidhar Sen, popularly referred to as Dharani Sen was born in the town of Gazipur, Uttar Pradesh in the year 1909. His family moved to Calcutta in 1918, when he was nine years old. Dharani Sen was educated in school and colleges in Calcutta and earned a bachelor's degree with Honours in Geology from Calcutta University. In 1935, he completed a Master's Degree in Anthropology from the same university. After completion of postgraduate studies in the department, he took up research work in the Department of Anthropology from 1935 to 1938. But he did not submit his thesis for a further degree. However, he was called upon to join the Yale-Cambridge expedition in the Northwestern part of the Indian subcontinent while he was carrying out his research work in the department. In 1936, the famous expedition in search of man and culture in India took place under the joint auspices of the Yale and Cambridge Universities. The team consisted of Drs. Helmut de Terra, Teilhard de Chardin, and T. T. Paterson from the Yale and Cambridge universities. Two young scholars were recruited from Indian universities. One was V. D. Krishnaswamy and the other was Dharani Sen.

It was a multidisciplinary study with a conjoined effort of geology, paleontology, and archaeology. The result of the expedition was brought out as the volume, *Studies on Ice Age in India, and Associated Human Culture* (1939). The expedition covered the sub-Himalayan terrain in the northwestern part of the Indian subcontinent, Narmada valley in Central India, and Kortalayar valley in South India, following a longitudinal line from North to South in the subcontinent. Dharani Sen with his bachelor's degree in geology and Masters in Anthropology was an asset to the team with knowledge about geology and geomorphology of the terrains, and an understanding of early man and his culture. During this period he was offered a scholarship at Cambridge University but because of some personal reasons, he was not able to accept it (Ghosh, 1974). The exceptional merit of Dharani Sen in Paleontology, glacial geology, and Palaeolithic archaeology impressed De Terra while he was a collaborator in the Yale-Cambridge expedition in Northwestern India. De Terra always remembered him and expressed his admiration often to another famous prehistorian of Harvard University Hallam L. Movius (Movius, 1974).

Professor Sen continued his work on prehistory after the expedition. He was associated with the Indian Museum for studying and arranging for the exhibition of the prehistoric tools collected and deposited in the Museum. He had been associated with Professor Nirmal Kumar Bose during this time. Between 1939 and 1940, together with Nirmal Kumar Bose, another stalwart in Anthropology and a student of Panchanan Mitra carried out a prehistoric investigation in the Mayurbhanj district of Odisha. They excavated Palaeolithic sites at Kuliana, near Baripada, which came out as a monograph in 1948, which is still considered as a text for the scholars in prehistoric archaeology (Bose and Sen, 1948).

In the year 1940, Professor Sen was invited to set up the geography department at Vidyasagar College in Calcutta. He joined the college and specialised in geography and geomorphology. In the year 1944, he joined the Department of Anthropology, Calcutta University as a guest lecturer. In 1948, Dharani Sen was appointed in the department as a full-time faculty. He continued teaching prehistoric anthropology until his retirement in 1974. For a short spell from the years 1952 and 1953, Professor Sen joined the Anthropology Department at Lucknow University. After that, he resumed his duties as a lecturer at Calcutta University. He was promoted to the post of Reader in 1963. In 1957, the advanced course in prehistoric archaeology started with Professor D. Sen in charge of the curricula. He structured the syllabus for general and special papers in prehistoric archaeology. He was elected sectional President of Anthropology and Archaeology of the Indian Science

Congress for the session 1953-1954. Professor Sen retired on August 31, 1974, from active service in the Department of Anthropology. After retirement, he was invited as a visiting faculty at Dibrugarh University in 1978 and Ranchi University in 1979. On February 14, 1980, Professor Dharanidhar Sen succumbed to a brief illness. He had left a good number of students, whom he had trained in prehistoric archaeology. Dr. Asok K. Ghosh was his first batch of students who took up Prehistoric archaeology and passed out in 1959. He followed into his teacher's footsteps and brought the sub-branch into its full glory.

Contributions of Prof. Dharanidhar Sen in building prehistoric anthropology in India

Dharani Sen joined F. E. Zeuner in the Mirzapur expedition of the Archaeological Survey of India in the period between 1949 and 1950. Sen's area of fieldwork was mainly in the states of West Bengal, Orissa, and Bihar including the present-day Jharkhand state. He had also conducted intensive field research in Punjab (Sen, 1938, 1955 and 1957). His work had been on Pleistocene geomorphology and Palaeolithic, Mesolithic, and Neolithic cultures (Sen, 1950, 1954, 1969, 1975).

During his long teaching and research career, he saw prehistory to reach an important academic status as one of the branches in Anthropology. Professor Dharanidhar Sen played a pivotal role in it. Dharani Sen developed a precise methodology for prehistoric investigation, analysis, and interpretation. He had used an integrated methodology of geoscience, archeology, and anthropology for proper interpretation and understanding of Indian Prehistory. He studied prehistory with a focus on man, his culture, and his capability for making culture and adjustment to the changing environmental condition through time and space. His study was not concentrated only in the past but included the ethnic study of geographically isolated groups for the further understanding of prehistoric life in the context of modern preliterate people. Professor Sen not only built the branch of prehistory in the world standard but also trained his students to carry out the study of prehistory further.

Professor Sen had put up a fine museum and a laboratory of prehistory in the department of Anthropology, Calcutta University along with creating a strong center of prehistoric research in Calcutta University (Ray and Mondal, 2020). The museums and the laboratories were properly planned with necessary facilities and with adequate space. The museum has got representative collections from various parts of the world, namely, from France, Europe; Mt Carmel, Israel; South Africa, and China. Huge collections made by archaeologists and prehistorians in India are also there. Artifacts were donated by scholars, such as C. W. Anderson, tools collected from Chakradharpur in 1917; Yale-Cambridge expedition collection from Soan Valley, and Krishnaswamy's collection from Attirampakkam and Vadamadurai. All these were placed in the prehistory Museum as a result of Professor Sen's endeavour. The archaeological survey gave samples of seals, bricks, pottery, conch shell, and several other materials from the Indus Valley collection on request by Professor Sen. Siwalik fossils from Quaternary deposits of the North-Western region were placed in the museum from Sen's collection. Since prehistoric tools are mostly made of stones and the stones are varied in nature, Professor Sen had arranged to display samples of rocks and minerals. Students could gain knowledge about the suitability of certain rocks for making tools. This may give an understanding of the suitability of the stone types for making different tools and development of manufacturing techniques at different cultural phases and also about the evolution of man's capability for choosing raw material for the tools he made.

Under his supervision and with the help of Himanshu Kumar Basu of Archaeological Survey of India, several miniature models of megalithic types of India were made for the students' understanding of megaliths. The museum was first set up in the old building by Professor Sen. It was moved to the new modern building within the same campus in Ballygunge Circular Road, Calcutta in 1964. With this shift, Professor Sen had more modern amenities and space to set up the museum in the new building on the third floor. He with the help of his student and later colleague Professor Asok Ghosh and subsequently with help of the present author had arranged the museum and its exhibition in a manner that both the visitors, scholars, and students were benefitted.

Field work is an essential part of prehistory. Fieldwork each year under the guidance of teachers is mandatory for students of Anthropology. Professor Sen had trained his students for fieldwork, both exploration and excavation. He had commissioned field kits for fieldwork in prehistoric archaeology. The equipment is still useful to students and scholars. After fieldwork, the collections needed to be identified, preserved, and cataloged. Professor Sen had arranged the prehistory laboratory in such a manner, that students may learn the method of recording, both before and after the fieldwork. Prehistoric Anthropology is the brainchild of Professor Dharanidhar Sen. All the students of the past and present in Anthropology are indebted to the great teacher.

There are several articles, a book, and volumes written and edited by Professor D. Sen both under single authorship and jointly with other scholars. Some examples are given by Sarkar (2019). A few are mentioned at the end of this article.

Professor Asok Kumar Ghosh

Professor Asok Kumar Ghosh was among the first batch of students to pass out in Anthropology with a specialisation in Prehistoric Archaeology. He had earned Ph.D. degree under the supervision of Professor Dharanidhar Sen. He had carried forward the task of building prehistoric anthropology to further glory, which was already established quite strongly in the discipline of Anthropology by his teacher Professor Dharanidhar Sen.

Professor Ghosh was born in Calcutta in 1934. His ancestral home was in the town of Jessore, the eastern part of undivided Bengal in British India. His father was in Government service, posted in Calcutta. He lived with his family in Calcutta. Dr. Ghosh was the eldest child of his parents. He had two brothers and two sisters. His schooling was in Calcutta. He graduated from Bangabasi College in Kolkata and took admission in anthropology for postgraduate courses at Calcutta University in 1957. It is informed by his friend and classmate Dr. Ajit K. Danda, former Director Anthropological Survey of India, that Dr. Ghosh had the ambition to study medicine but this ambition was not fulfilled under unavoidable circumstances. Although he took up anthropology for his postgraduate studies, it is said that he had no idea about the subject (Bellwood, 1988: xiii - xv). In 1959, he passed M.Sc. in anthropology and scored first-class first marks with specialisation in advanced prehistoric archaeology. Specialisation in physical, social, and prehistoric anthropology started for the first time in the Department of Anthropology, Calcutta University in 1957. Asok Ghosh took up prehistory as a special paper in his final year of M.Sc. The subject was new to him but he liked it. Soon after completion of Masters Degree in anthropology, Ghosh began research in advanced prehistory under the guidance of Professor Dharani Sen. He was awarded Ph. D. Degree in 1964 for his work on the Palaeolithic culture of Singhbhum district, his thesis came out in the form of a monograph in the *American Journal of Philosophy* (Ghosh, 1970). In 1963, he joined as a faculty in the Department of Anthropology, Calcutta University. Dr. Ghosh received Prem Chand Raichand Scholarship from Calcutta University and was awarded D.Sc. Degree for his work in the prehistory of Eastern India in 1975. He became a Reader and subsequently Professor until suddenly he died in April 1997 at the age of 63 years.

Achievements of Professor Asok Kumar Ghosh

Professor Ghosh got his training in prehistory and quaternary geology from Professor Dharani Sen. He went to Harvard University with Fulbright Fellowship and worked with Professor Hallam L. Movius. He also had a close association with renowned scholars of prehistory, such as G. H. R. Von Koenigswald and Francois Bordes. Professor Ghosh considered them as his teachers. Asok Ghosh had great reverence for Professor H. D. Sankalia. Professor Sankalia admired Professor Ghosh and may be considered as another of his mentors after Dharani Sen. He had a very cordial relationship with his peers Professor G. C. Mohapatra of Punjab University; Professor V. N. Misra, Professor S. N. Rajaguru and G.L. Badam of Deccan College Pune; D.P. Agrawal of Tata Institute of Fundamental Research, Navrangpura, Ahmedabad; and Professor K. C. Tripathy of Utkal University, Bhubaneswar. There are a large number of scholars from other disciplines who were quite close to Professor Ghosh. Ghosh believed in a multidisciplinary study in anthropological research.

Professor Asok K. Ghosh was a member of several learned bodies both in India and abroad. He was an executive committee member of several societies, namely, of the International Union for Prehistoric and Protohistoric Sciences (UISPP), International Geographical Union (IGU), International Association for Quaternary Studies (INQUA), and Indo-Pacific Society for Prehistoric Association (IPPA). He was elected Sectional President for 62nd Indian Science Congress in the Anthropology and Archaeology section in the year 1975. The presidential address was entitled "Man Evolving – in India" and was highly acclaimed by anthropologists and archaeologists.

Contributions of Prof. Asok Kumar Ghosh in developing prehistoric anthropology in India

Professor Asok Kumar Ghosh believed in the holistic study of Anthropology. His interest and research covered all the main branches of anthropology, namely, the physical, socio-cultural and prehistoric archaeology. He had supervised a doctoral thesis on prehistory, human evolution, and domestication of plants, education, communication, tribal studies, and women studies. He had done fieldwork in the Punjab area, Narmada valley, and in the Peninsular region of the southern part of India, but his major field research was in Eastern India.

Ghosh had developed a prehistoric study of India into a global standard. He has brought in revolutionary changes in the terminological concept in anthropology. Ghosh preferred the term Palaeoanthropology instead of prehistoric archaeology. His logic for this may be understood in the quote from his writing, "Palaeoanthropology is the meaningful understanding of human evolution in the realm of bio-cultural perspective and to follow the evolution process of man and his culture objectively, substantiated with relevant data." (Ghosh, 1974: 171). Most important of his contributions in prehistory is his critique of terminological concepts in prehistoric cultural divisions and their nomenclature. He had shown that neither European nor African terminologies can be applied for the Palaeolithic subdivisions in India because cultural milieu differed from one continent to the other. He followed ecological anthropological theory and New Archaeology for framing the nomenclature. He proposed the use of typo-technological attributes to name the different phases of Paleolithic cultures.

Subsequent stages of Palaeolithic culture were named by him as Pebble-Core, Flake, and Flake-Blade stages. This was done based on the dominance of the form of raw material or blanks for making tools in subsequent stages of the culture (Ghosh, 1987).

Most outstanding of his contributions is intensive research on the Palaeolithic culture of the Singhbhum district in Jharkhand state, erstwhile Bihar. The area covered is Saraikella, Kharswan, Dhalbhum, Kolhan, Porhat, and Saranda. He explored the valleys of River Subarnarekha, its tributaries; and valleys of Rivers Koel and Baitarani. He had put forward a clear geo-stratigraphy of the district and had placed the Palaeolithic cultures in the proper geochronological framework. He reconstructed the past climate of the quaternary period of the region from the stratigraphic studies. The research has given a proper understanding of man, environment, and subsequent adaptation of man with his culture to the contemporary environment. Going through the prevalent terms of the cultural sequence in Europe and Asia he coined his terminology for the cultural phases of Singhbhum. In India, both pebbles and cores were used for making tools at the lower Palaeolithic level. With the discovery of the prepared core technique, flakes became the main blank for making tools. A refinement of technique and gradual size diminution took place in the subsequent evolution of the culture. He felt that that early cultures developed in response to the respective environmental condition and simultaneously with the development of the biological evolution of man, change and development of culture took place through time and space.

Professor Ghosh had reconstructed the Palaeolithic culture of West Bengal in the districts of Medinipur and Bankura in the fringe area of the Eastern plateau. Bengal basin was not suitable for human habitation during the Pleistocene period. He had also built up a synthesis of the Palaeolithic culture of India in the context of South Asia and Southeast Asia. This he did between the years 1969 and 1975. This was the result of his exploration and excavation in South and Southeast Asia. Data on Paleolithic cultures of South and Southeast Asia were also collected from museums and institutions in India and abroad. Professor Ghosh followed a multidisciplinary and conjunctive approach for his study. He emphasised bio-cultural dimensions. He studied regional patterns of Palaeolithic cultures of India and made a comparison with the cultures of South-east Asia.

For an understanding of the emergence of man in India, he studied the late Tertiary humanoid creature, *Ramapithecus* (Ghosh and Sen, 1981). He had taken into consideration the handaxe and pointed out its presence in the lower Palaeolithic tool kit of India (Ghosh, 1973) as opposed to Movius's view about its absence in South Asia. Type concept according to him was a major issue. He had looked for Mousterian culture in India and pointed out that the Mousterian element in India may be called Mousteroid because of its typo-technological difference from the true Mousterian of France (Ghosh, 1974).

The identification of geo-stratigraphy, chronology for the deposits, and reconstruction of the past environment from the nature of the deposits and its composition together with cultural remains from the stratigraphic sequence and ordering of Palaeolithic culture in Eastern India may be considered a seminal contribution to the discipline. He also had experimented with tool-making technology. Some tools made by him are displayed in the prehistory museum of the department of Anthropology as samples for 'experimental prehistoric archaeology'. The subject has since then developed in its full form in the department of Anthropology, Calcutta University (Polley and Ray, 2009).

Professor Ghosh made contributions to the Megalithic burial system of prehistoric and present-day context and explained the religious aspect of the ritual (Ghosh, 1975). Asok Ghosh had done research on the man and plant relationship, especially in the tribal area. His purpose was to find out a balance between the ecosystem in the form of utilisation of plant resources by man. The utilisation of plants was considered from the viewpoint of utilisation for medicine, food, socio-religious purposes, for the construction of a structure, and for making tools. Types of plants were also taken in the data for research. Professor Ghosh has supervised several doctoral pieces of research. There were works done on Flake-blade elements of India, Mesolithic culture, and adaptation with the tool kits to the contemporary environment. Both the thesis was in the line of Bordes and Binford Schools with attribute analysis. In the same method, he supervised work on Siwalik hominoids. He had taken up supervising work on a cultivated variety of rice. This was to unveil the mystery of the domestication of rice by the Neolithic people in eastern India. He had discovered some rock art from the Ghatshila region in Jharkhand and had guided a thesis on prehistoric rock art.

An extensive exploration of Sanjay River Valley, a tributary of River Subarnarekha was done. A large number of prehistoric sites were discovered. These were of Palaeolithic, Mesolithic, Neolithic, and Chalcolithic cultural sites. (Ghosh *et al,* 1984). This was done under the collaboration of the Australian National University and Calcutta University. Asok K. Ghosh had a good number of friends in the fraternity of anthropology and archaeology both in India and abroad. It is much apparent in the volume called *Man and His Culture* (1988). The book was compiled to felicitate Professor Ghosh and was edited by Peter S. Bellwood of Australian National University.

Professor Asok K. had not written a book on prehistory but he has edited several books on various subjects of Anthropology. Professor Ghosh had carried on the legacy of Professor Dharani Sen and taken the study of prehistory to its present glory. He was a dedicated teacher and has trained several students who had carried out research and study of prehistory in India.

Homage

Professor Dharanidhar Sen and Asok Kumar Ghosh, both were great teachers, scholars, and researchers. They had built Prehistoric Anthropology, the branch of Anthropology, in world standard. The editors of this volume have appropriately called them the architects of Prehistoric Anthropology. The next generation and the present generation of students, scholars, and teachers of Prehistoric Anthropology are indebted to these two great prehistorians. At present Indian scholars follow the methodology and vision set forth by these two teachers.

References

Bellwood, Peter S. 1988. *Man and His Culture: a resurgence.* Books and Books. New Delhi and Calcutta.

Bose, Nirmal K., and Sen, D 1948. *Excavation in Mayurbhanj.* Calcutta University Press, Calcutta.

Ember, Carol R. Ember Melvin, and Peregrine N Peter, 2002. *Anthropology.* Pearson Education Pvt. Ltd., Singapore.

Foote, RB. 1866. 'On the occurrence of stone implements in lateritic formations in various parts of Madras and North Arcot Districts'. *The Madras Journal of Literature and Science,* Third series part 2: 1-41.

Ghosh, Asok K., 1970. 'The palaeolithic cultures in Singhbhum'. *Transactions of the American Philosophical Society.* N. S. 60: 1- 68.

Ghosh, Asok K., 1973. 'Handadzes in the palaeolithic culture of India'. *Asian Perspective,* 15: 156 -166.

Ghosh, Asok K., 1973. 'Chronocultural perspective on the palaeolithic culture in India', in DP. Agrawal and A. Ghosh (Eds): *Radiocarbon and Indian Archaeology.* pp. 23 – 51. Tata Institute of Fundamental Research, Bombay.

Ghosh, Asok K., 1974. 'Preface', in *Perspectives in Palaeoanthropology: Professor D. Sen Festschrift,* Firma K. L. Mukhopadhyay, Calcutta.

Ghosh, Asok K.1974. 'Palaeoanthropology in India'. In Dharani Sen. (Ed): *Indian Anthropology Today.* Department of Anthropology, Calcutta University, Calcutta.

Ghosh, Asok K., 1974. 'Denticulates in India: examination of a typical concept'. *Journal of the Hong Kong Archaeological Society.* 5: 47-56.

Ghosh, Asok K., 1975. 'Reconstruction of prehistoric religion from megaliths in India', *Proceeding of the 1st symposium of the International Association Prehistoric and Ethnographic Religion.* (Ed) E. Anati, pp. 1-16. Vulcamonica: Centro Camuni di Studi Prehistorichi.

Ghosh, Asok K. 1987. 'Palaeoanthropology or prehistory: selection of terminology in Indian context'. In A. Ghosh, BM. Pande and BD. Chattopadhyay (Eds): *Archaeology and History: In memory of Sh.* pp. 3-10, Agam Kala Prakashan, New Delhi.

Ghosh, Asok K., and Sen Amiya K., 1981. 'Fresh light on phyllo- taxonomy of Siwalik Hominoids', *Proceedings of the Field Conference Neogene Quaternary Boundary, 1979.* pp. 55-61.

Ghosh, Asok K., Ray Ranjana, Chatterjee PG., Nanda Poresh, and Bellwood Peter S.. 1984. 'Archaeological reconnaissance in the Sanjay Valley, Singhbhum district, Bihar'. *Indo-Pacific Prehistory Association.* 5:29 -38.

Movius, HL. 1974, 'Foreword'. In *Perspectives in Palaeoanthropology: Professor D. Sen Festschrift,* Edited by Asok K. Ghosh. Firma KL Mukhopadhyay, Calcutta.

Paddayya, K. 2013. *Essays in History of Archaeology: Themes, Institutions, and Personalities.* Edited by D. Sen, Archaeological Survey of India, Government of India.

Polley, K., and Ray Ranjana, 2009. 'An experimental study on the manufacturing process of the lower paleolithic implements from quartz nodules'.

In R. Ray and V. Jayaswal (eds): *Status of Prehistoric Studies in the Twenty-First Century in India.* pp. 49-54, BAR International Series 1924. Oxford.

Ray, Ranjana, 1993. Editorial. *Journal of the Department of Anthropology, University of Calcutta.* No. 1: 1-4.

Ray, Ranjana, and Mondal Debasis K., 2020. 'Development of the discipline of archaeologicalanthropology/palaeoanthropology/prehistoricarchaeology in India'. In Biman Kumar Das Gupta, Samira Dasgupta, and Amitabha Sarkar (Eds): *Retrospect of 100 years of Indian Anthropology*. (1920-2019), pp. 87 – 102, Aayu Publications, New Delhi.

Sarkar, Amitabha, 2019. 'Dharani Sen (1909- 1980)', in (ed.) Amitabha Sarkar and Samira Dasgupta (Eds): *Doyens of Indian Anthropology (1920 -2019).* pp. 60-63, Agam Kala Prakashan, Delhi.

Sen, D. 1938. 'A short note on the paleolithic implements supposed to have been obtained from the Siwaliks'. *Anthropological Papers, Journal of Letters, University of Calcutta.* 5: 71-76.

Sen, D. 1948. 'A note on some celts and chisels from West Bengal', *Science, and Culture*, 48: 252-253.

Sen, D. 1950. 'A celt site in Singhbhum', *Man in India*, 30: 1&2.

Sen, D. 1954. 'Lower palaeolithic culture complex and chronology in India'. Proceedings of 41st Indian Science Congress. 2: 113-131.

Sen, D. 1955. 'Nalagarh palaeolithic culture'. *Man in India.* 35: 176-184.

Sen, D. 1957. 'Soanian and the pebble tool Complex in India'. *Man in India.* 37, 2: 157-159.

Sen, D. 1969. 'Profile of a pre-literate culture in Sanjai Valley, Singhbhum', *Journal of Indian Anthropological Society*. 4, 1&2: 17-29.

Sen, D. 1975. 'Dugni— profile of a neolithic site'. *Journal of Indian Anthropological Society,* 12, 2: 159-164.

Sen, D. 1974. *Proceedings of the seminar: Indian Anthropology Today.* Department of Anthropology, Calcutta University.

Sen, D. and Ghosh Asok K., 1966. *Studies in Prehistory: Bruce Foote Memorial Volume.* Firma KL Mukhopadhyay, Calcutta.

14

M.N. Srinivas and his Ineffaceable Contributions in Social Anthropology

Jyoti Prasad Saikia

M.N. Srinivas, one of the founding fathers of Indian Sociology, is widely acknowledged as a pioneer of modern Sociology and Social Anthropology in India. Srinivas was born on 16 November 1916 in Mysore city of India. He contributed a lot to make both Sociology and Social Anthropology richer throughout his life and specially wrote extensively on Indian society. His contribution to Sociology and Social Anthropology is not only praiseworthy but also unique in terms of its essence. His scholarship inspired many students of these domains and taught them to accept any kind of challenge to acquire the most effective paradigm for understanding Indian society. He was not an armchair intellectual and never tried to write anything with utopian understanding. He constructed his idea about Indian society based on field study. He always sought to catch the flowing and vibrant spirit of the subject for searching and constructing new knowledge. In connection with the methodological practice, he strongly advocated ethnographic research based on participant observation.

Srinivas studied Sociology under G.S. Ghurye, one of the stalwarts of the sociological discourse of his time, and completed his academic research for pursuing a Ph.D. on the topic '*Social Organisation in Mysore families*' in 1944. After that, he expanded his research activities, and in 1945, he went to Oxford where he further analyzed his Coorgs material for his D. Phil thesis in Social Anthropology under the supervision of A.R. Radcliffe Brown and E.E. Evans Pritchard. Subsequently, the revised version of his work was published as *'Religion and Society among the Coorgs of South India'* (1952). This landmark volume gave him a new identity among the intellectuals as a functionalist with a scholarly reputation.

M.N. Srinivas was appointed as a lecturer in Indian Sociology at Oxford and started empirical studies in Indian society. He carried out fieldwork in the Rampura village of Mysore, which is the content of the great book '*The Remembered Village*' (1976). Interestingly, this book was written largely from memory at Stanford in 1970 after the entire notes of fieldwork had been destroyed by a devastating fire. But after working for three years in Oxford, he decided to come back to India and joined in M.S. University of Baroda as a Professor of Sociology in 1951. M.N. Srinivas served in this University for eight years as Professors and created an academic atmosphere there consisting of a good number of fellow teachers, scholars, and students. In the later part of the 1950s, he was cordially invited to teach in the Delhi School of Economics and he joined this Institution as Chair Professor of Sociology in 1959. The presence of Srinivas as a Professor in the Delhi School of Economics enlightened both the teachers and students and escalated the academic spirit of the Institution to search for new knowledge of the concerned domain. His cognizant quality to find out insightful understanding of sociological issues attracted many students throughout the world to the Delhi School of Economics. It, no doubt, helped the Institution to initiate academic enterprises. André Beteille, a universally acclaimed sociologist, also joined the department in the same year. Beteille writes, 'Srinivas's reputation and reputation of the Delhi School of Economics attracted a succession of very able and dedicated students from all parts of the country and from overseas. The place became a hive of intellectual activity, and the weekly research seminars over which Srinivas presided were among the best I have attended anywhere in the world' (Beteille, 1996:239). However, Srinivas was also not free from the criticism for his galloping outstanding intellectual activities and a few strived to debase his erudite credibility in building the image of the department on apex.

He categorically ignored all the disparagement and concentrated on his works. Chris Fuller, well-known Professor, and anthropologist, rightly mentions that 'However this department is judged today as a world-class department that is still the best in India, or one that is decaying along with its buildings - few among even its severest critics would dispute Srinivas's success in creating a major center of modern Sociology and Social Anthropology in Delhi' (Fuller, 1999: 15).

Srinivas was a person who believed only in works and completely ignored all kinds of 'academic gimmick' in his glittering academic life. He always carried out a placid personality and never started any assignment without deep-rooted insightful thought. He kept trust in hard work and true cognition to involve in meaningful academic as well as public activities. According to him, one can contribute his best work from anywhere if the intention is correct for good cause. In his days, Srinivas used to move from one place to another place devoting him to the academic endeavour and created renaissance with novelty in the grandeur of intellectual exercise where he worked.

Srinivas returned to Karnataka, his home state, to take responsibility for a splendid and leading role in the newly established 'Institute of Social and Economic Change' in Bangalore in 1972. He accepted an affectionate official retirement from the same Institution in 1979 but continued his academic activities in the 'National Institute for Advanced Studies' till the last breath of his life. Although, at the later period of his life, he stopped his pen due to his deteriorating health condition, however, still his works are extremely pervaded throughout the world. There is an all-encompassing fragrance of his contribution to Sociology and Social Anthropology everywhere.

Srinivas was a 'colossus' in sociological discourse. A long list of his publications gives him an international academic reputation and among them, the concept of 'dominant caste', 'vertical and horizontal solidarity', 'westernisation' is outstanding. Even Srinivas is known as a perspective commentator and there has been a very strong emphasis on policy and politics, as well as on comparative ethnography in his most influential collection of essays (1962-1996). His theory of Sanskritisation raises some significant questions such as 'Is the process of Sanskritisation unilinear? In this context, Professor A.M. Shah negates such inhibition.

M.N. Srinivas's contribution to making Sociology in India is stupendous. When in the early fifties, some of the social scientists propagated that American Sociology has created the most important theoretical paradigm to study Sociology; Srinivas strongly opposed this statement and contested it with a different point of view and a different position. Srinivas opines that 'the acceptance of this Sociology would be a national intellectual disaster of the first magnitude' (Srinivas, 1952:36). Of course, before him, some of the distinguished sociologists and anthropologists also expressed their concern about the Indian perspective to study our society. They, particularly, G.S. Ghurye, D.P. Mukherjee, and Radhakamal Mukherjee, seriously applied very distinctive Indian materials for making the bases of the Sociology and Anthropology in India. Even in 1952, Srinivas affirmed his role as constructing a type of Sociology that 'we want' (Srinivas, 1952:36). Srinivas strived to make the proper frame of sociological principle based on true experiences gathered in Indian society. Therefore, although initially, he was working at Oxford University with some British and American anthropologists and sociologists, however, he confined himself with the Indian experiences to continue his research activities and selected south India as a field of study. He thought that 'Sociology to move away from the study of tribes, and the enormous importance this perspective gave to 'culture' (Patel, 1998:49). On the other hand, Srinivas focused on Radcliffe Brown's concept of 'structure' and emphasised to study as a 'totality' which always integrates the different groups in its inter-relationship. Professor Sujata Patel, a well known Indian sociologist, comments that 'given these antecedents, Social Anthropology in the Srinivasan project became coterminous with Sociology. To this connected his vehement rejection of the then fashionable understanding of Sociology and its methodology popularised by American Sociology - that of doing surveys, through opinion polls and questionnaires - and substituting it with the methodology of fieldwork. Where would Indian sociologists attempt to initiate fieldwork?'(Patel, 1998:49). In this context, Srinivas talked about the ethnographical investigation which has been initiated in the village. Therefore, Srinivas was instrumental to initiate the village study in India.

Srinivas is regarded as the pioneer of the empirical investigation of village society as a microcosm of Indian society. No doubt, village studies in India had been started in 1861 when Sir Henry Main published his book on *'Ancient Law: Its Connection with the Early History of Society and Its Relation to Modern Ideas'*, focusing on the land system in India, but in the true sense, it could not provide detailed data about various aspects of rural life. Even the study was not based on any empirical reality and theoretical explanation. Srinivas accelerated the way to cultivate a new knowledge of Sociology through proper initiation of field study. He published an eye-catching and thought-provoking book 'Indian Village' (1955), consisting of a series of ethnographic papers on Indian villages. After that, he published his most valued writings on Sanskritisation and Westernisation in 1956. Apart from these notable works he also boosts his academic reputation by introducing the concept 'dominant caste'. Significantly these writings came together in his praiseworthy books *'Caste in Modern India and Other Essays'* (1962) and '*Social Change in Modern India*' (1966). In contemporary village studies, scholars and students throughout the country accept field study as the most relevant and fruitful methodology. It is the significant credibility of Srinivas to establish his way of thinking adequately for the village study. His methodology helps the research scholars to gather many first-hand experiences of human life in the village society. It also makes the investigators in the field sharper to involve in their activities.

Srinivas believed that sociologists should play an all-encompassing role in society. He observed the sociologist as a mediator who can only understand the process of change. According to Prof. Srinivas, sociologists can communicate this to the government and the public in a proper way. Srinivas opined that 'the sociologist has not only to record the changes initiated by and through adult franchise and the increasing democratisation of society but to offer comments on its impact on the traditional structures which were changing as the result of the forces of modernisation' (Patel: 1998:50). In the view of Srinivas, the sociologist must make the mean for conveying the message to common people about changes taking place in Indian society. However, some of the severest critics of sociological discourse are not to accept Srinivas's statement and they remarked that it is a very hard task to say whether sociologists should provide their helping hands to make the public conscious about social change or not. Some critics believe that sociologists should only analyze the social phenomenon, but Srinivas advocated the social responsibility of academicians and tried to create a mediator in the sociological enterprise to communicate with the public and government for providing information about cause and consequences that take place in human society. He introduced the human element in the process of change and thereby inculcated an attitude of patience sorely lacking among the contemporary elite in India. In light of this, Sujata Patel rightly gave her comment that 'Srinivas's Social Anthropology project hinged on very pragmatic considerations and spelled out a critical and active role for social anthropologists in the process of post-independent nation-building' (Patel, 18:52).

Srinivas always tried to make Sociology accessible to all. He wanted to interact with the common people through articles, newspapers, essays, and talks. He constructed a rational view of Sociology in India through the affective interface with common people. Although Srinivas wanted to make Sociology popular among common people, however, still it is confined to the academic institution of Higher Learning in India. Till today no appropriate attempt has been made by sociologists to popularise field study to realise the real plight of various human groups in India. The Departments of the Sociology of the higher-learning Institutions throughout the country have been mostly encouraging 'book view' rather than 'field view' in the sociological investigation at both undergraduate and postgraduate levels. But Srinivas always appealed to the scholars and students to replace the American's methodology with field study. He was a very strong advocate of empiricism and opined that so long as the tradition of fieldwork continues in Sociology and Social Anthropology; both the disciplines would flourish in India. It is most relevant and functional to understand the various aspects of human life in India. The application of 'participant observation' is an extremely useful technique in a field study. Srinivas gradually sharpens this technique to the level of philosophy. Even Professor M.N. Panini, a luminous student of Srinivas, explored the resemblance between Gandhi's idea of Satyagraha and participant observation. He mentions that 'although Srinivas never articulated it, he practiced the philosophy of participant observation in his personal life' (Panini, 1999:175). Srinivas thought that participant observation is competent enough to teach the sociologist a few lessons in humility. He considered it as an open, non-intrusive learning process. He extremely advocated for the establishment of deep friendship with the respondents during field study to explore the facts. Establishing rapport during field investigation is required to achieve the most substantive findings of an ethnographic study conducted by sociologists and social anthropologists. As the inhabitants of villages in India always prefer strong human bonds based on traditional values; they like to make friends first to disclose obscure practices of their everyday life. It is very difficult to gather proper information about every aspect of their life following some methods and techniques during field investigation. Srinivas realised this reality and therefore preferred participant observation with deep friendship in the village study. He has deserved a high appreciation as he made a new path to initiate a village study in India using 'Indian experiences'. For Indian sociologists and social anthropologists, village study is most significant to understand Indian society as a whole. Manish Thakur rightly observed that 'village studies, to be sure, were meant not simply to add to the empirical corpus of knowledge about the Indian village, but also to father a distinctive understanding of Indian society and culture' (Thakur, 2013:139).

The storytelling ability of Srinivas established his excellence in writing reports of any empirical study. Srinivas explained the fact gathered during field study as a novelist to his readers. He is highly acknowledged for his ability of storytelling in sociological work. T.K. Madan also compared him with eminent novelist R.K. Narayan. His sociological sensibilities shaped his style; in his autobiographical writings, a social fact would all of a sudden pop out of a descriptive narration or his description would itself seem to point to a sociological insight he wished to share with his readers (Panini, 1999: 175). Of course, Srinivas never estranged from the disciplinary boundary and he adopted the novelist's style of interpretation of facts that Sociology demands. It is necessary to communicate with the common people regarding social change take place in human society. If the readers accept the sociological book as 'bedtime reading' or 'leisure time reading', it is not mean that book is not the result of serious sociological work. Srinivas's books depict his hard work and insightful understanding of human society. In this context, M.N. Panini mentions that he had seen the meticulousness with which Srinivas had classified his field notes, indexed them, and had provided cross-references for each pile of cards of which he had transferred his data (Panini: 1999:175). This statement of M.N. Panini, who got the privilege to give a close eye on Srinivas's work as his close kin and his ward for some years, is one of the absolute evidence to recognize the quality of books written by Srinivas. It is, therefore, true that Srinivas's books are not only readable but also most insightful. Srinivas's book represents 'the best of Indian ethnography and it makes the reader engage, both intellectually and emotionally, with narration, making it possible for us to transcend the boundary lines distinguish academia from literature. It is no wonder it has been judged as quality' (Nakane, 1978:33). Srinivas opines that we need to use ethnography and it will remain relevant in sociological discourse. Unfortunately, Srinivas's ethnography was also continued within the strict boundary of colonial ideology. His ethnography was not emancipated from the colonial ideological legacy. It created space coterminous with the village and also made ethnography as episteme. Kamala Ganesh nicely mentions that 'his emphasis on ethnographic fieldwork left their distinctive imprint on his writings on family and kinship (Ganesh, 2013:300). Indeed, his methodology was not like Ghurye's other students, such as I.P. Desai, Kapadia, and Karve. A galaxy of sociologists and social anthropologists have extensively criticized, evaluated, and commented on his methodology. T.K. Oommen, well known Indian sociologist, also labeled Srinivas as one of the proponents of 'Methodological Hinduism' (2008:78). Srinivas used 'participation observation' as a methodology to understand Indian society. He never strived to make only Hinduism an object of study but also Indian society. When T.K. Oommen uses the term Methodological Hinduism', perhaps he means that it is mainly through the study of the Hindu religion by using the method of participant observation. According to him, Srinivas exclusively applied Hinduism to understand Indian society. Ananta Giri also argued that though India is a plural society, however, Srinivas did not study any other religion except Hinduism. Even Srinivas's praiseworthy collection, '*Social Significance of Religion in India*' does not discuss much the dynamics of non-Hindu religions in India (Giri, 2010:61). But it is not a correct statement. It is very difficult to comment on T.K. Oommen's observation as he held responsible that Hinduism became an object of Srinivas's study and it became methodological as opposed to only textual and self-valorising. It is to be understood as a set of fundamentals of belief and practice. It is said that 'a notion of the supernatural is not central to it, and the idea of moral law that may be considered substitute is highly relativistic (Madan, 2006:218). These academic debates have continued for a long time. Srinivas himself acknowledged them and wrote about the 'amorphousness' and 'complexity' of Hinduism and the difficulty of defining it (1952, 1958; Srinivas and Shah, 1968). On the other hand, a researcher in Sociology or Social Anthropology will have to choose any space for his empirical study. Sometimes selected spaces may have a label of religious or ethnic identity, but it does not mean that researchers knowingly valorise this identity. Srinivas was not the kind of sociologist and social anthropologist who praised any 'ism' to make label his intellectual affront with 'other's affiliation'. He only tried to explore the reality of society by keeping his eyes with a focus on the everyday activities of the people. On the other hand, the method is considered as an epistemological process. It is looked at only as a tool. When a researcher decides to use the tool for gathering information from the field, he or she never thinks of any self-critical approach.

Srinivas was the most dedicated researcher during his time and never presented himself as one of the moralists or philosophers. Andre Beteille argues, as a social anthropologist, he valued observation, the description above introspection, and speculation. He knew that introspection had been valued far above observation in the Indian intellectual tradition. (2003: xxiii-xxiv) However, there are differences in the appropriateness of the methodological application in Srinivas's study. In this context, a question has been raised that 'Did Srinivas valorize Hinduism?. 'Some of the critic's comments, that his approach is more complex and multi-dimensional. In some of his passages, we can find an element of valorisation of Hinduism, but in others, it is an engagement of non-valorisation and critique' (Giri, 2010:216). Overall, the debate centering on Srinivas's methodology has brought demand for Srinivas's methodological application in contemporary sociological and anthropological study. The scholar of Sociology and Social Anthropology are still keen to use 'participant observation' as the most effective method to understand the various aspects of human society. No one can reject the relevance of his methodology in social sciences research with poor arguments. Even his study attempts to provide empirical details to make a new theoretical explanation about human life in Sociology and Social Anthropology. He used 'participant observation' as a very simple method and it never compels the researcher to move away from his objective of the study. G. Mishra rightly says that 'the most important method is the methods of inquiry were certain simple but critical question raised and answered' (2004:274). Thus, the methodological practice of Srinivas has significant implications for methods in social sciences. T.N. Madan also argues, 'Srinivas made a strong plea for empiricism in the social sciences and the method of 'participant observation' in anthropological research. Successful fieldwork, he maintained, required total commitment, even the holding in abeyance of family and personal obligations' (2006:215). Considering this argument, his methodological stance has provided him the most dignified academic recognition forever. Srinivas's lesion to new generation researchers makes a concrete way for the good enterprise of ethnography. Sujata Patel opines, 'an enterprise of ethnography should alert us to explore the details that link relationship between cultural products, social behaviour and processes as they have been articulated in the context of received, reconstructed and emerging hierarchies in the global world'. His enthusiasm for a field study to find out the most substantive findings of his research is the most positive and potent scholarship in his century. Still, field study is an important subject of sociological research. It has merit for first-hand experiences that led to critical thinking. A good number of contemporary sociologists have been associating with field study in the context of their research. Srinivas must be acknowledged for his effort to popularise the field study among the sociologists in India. Of course, contrary to the common perception, Srinivas never ignored the theory also. He used to say that theory should be articulated through facts. According to him, if no attempt has been made to explore the fact, then the proper theoretical explanation will not be obtained about the concerned subject of human society. Hence, he strongly preferred the 'field view' rather than the 'book view'. Srinivas was most apprehensive of 'bibliocentrism'; he was equally wary of 'paleocentrism'. According to him, both are two sides of the same counterfeit coin. He believed that the aridity of the book's view fails to contract with lived reality. Srinivas always strived to highlight a view of society after exploring reality through participant observation. He distinctly clears his stance in favour of field study to acquire appropriate knowledge about human society.

M.N. Srinivas had tremendous credibility as a sociologist and social anthropologist. He was an indefatigable and exemplary researcher and dedicated his life to true up-gradation of the subject like Sociology. B.S. Baviskar, who was in the first batch of Srinivas's students in the Department of Sociology at Delhi University, opined that Srinivas was a born sociologist.

Srinivas had many qualities that created such an impression on others. He always liked the company of other people and enjoyed meeting with them. He was a person who laid much emphasis on rules in his academic career. He strictly preserved a sense of ethics but was never judgmental. As a human being, he had enough respect for others and never tried to faze at any cost. T.K. Madan confessed that at the beginning of his research career he came to respect Srinivas deeply for his seriousness as a scholar and his unfailing courtesy, charm, and wit as a human being (2006:217). Srinivas will remain as a colossus in the social sciences domain for his great contribution. Though the debate is still going on whether he is a sociologist or anthropologist, however, his contribution would be admired by all scholars, students, and academicians who belong to both disciplines in years to come. Once Andre Beteille asked whether he still believed in the unity of Sociology and Social Anthropology and response to him, Srinivas strongly replied that there is no real difference in the endeavour between Sociology and Social Anthropology. Srinivas himself commented that 'I do not believe that distinction has much value as far as the study of Indian society and culture is concerned' (Srinivas, 1999: Vol. 5). We are to recall and remember Srinivas as the most charismatic personalities in the academic world.

References

Fuller, Chris 1999. An interview with M.N. Srinivas, *Anthropology Today*, 15.

Nakane, Chie, 1978. The Remembered Village: memory 'maximized', *Contributions to Indian Sociology*, 12,1.

Panini, MN, 1999. M.N. Srinivas and Sociology, *Economic and Political Weekly*, January 22, 1999.

Patel, Sujata, 1998. The Nostalgia for the village: M.N. Srinivas and the making of Indian Social Anthropology, *South Asia*,11,1.

Srinivas, MN, 1952. *Religion and Society among the Coorgs of South India*, Clarendon Press, Oxford.

Srinivas, MN, 1955. *India's Villages*, West Bengal Government Press, Calcutta.

Srinivas, MN, 1962. *Caste in Modern India and Other Essays*, Asia Publishing House, Bombay.

Srinivas, MN, 1966. *Social Change in Modern India*, University of California Press, California.

Srinivas, MN, 1976. *The Remembered Village*, Oxford University Press, Delhi.

15

Contributions of S.C. Dube Towards Anthropological Studies in India

Anannya Gogoi

Life and professional journey

Prof. Shyama Charan Dube is an eminent luminary in a league of scholars who have made tireless contributions to build the discipline of Sociology and Anthropology in India. Prof. Dube belongs to a generation of scholars who were engaged in the difficult task of framing the concepts and content of both the disciplines during the phase of development of social, political, and economic institutions in India after independence. The contributions of Prof. Dube had made an intrinsic effect on the expansion of the practice of sociology and social anthropology. They helped to address the social specificities in the context of Indian society, its problems, and concerns. These issues and areas are different from western societies and required a fresh approach to study from the prism of social sciences. Prof. Dube's academic and professional journey is one of purposeful versatility and can be understood by looking at the biographical profile of his life.

Prof. S.C. Dube was born on 25th July 1922 at Narasinghpur in Madhya Pradesh and passed away on 4th February 1996 at the age of 73 years. He completed his Master's Degree in Political Science from Nagpur University and pursued his Doctoral research on the Kamar, a tribe of shifting cultivators in Madhya Pradesh. This work was the beginning of his long term engagement with the field as well as with the experimentation with different methodologies of field-based studies. At the beginning of his career, Prof. Dube joined as a lecturer at Bishop College, Nagpur, Maharashtra, and later moved to Lucknow University to join the Department of Political Science. Rather than strictly confining himself to one compartment of social science discipline, Prof. Dube extended his practice of social sciences. For example, during his stay at Lucknow University, he engaged with Prof. D. N. Majumdar and assisted him in the publication of the journal titled Eastern Anthropologist (Chauhan, 1996).

The meticulous shifts in the pursuit of different scientific practices are yet again noticed when Prof. Dube moves to Osmania University to join as a Reader in the place of Von Fürer Haimendorf in the Department of Sociology. Prof. Dube henceforth expands his work in the study of Indian society by engaging with students, scholars, and social scientists both in his institution as well as institutions from other countries. He was a visiting lecturer at the School of Oriental and African Studies SOAS, London where he met Raymond Firth. The intellectual interaction between these two scholars led to the publication of the book *'Indian Village'* in 1955 based on the field-based work conducted by Prof. Dube in Shamirpeth, near the city of Hyderabad in India (Nagla, 2008). This work is one of a few that marks the beginning of a new phase of village studies both in the academic life of Prof. Dube and in the empirical studies of villages in India in general (Dube, 1973).

Two major events in his academic journey in the realm of anthropology are Prof. Dube's engagement with the Anthropological Survey of India from 1956 to 1957 at Nagpur and his subsequent appointment as a Professor of Anthropology at the University of Saugar in Madhya Pradesh from 1957 to 1978. While holding these positions he made extensive contributions to the development of the discipline of Anthropology. He spends a substantial part of his professional life at the University of Saugar and had initiated a course titled 'Anthropology Today'. It was an important step to expand the reach of the discipline among the students of the university as well as other educational institutions. Thus, from Political Science to Sociology to that of Anthropology, Prof. Dube's versatile academic engagement denotes his thirst for knowledge through interdisciplinary engagements. Other institutions where Prof. Dube engaged as a visiting professor or lecturer include the London University 1952 -53, London School of Economics, and the Anthropology of Far Eastern Studies at Cornell University 1955-56. These visits were an integral part of his journey into the realm of the practice of social sciences.

Another dimension of Prof. Dube's career is his lifelong engagement with the practice and study of community development. Prof. Dube was very much interested in the Community Development Programmes initiated by the Government of India at that time to revive the social, political, and economic structure of Indian in the post-independence phase. This field of interest of Prof. Dube was reflected in his active service in various positions both in academic as well as non-academic institutions. He acted as the Principal and Director of Research, National Institute of Community Development, Mussorie from 1961- 64 and was the Director at the Indian Institute of Advanced Studies, Shimla 1972- 77. He was also engaged in various projects related to the United Nations Organisation (UNO) and the United Nations Educational, Scientific and Cultural Organisation (UNESCO).

Significant positions held by Prof. S.C. Dube also includes his joining as the Vice-Chancellor of Jammu University 1978-1980. (Gupta, 1996); Advisor, National Institute of Rural Community Development; President of Indian Sociological Society, 1975-76, ICSSR National Fellow1980-1993; Chairman, Madhya Pradesh University Grants Commission; Editor of *Bharatiya Samaj Pachichaya Mala.* These designations not only throw light on Pro. Dube's professional and academic hard work but also speak of his continuous effort in the practice of the development of institutions and society. These diverse services emphasise that he was successfully managing his role in academics, research, development as well as administration. However, this list cannot be exhaustive of all the laurels that Prof. Dube has earned in his lifetime.

Works of Prof. S.C. Dube

Similar to the professional accolades of Prof. S. C. Dube, one cannot exhaust the list of his academic contributions in the analysis of Indian society expressed in the form of the written word. As discussed earlier one of his first contributions was *The Kamar* (1955) based on his Doctoral research. The work depicts his growing association with the field of study beyond the textual image of Indian society. Indian village 1955 is a watershed in the progress of village studies in India. This work of Prof. Dube along with a few others *'Village India'* by Mackim Marriot and Indian Villages by M.N. Srinivas marked a departure from the earlier anthropological studies on villages in India conducted during the colonial period (Dube, 1973).

Along with contributions to village studies, Prof. Dube also authored and compiled works on the study of tribes, modernisation and social change, and community development. These include: *India's Changing Villages: Human Factors in Community Development* 1958; *The study of complex cultures* 1965; *Institution Building for Community Development* 1968; *Explanation and Management of Changes* 1971; *Contemporary India and its Modernisation* 1974; *Tribal Heritage of India* 1977, *Understanding Society* 1977, *Modernisation and Development: The Search for Alternative Paradigms* 1988, *Tradition and Development* 1990, *Understanding Change: Anthropological and Sociological Perspectives* 1990; *Indian Society* 1990. These studies describe the image of the structure of the Indian society and the changes occurring in it at a macro level.

On the other hand, the field-based studies have highlighted the micro-processes at the ground level. Some of these works are: Thinking of caste in Telangana Village 1955, Dominant caste and village leadership 1961, Antiquity to modernity in Tribal India, Public Services and Social Responsibility, Field Songs of Chhattisgarh, On crisis and Commitment in Social Sciences. Secularisation in Multi-religious Societies, Development perspective for the 1980's 1983.

Prof. Dube has also published in the vernacular languages to make the knowledge on Indian societies available to the students and scholars from different sections of society. Some of these publications are *Manav Evam Sanskriti, Bharatiya Gram, Vikas Ka Samajshastra, Sankraman ki Peera*. From the above shortlist of the works done by Prof. Dube, we can understand the extensiveness as well as the intensiveness of his thoughts and his anthropological and sociological studies.

Revisiting major themes in the contributions of Prof. S.C. Dube

Prof. Dube's works have extended from that of study of tribes to that of rural studies to studies in social change and modernisation. Many eminent scholars and students from the social sciences, especially from Anthropology and Sociology have already reviewed and compiled Prof. Dube's work (Nagla, 2008; Gupta, 1996; Chauhan, 1996; Beteille, 1996). The current practice of social sciences is incomplete without the citation of works by scholarly geniuses like Prof. Dube. This repository of contributions by him has inspired generations of scholars to look at society and its various compositions from different perspectives and find new facts about the same. Hence the narration of his contribution is only a humble attempt to repeat the already appraised and cherished works.

Tribes and village communities

The work on tribes and village studies conducted by Prof. Dube was part of new development in the social anthropological understanding of these communities in India. These studies looked at the social structure of Indian Villages from a prism unlike that of the earlier colonial researchers. The village community was looked like a self-sufficient unit in many of the earlier studies but Prof. Dube's work investigated the facts that are contrary to this assumption and asserted that the Indian village and other communities in the modern era cannot operate as an isolated self-sufficient unit. The component social organisations are a part of the larger social processes experienced by society (Dube, 1990). He considered the social structure of the village to be as susceptible to change as that of the other social dimensions in Indian society. Society in India during the post-independence period of that time was adapting to new socio-political and economic forces such that as sovereignty, modernisation, secularism, and the drive towards development. Prof. Dube embedded his field of study in these changing social situations to understand them and formulate a new image of the Indian social structure.

The methodology used for these studies were also not as categorical and exclusive as that of the studies conducted by earlier scholars, particularly by the colonial scholars. Prof. Dube draws theoretical insights and methods not only from his association with anthropologists like Robert Redfield and Raymond Firth but also from a diverse range of scientific paradigms. To understand the social organisation of the villages and the larger Indian society he used the structural-functional approach. He drew insights from the historical understanding of Indian society. Further, he also focused on Indology for an alternative understanding of the social organisation in India. Besides the above approaches, he was always a pioneer of the theoretical and methodological approaches from Anthropology and Sociology in general (Dube, 1990). Such a multidisciplinary orientation in methodology helped to provide a fresh understanding and description of social institutions and practices of the Indian society.

Prof. Dube's work was extensive enough to incorporate the study of a wide range of social institutions in the villages such as religion, economy, kinship, and caste (Nagla, 2008; Dube, 1990). Further, he also dwelled on the philosophical understanding of the values and attitudes that give rise to these institutions and regulate the changes that happen in them in due course of time. The empirical studies and analysis done by him in these areas demonstrate his anthropological and sociological brilliance.

Influence of community development programme

Yet another example of his versatile genius is Prof. Dube's interest in the Community Development Programme initiated by the Government of India. Prof. Dube was very much concerned with the process of nation-building during the post-independence phase in India. For him, the social science practice in India cannot abstain from the understanding of changing paradigm of values that center on the project of nation-building (Dube, 1973). Social science research should contribute to enhancing the knowledge of the existing social structures, the issues, and challenges in their development and in building up measures for better developmental projects. Thus, Prof. Dube questioned the maintenance of complete value neutrality in the social sciences. He posited that a social scientist cannot take a neutral stand when the society itself is taking a definite path of progress and development.

His interest in community development, therefore, led to the extension of empirical studies, documentation, and analysis in the social anthropological discourse. Prof. Dube conducted studies on the role of the community in social change and progress. Further, he also raised concerns about the role of traditions in community development and challenges related to it. For this, he emphasized the study of the normative order of society and its influence in the process of development. Finally, the role of the state in addressing this normative order with a new approach that is different from the colonial rule was also a dimension of the studies conducted by Prof. Dube with inspiration from the Community Development Programme. This extensive and active practice of social research found expression when he was engaged in the Cornell India project in Saharanpur, Uttar Pradesh.

Thus, Prof. Dube keenly sought the relevance of social science disciplines such as Anthropology in the analysis of the emerging issues of the process of nation-building and social development in India, while conducting his studies.

Social change

A running theme that emerges from most of the contributions of Prof. S.C. Dube is that of the understanding of social change. His interest in the process of nation-building not only included the issue of development but also of cultural and social change. As mentioned earlier one of the dimensions of understanding social organisations for Prof. Dube was the analysis of the relationship between the world view, values, and attitude of the community and that of social progress. Therefore the understanding of social change, particularly modernisation of Indian society was a large part of his contribution to social anthropological understanding.

In works such as India's Changing Villages (1958) and Contemporary India and its Modernisation (1974), Prof. Dube looks into the interaction between tradition and modernity in specific communities as well as in the larger social structure of India. Social change in different social contexts such as the rural and the urban are emphasised. He explores the factors of social change and modernisation, focusing on both technological development and social transformation. Areas of social change such as religion and secularism, youth and education, bureaucracy, and the state are discussed in detail (Dube, 1974). Prof. Dube's concern for the reconstruction and development of the Indian society is reflected while he is narrating about these aspects of social change.

Further, different contributions also highlight the issues and challenges that are there in the process of social development. While discussing these issues Prof. Dube identifies and describes the emerging social problems of that period of Indian social history. He also dwells on the impact of social change on the social structure, social institutions, and social interactions. The result of the interaction of these forces of change is the rise of sub-cultures and restructuring of the accommodation processes in Indian society.

The analysis of changing Indian society and the embedded communities and institutions in his different works reflect the versatile expertise of Prof. S.C. Dube. His training in social anthropology contributed to his intensive engagement with the field. At the same time, sociological imagination (Dube, 1973) had inspired him to conceptualise social change and modernisation and his training in political science earlier had influenced his work regarding the issues and problems of development.

Conclusion

A comprehensive concluding remark on the contribution of Prof. Dube will be invalid from a student of social science. However, the major strands of knowledge that are visible to the students can be drawn from two dimensions of his contribution. First is his extensive study of Indian society at different levels. These include the study of the social structure at the macro, and micro level, institutional level, community, practices, and philosophy of Indian society. For this exercise, Prof. Dube practices the use of empirical studies rather than relying on modeling and grand theories.

The second dimension is very much embedded in his engagement with the project of community development as a practice and also as a subject of study. In this dimension Prof. Dube attempts to redefine the objectives and methodology of the social sciences, particularly social anthropology, to capture the specificities of the Indian social context which was undergoing substantial changes. The social anthropological work by Prof. Dube contributes to the understanding of the current challenges of that era in juxtaposition to the prospects for the nation.

The social anthropological study of Indian society by Prof. Dube also helps to change the colonial imagery of the field in India as the 'other' by providing empirical contestations from an insider's perspective. Thus, it helps in the re-imagination of the Indian Society with fresh interdisciplinary approaches and methods. It helps in the understanding of the process of modernisation from an Indian lens rather than as a part of the process of westernisation.

Thus, the contribution made by Prof. Dube to Anthropology, Sociology, and Social Sciences, in general, is profound. The influence that Prof. S. C. Dube and his work have on every scholar and student who has met him, read his work, or have worked with him still lingers on in the Indian academia as well as elsewhere else. This written piece is only a humble remembrance of the eminent scholar from the perspective of a student of social science.

References

Beteille, A. 1996. 'Shyama Charan Dube (1922-1996)'. *Economic and Political Weekly*, 811.

Chauhan, BR. 1996. 'Obituary: Shyama Charan Dube (25.7.1922 - 4.2.1996) Former President, Indian Sociological Society, 1975-76'. *Sociological Bulletin*, 130-133.

Dube, SC. 1990. *Indian Society.* National Book Trust, New Delhi.

Dube, SC. 1974. *Contemporary India and Its Modernisation.* Vikas Publishing House, Delhi.

Dube, SC. 1973. *Social Sciences in Changing Society D.N. Majumdar lectures 1972.* Lucknow University: Ethnographic and Folk Society, Lucknow.

Gupta, SK. 1996. 'Obituary: Professor Shyama Charan Dube (1922- 1996)'. *Indian Anthropologist*, 85.

Nagla, B. 2008. *Indian Sociological Thought.* Rawat Publications, Jaipur.

Shukla, S. 1996. 'Intellectuals, nation, and the people'. *Economic and Political Weekly*, 2707.

16

Nirendra Chandra Choudhury: A Silent Anthropologist

Sekh Rahim Mondal

Introduction

Professor Nirendra Chandra Choudhury, popularly known as N.C. Choudhury was not only a doyen of Indian anthropology but also an eminent teacher and institution builder. Prof. Choudhury was known for his versatile knowledge of classical anthropological and sociological theories as well as for fieldwork experiences among varied tribal and non-tribal groups of various parts of India. He was both the theorist and at the same time empiricist. His work on action anthropology and sociology was acknowledged both in India and abroad.

This chapter is a humble attempt to highlight in brief the life and works of Professor N. C. Choudhury as a tribute to remember him on hundred years of teaching in anthropology in India. The chapter is based on facts gathered from published works and facts obtained from his wife Dr. Namita Choudhury. All these are supported by the author's own experience out of his close interaction with Prof. Choudhury as like as a student and as a colleague for a long time.

Early Life, Education, and Carrier

Nirendra Chandra Choudhury was born on 21 January 1924, in Banaras in Uttar Pradesh. He was the sixth son of Sri Nishikanta Choudhury and Dakshina Debi. He was brought up in an environment of a typical Bengali joint family; this helped him to learn the art of sharing, sacrificing, and caring. He lost his father at the age of 14 years and grown under his mother and elder brothers. At a very young age, he was bound to share the family responsibility and this was reflected in his education and career.

N. C. Choudhury completed his basic education from the Anglo-Bengali school of Banaras, located near the *ghat* of Ganga. He passed I.Sc. from the college of Banaras in 1943. After completing I.Sc. he took admission to B.Sc. under Kashi University, but unable to continue for familial responsibility. This was a very tough period for him. At that time, he got mental support from his mother and other family members. During this period, he was exposed to Swami Achalananda (Kedar Babu) of Ramkrishna Mission Ashram and Satish Chandra Mukhopadhyay, a journalist (Editor of Dawn); those who helped him in many ways to move forward. Prof. Choudhury was very much influenced by the ideas of Ramkrishna Paramhangshodeb and Swami Vivekananda, and which was continued throughout his life. At a young age, he was very fond of playing football and cricket. He learned the art of rustling, chase, and card playing. However, his playful character underwent a complete change when he joined in service.

In 1944, N. C. Choudhury joined the traffic and account section of the Indian Railway. In 1944, he left the Railway service and joined as a Field Assistant in the Department of Anthropology, Government of India, now known as Anthropological Survey of India (ASI). It is to be noted here that at that time, the Head Office of ASI was shifted from Calcutta to Banaras for a brief period due to the World War situation.

Later, the ASI office was again shifted to Calcutta and he left Banaras with a hope for a new destiny. While working as a Field Assistant in ASI, he was able to attract the attention of Dr. B.S. Guha, (Director) encouraged him to study further. With the support and permission of Dr. Guha, Choudhury took admission in B.A. (Honours) course in anthropology under the University of Calcutta. In 1951, he passed B.A. (Hons) examination and got the position of first in first class. This was the turning point of his academic and professional life.

Again with the permission and support of Dr. Guha and many others of ASI, he took admission for P.G. Course of Anthropology at the University of Calcutta. He completed his master's degree in 1953 and secured the position of first in first class. During his P.G. classes, he came in close contact with many experienced teachers of the department like Prof. K.P. Chattopadhyay, Prof. T.C. Das, Prof. M.N. Basu, Prof. N.K. Bose, Prof. G.S. Roy, and others, who motivated him in many ways to develop his research interest in the discipline.

After completing a master's degree, Choudhury again joined ASI as Field Assistant and engaged with a variety of research activities of the office. His inquisitive mind, sincerity, and dedication took him to come to closure with Prof. N.K. Bose. In 1954, N.C. Choudhury was promoted to the post of Preparator of Ethnographic Materials, and then gradually obtained the positions of Senior Technical Assistant and Research Associate. In 1955, he was selected for the post of Curator for the Anthropology Gallery of the Museum. At this stage, his external linkages were started to grow up. He was exposed to Prof. L.K. Hsu of North Western University (NWU), Illinois, who at that time was the Visiting Fellow of ASI. Prof. Hsu was very pleased to see Choudhury's anthropological works and suggested him to do a Ph.D. in his University. With the permission of the Ministry and the support of Prof. Hsu, Choudhury went to NWU, Illinois as a Full Bright Fellow to do his Ph.D. research in 1957. He married in the year 1956. His wife is Dr. Namita Choudhury who is the daughter of N. Dutta Majumder and a Sociologist. At this stage, N.C. Choudhury got encouragement and valuable support from Prof. Surajit Chandra Sinha, who also had his Ph.D. from the N.W.U. Illinois. N.C. Choudhury completed his Ph.D. under the supervision and support of Prof. M.J. Herskovits and L.K. Hsu in 1960. His Ph.D. thesis of N.W.U. was titled "*Acculturation of Mundas: A Study in Differential Change and Caste Formation.*" After completing the Ph.D., Choudhury decided to return to India.

Dr. N.C. Choudhury came back to India and joined again in ASI with some innovative ideas. In 1962, he organised a major science exhibition for children on "*Evolution of Man and Culture*". With the support of Prof. N.K. Bose, Choudhury involved the artists of Kumartuli (Calcutta) to prepare the clay models for display in the exhibition.

The exhibition project achieved a grand success. After its successful completion, he was actively involved in the Museum movement and got the recognition of "a Man of Museum".

The period between 1962 - 1975 was the golden era for Dr. Choudhury in ASI. During this period he was able to traverse the most important hierarchical positions of ASI ranging from Superintending Anthropologists to Deputy Director and finally to the post of Director in Charge.

Although N.C. Choudhury was primarily associated with the research institutions like ASI since the beginning of his professional life, he had an interest in teaching and research supervision. Along with his official (ASI) duties, he served the department of Museology, University of Calcutta, as a guest and visiting faculty. At one point in time, he was thinking to join the University of Trinidad, but it was not materialised for familial reasons.

During the last phase of the 1970s, N.C. Choudhury decided to shift to the teaching profession. The opportunity came to him when Prof. Amlan Dutta, then Vice-Chancellor of the University of North Bengal (NBU), invited him to set up the new interdisciplinary department of Sociology and Social Anthropology in the said University. N.C. Choudhury left ASI and joined North Bengal University in 1976 as a founder Head to establish the new department. In the same year, he took all the initiatives to start the P.G. classes as well as to promote research programmes with only three colleagues and six students. With his active leadership, the department got a national and international reputation within a decade. The department later bifurcated into two separate departments – Sociology and Anthropology in the year 2001. Prof. N.C. Choudhury retired from North Bengal University in 1989. Nearly ten scholars did their Ph.D. under the active supervision of him.

While in NBU, N.C. Choudhury not only was the Professor and Head of the Department of Sociology and Social Anthropology but also served as a Dean of the Faculty of Arts and Social Sciences. In the early 1980s, Choudhury became interested in action anthropology/ action sociology and this was continued until he was academically active. He had the belief that there is no use to be an armchair anthropologist unless the knowledge is applied for the development of society. With this idea in mind, during his last phase of University service, he was involved with the evaluation project of the impact of the existing irrigation scheme in the Terai region of North Bengal in 1986. The project was supported by the Dutch Government-sponsored body in collaboration with the Department of Agriculture, Government of West Bengal. Just after his retirement, Prof. Choudhury was deeply involved with the irrigation project until its completion in 1994. For the sake of this project, he formulated a solid research team with the passed out students. He had conducted a wide range of field surveys at several parts of Terai, Duars, and Cooch Behar with his research team for examining the socio-economic impacts of irrigation from the perspective of rural development. The project report prepared by him got wide recognition and for which the University of Amsterdam invited him in 1995 for delivering a lecture on the findings of the project.

After his retirement, Prof. Choudhury used to live in the NBU campus with his wife and finally shifted to Calcutta in 2002. After the end of the irrigation project, Prof. Choudhury gradually withdrew from the academic arena and was involved with reading books, watching T.V., visiting local R.K. Missions, and extending social services to the local village peoples. In his post-retirement life, he used to spend time with local villagers with whom he had developed close relations by helping them in various ways. Most of the local villagers used to utter kinship terms like Baba to address him.

Research and academic works

Prof. Choudhury conducted as well as supervised a series of field-based research works in both ASI and NBU. He did fieldwork both among tribal and non-tribal groups living in islands, plain lands, mountains, urban spaces, and frontier regions. Among his field-based researches, the most important are Mundas and Oraons of Chotanagpur, Noctes of Arunachal Pradesh, Onges of Little Andaman, Lois of Manipur, to name a few. His active involvement with the ASI Area and Border Studies Programmes of Manipur and Nagaland are still used as reference materials to many scholars.

After joining NBU, Prof. Choudhury took special initiatives to study small tribal and ethnic groups of North Bengal, particularly the

Meches, Rabhas, and other less-known communities of the region. His research interests were also focused on socio-economic problems and developmental issues of rural North Bengal. He had assigned research topics on those subjects to many of his research scholars. He also encouraged his colleagues to take up research projects on the local communities and their problems.

Contributions to the domain of knowledge

Prof. N.C. Choudhury left behind a rich tradition of anthropological studies in India. He immensely contributed towards field studies among various tribal and non-tribal groups living in varied eco-cultural zones. His primary focus of the study was the dynamics of social structure and culture. The study of acculturation among the tribes was his special fascination, and through which he was able to discover the new social formation (caste-like and class/like) among some tribal groups of Eastern India. His knowledge about the tribal life of Northeast India was very significant which he acquitted through intensive field studies at several parts of this region. He had vast experience in the tribal mosaic of the country. He also contributed to the study of the folklore of indigenous communities. His concept of "Small Tribe" or "Minor Tribe" is getting popularity in Indian anthropology today. He holds the view that the "small" or "minor" tribes of India are facing unique problems of social and cultural adaptation due to the strong influence of dominant communities living around them, be they tribe or non-tribe. The nature of such a situation pushed them in a different position to maintain their distinct identity. Through his experience of the area and border studies he developed the idea of "Frontier Society" and "Frontier Culture". He meticulously noted the economic and cultural ties of the frontier peoples. In his view, peoples living in frontier areas share the social and cultural elements of both sides of the border and which helped them to integrate despite their different political identities. He had also examined how the frontier people adjust themselves under the pressure of adjacent civilisations. In his view, economic and cultural ties between both sides of the border people helped them to develop such an adaptation. In the last phase of his academic life, Prof. Choudhury got interested in action research and which he fulfilled through a research project on the impact of irrigation in the rural society of North Bengal. He along with his other friends he started to publish a journal on "Action Sociology" from Patna University, to which he had contributed some impact papers. He was a strong believer in alternatives in development as viewed by the people for whom it is planned. This reveals his postmodern views. He was interested to apply anthropological knowledge to the social development of poor and backward sections of Indian society.

Prof. Choudhury not only conducted several field studies but also left behind the rich tradition of doing long-term fieldwork through appropriate methods and techniques suitable for the need for research. Being influenced by T.C. Das and N.K. Bose, he had acquired the art of free dialogue for establishing a good rapport with the various kinds of village people. He was very fond to adopt the story-telling method for the collection of field data. His fieldwork experiences quite often he used to share with his students and colleagues, which later helped them in many ways to handle their respective field situations.

Throughout his entire professional carrier, Prof. Choudhury held many important positions both in ASI and in University. He had initiated, directed, and completed many research projects. He developed the Department of Sociology and Social Anthropology at North Bengal University in the frame of interdisciplinary perspective. He supervised almost ten scholars for their Ph.D. degree. The topics of research allotted to his scholars were of varied nature, consisting of the issues and problems of tribes, castes, peasants, social problems, social movement, state of education, cultural ecology, industrial wearers, women's studies, health issues, etc.

He emphasised the need for proper grooming of the students both in theoretical as well as in empirical works. He was an excellent teacher. He used to teach the courses on classical social thoughts and theories, social structure and organisation, and social and cultural change. Even at a very senior age, he accompanied the field trips of P.G. final year students along with his young colleagues. He had the habit of spot assessment of the progress of the fieldwork of the students. He was the hard taskmaster and this was his way of guiding the students.

Prof. Choudhury was not only a good teacher but also a meticulous examiner. He was also known for his critical assessment of research works. His ability for inspiration and motivation and the way to connect the hearts of the students is still a role model for many teachers.

Epilogue

Prof. N.C. Choudhury was not only a scholar but also a very good teacher and institution builder. He might have not published much, but immensely contributed in the domain of anthropological and sociological knowledge. He had a hard life since childhood, continued throughout his professional life, which he had faced challengingly. He was very fond of value-oriented research and advocated for work on socially relevant issues, to meet the needs of common people. In his view, knowledge is useless unless it is used for the good of humankind, especially of the oppressed.

Being trained by both Indian and American mentors, Prof. Choudhury followed the traditions of both social and cultural anthropology in his research. On one hand, his focus of the study was social structure and social institution, while on the other hand, he had examined the cultural attributes of tribes and non-tribes. These traditions even reflected in the formation of the course curriculum of the Department of Sociology and Social Anthropology of NBU which he set up with great hope for interdisciplinary study and research.

Prof. N. C. Choudhury had produced several good students and scholars who have established their name as a teacher in Anthropology as well as in Sociology and even in administration and bureaucracy. He not only guided his students in the realm of academics but also socialised them into productive and socially sensitive human beings. He would always advise and encourages his students and colleagues to publish their research works, so that they may get away from the arena of academics. His students, colleagues, and friends did have a sweet and special kind of relationship with him, which they still cherish. He left for his heavenly abode on 18 October 2013.

Some of his major publications

Choudhury, NC., 1961. *Acculturation of Mundas: A Study in Differential Change and Caste Formation,* Unpublished Ph.D. thesis, Department of Anthropology, North Western University, Illinois, USA.

Choudhury, NC and Dasgupta Biman, 1975. 'The Lois of Manipur: A study of inter-ethnic relation', *Journal of Indian Anthropological Society,* 10: 153-158.

Choudhury, NC., 1977. *Munda Social Structure,* Farma KL Mukhopadhyay, Calcutta.

Choudhury, NC., 1982. 'Meches – A small tribe', in B.D. Choudhury (Ed.): *Tribal Development in India,* Inter India Publication, New Delhi.

Choudhury, NC., 1986. *Impact of Existing Irrigation Schemes in the Terai Region – An Evaluation Report;* Department of Sociology and Social Anthropology, University of North Bengal.

Choudhury, NC., 1987. *Action Sociology in India,* Seminar Proceedings, Department of Sociology, Patna University, Patna.

Choudhury, NC., 1988. *North Bengal Terai Development Project,* Project Coordination Reports, Euro consult the Netherlands.

Choudhury, NC., 2003. 'From heroines to beneficiaries and from beneficiaries to heroines' in *Impact of Irrigation Project on Gender in West Bengal,* Report of the Evolution Mission, Euro consult, Netherlands.

Choudhury, NC., 2007. 'My days with tribes: Reminiscences of fieldwork', in A.K. Danda and S. Roy (Eds.): *Methodological Question in Social Anthropology,* Indian National Confederation and Academy of Anthropologists, Jhargram, West Bengal.

17

Surajit Chandra Sinha: A Legend in Anthropology of India

Sekh Rahim Mondal

Introduction

Professor Surajit Chandra Sinha is considered a legendary figure and a veteran architect of Indian Anthropology. He is known for his significant contributions in the theoretical, conceptual, methodological, and empirical domains of the discipline. He was both a theorist and an empiricist. His anthropological journey started from the studies of tribes, followed by castes, peasants, and various other social groups of towns and cities, and finally ended with the comprehension of Indian civilisation.

In this chapter, the author intends to highlight in brief the life and works of Professor Sinha as a tribute to remember him on the very occasion of hundred years of teaching Anthropology in India. The chapter is based on facts gathered from a review of published materials, supported by the author's own experience out of his close interaction with him as one of his teachers in Anthropology.

[II]

Early life, education and career

Prof. Sinha was born on 1 August 1926 and died on 27 February 2002. He was the eldest son of Maharaja Bhupendra Chandra Sinha of Susang in the Mymensingh Division of then East Bengal, now Bangladesh. His mother was the daughter of Jogendra Nath Mitra, a Zamindar of Sithlai in the Pabna District of East Bengal, which is also now in Bangladesh. His paternal uncle Maharajkumar Mani Sinha was a well-known communist leader of East Bengal (Pakistan). At a very young age, Sinha followed the footsteps of his paternal uncle. Sinha's maternal uncle Kumar Jatindra Moitra and his younger sister Purba Dam were the distinguished experts of Rabindra Sangeet. Sinha married Professor Purnima Sengupta (Sinha), an eminent physicist as well as a music scholar. Sinha's family was considered as the most important Zamindar family of undivided Bengal, thus had close contact with the Government House of Calcutta in British India. Sinha's family and his kin members had a very close relation with Tagore and Santiniketan.

Sinha had his basic school education in Mymensingh but completed his high school education in Kolkata. He was a student at Ballygunge Government High School. Sinha graduated from Presidency College in Geology (Honours) with record marks. He obtained his Post Graduate degree from the University of Calcutta in Anthropology, with a specialisation in Social-cultural Anthropology, and stood first in first-class with record marks. It is interesting to note that Sinha initially took admission to Physics (Honours) in Presidency College but later shifted to Geology (Honours).

At the Post Graduate level, Sinha was trained in fieldwork by Prof. T.C. Das who introduced him to work on the Bhumij community of then Bihar state for intensive research. Sinha's other mentor was Prof. N.K. Bose, with whom he was first meat during the viva-voce examination for his M.Sc. Dissertation as an external examiner.

Sinha completed his Ph.D. in Anthropology from North Western University, Illinois, the USA as a Full Bright Scholar. His thesis was on "Bhumij's of Barabhum". During his Ph.D. research, he had a very close interaction with the Professors and Scholars of both North Western University and the University of Chicago. Sinha was very fond of Prof. Redfice's ideas of "Great Tradition" and "Little Tradition", "Folk Community", "Peasant" and "Civilisation". All concepts he had used in his research but given emphasis to contextualise them in the Indian context.

It is to be noted here that while in USA Sinha did unique field research in an American village on the religious life of the village people. Based on this study he published a unique paper titled "Religion in an Affluent Society", which was published in *Current Anthropology* at an early age.

After completing his Ph.D. degree in the USA, Sinha back to India and continued to conduct field-based research in various parts of India. His main interest was on tribal and peasant lives in Central India, which he started to examine and analyze in the framework of Indian Civilisation. (N.K. Bose Memorial Foundation,1978; Sarkar and Dasgupta, 2019; Sinha, 1966a).

There are several views behind Sinha's interest in Anthropology and tribes. Some hold the view that being a member of the Jamindar family; Sinha had the habit of visiting hills, forests, and villages through which he goes interested in tribes and peasants. While others hold the view that being the initial student of geology, he used to travel to hills and forest areas and thereby got an interest in tribes and peasants of the place. Still some other holds the view that it was his mentor N.K. Bose motivated him to study Anthropology and tribes.

[III]

Research and administrative experience

Throughout his entire professional life, Sinha occupied several important academic and administrative positions in Anthropology. He was associated with Visva Bharati, Indian Institute of Management (Calcutta), Anthropological Survey of India, and ICSSR Centre for Studies in Social Sciences (Calcutta). He also served as Vice-Chancellor (*Upacharya*) of Visva-Bharati, Santiniketan. Besides, he was also associated with the various Governmental Bodies as well as with the Academic and Research Institutions as experts and advisory committee members.

Sinha had initiated, directed, and completed many significant research projects either alone or with his strong research teams. The most important of them are: "Ethnic Groups; Villages and Towns of Pargana Barabhum" (1966); "Research Programmes in Cultural

Anthropology and Allied Disciplines" (1970); "Cultural Profile of Calcutta" (1972); "Tribal Thoughts and Culture" (1976); "Weaker Sections in India" (1993); "Ascetics of Kashi" (1978); "Tribes and Indian Civilisation" (1982); "Tribal Politics and State System in Pre-Colonial Eastern and North-Eastern India" (1971); "Science, Technology and Culture" (1970); etc. Most of these project works published in edited volumes under his leadership.

So far as information is available, Sinha supervised 18 scholars, who completed their Ph.D. degrees under his able guidance. Most of his research students occupied important positions in their professional life in Research Institutions and Universities.

After he retired from professional life, Sinha started to minimise his involvement in Anthropological affairs. During his post-retirement life, he was involved in extending social services and associated with the teaching-learning process of school children, primarily of tribes and other marginal groups of the Santiniketan area. While doing so, he was inclined to know the environment, society, and culture of *Rarh* areas (middle part) of West Bengal.

Sinha had very wide connections and linkages with many reputed research and academic institutions of India and abroad. He was associated with many Anthropological bodies of national and international repute. He had several reputed Anthropology and Sociology friends in India, the USA, France, Germany, Great Britain, and Japan, etc. Sinha was well known for his multi-disciplinary outlook and very fond of inter-disciplinary interactions in an academic exercise. He had several friends from various disciplines in both India and abroad (N.K. Bose Memorial Foundation, 1978).

[IV]

Contributions to anthropology: Studies on tribes, castes, and peasants

Sinha's areas of research interest were tribes, peasants, and castes. Through his studies, he had shown that tribes and castes in India are not separate and isolate social categories; rather they are the parts of the greater India Society and civilisation. This he had shown in an evolutionary scheme under which the formation of early societies and even states in India took place. His original contribution to Indian Anthropology is reflected in some of his important publications. These are- "Tribal Culture in Peninsular India" (1957); "State Formation and Rajput Myth in Tribal Central India" (1962); "Tribe-Caste and Tribe-Peasant Continuum in Central India".

His primary focus of the study was tribes, particularly the Bhumij's of Central India. Later his focus of study shifted and extended to castes and peasants in India. He worked on various categories of tribes in different ecological, social, and cultural contexts. He studied the Hill Marias living both in isolation and in contact zones to examine their socio-cultural processes. He examined Bhumij's concerning environmental, social, and cultural contexts. He also examined the castes and peasants in varied dimensions. His interest was not simply for the ethnography of tribes, castes, and peasants, but how those social categories are related as well as integrated into an interlocking system of co-operation towards farming a complex greater society, and civilisation in India. His most unique and popular concept of the "Tribe-Caste-Peasant continuum", is an eye-opening idea, which he developed through his field studies.

Sinha sincerely worked on tribal mobilisation, tribal movement, tribal transformations, and finally tribal-state formation. He had examined the process of tribal social transformation in the direction of caste and class, which he conceptualised as a "tribe-caste-peasant continuum". His other concepts like "Bhumij-Rajput Continuum" and the "Bhumij-Kshatriya" continuum are also the outcome of such a transformation process of a tribe (Bhumij), who sustained through settled cultivation. His prime concern was how tribes became integrated with the regional peasant economy and the local caste system. He was inclined to show how the ascribed primordial tribal identity got fused with the achieved peasant identity through common habitat, economy, social system, and ideological beliefs. Through his studies on tribal transformation and tribal-state formation, Sinha was able to show tribal society is not always a simple and homogeneous social category and devoid of social stratification, which is usually stereotyped.

Sinha's unique ideas of tribal-state formation and Rajputanisation, clearly shows that the "Sanskritisation" (a variant form of

Brahminisation) received less significance, rather "Kshatriasation" and "Vaishnavisation" got much importance among the tribal groups of central and other parts of India. His famous concept of "State formation" among many agricultural tribes in India, indicates that how social complexities have emerged among the simple tribal groups in course of history and gradually imbibed the characters of class stratification, political domination, class-consciousness within the traditional egalitarian tribal social ethos. According to Sinha, there has also been a synthesis between tribal and caste worldviews and that binds them to live together in the regional social order. He held the view that tribes and tribal societies are not static as it is believed to be, but are highly dynamic as like as other nontribal communities living around them due to social contacts and functional necessities.

In Sinha's opinion, tribal lie and tribal peasant cultural attributes are nothing but the little traditions and those constituted the important dimension of Indian civilisation.

Sinha's comprehension of "peasant" as a social category in India is also very important. He had hesitation to accept "peasant" as simply an economic category, living only concerning land for their sustenance. In his view, "peasant" is a social category having both economic and socio-cultural attributes in rural settings. Peasant constituted a highly heterogeneous and diverse social group of people's cuts across ethnic, caste, and even religious boundaries. His major focus was to understand the Indian peasantry as an interconnected and interlocked social category based on reciprocal roles and relations among and between the various heterogeneous social segments living in a local context. He considered that peasants are engaged in intensive agriculture, which requires varieties of services to be provided by various groups in a particular ecological and social setting. To him, peasants form a unique social entity going beyond ethnic, caste, and religious affiliation, which is one of the building blocks of Indian society and civilisation as well. Sinha discovered, analyzed, and interpreted the elements of transition and transformation of tribal cultural elements in the direction of peasant cultural attributes out of interaction and amalgamation between tribes and castes. He had the notion that tribal villages are not simply the isolated localities but are functional spaces and units maintaining inter-local, inter-regional, and even trans-regional connectivity by several means. To him, these connectivity's are not one-dimensional but multi-dimensional which sustains the process of integration as well as acculturation.

Sinha meticulously examined the relation of castes with classes in India. This is reflected in his vision of *Bhadralok* (Babu Class) and *Chhotolok* (non-Babu Class) based on social stratification in Bengal. This according to him is the product of long-range historical stratification of caste hierarchy in changing the social context of Bengal; based on wealth, education, power, and honour in the society. In his view, this form of social stratification in Bengal is nothing but a secular adaptation of traditional varna-jati-based caste stratification in this province. (Redfield: 1956; Sinha: 1955, 1957, 1965, 1967, 1969a, 1969b, 1978).

Studies on Indian Civilisation

Sinha is well known for his new approach and perspective of understanding Indian civilisation. According to him, Indian civilisation is multidimensional, having both sacred and secular dimensions. In his view, civilisation is a complex whole, which is the result of the synthesis of many societies, cultures, values, and traditions, and all these are historically integrated, synthesised, and syncretised. He boldly stated that India is a vast land where varieties of peoples with varied cultures are living together since historical times concerning one another for economic and social necessities. As a result, somewhere the elements of their socio-cultural life converge at the same time diverge for maintaining its historically and functionally grown social relations, contributed by several ethnic, linguistic, and socio-religious groups.

Sinha's approach of civilisation study was to see the social process that relates to various social categories of peoples of the country viz. tribe, caste, peasant, and urban population and binds them to live together in harmony for their social requirement. Coexistence, co-operation, competition, and occasional conflict are historical truth in Indian society. There has been an inherent social mechanism in the country, which helps in minimising the conflict for living together for each other's necessities.

According to Sinha, composite nationhood and multi-cultural ethos have shaped the cultural traditions of India. This vast country constituted one ground civilisation to which all groups living in this country have made their significant contributions in different ways. (Sinha, 1974, 1976, 1978a; Sinha and Saraswati, 1978).

Decolonisation and indigenisation of the discipline

Sinha was very anxious about the colonial legacy and western domination in Indian Anthropology. Even though at the initial stage of his career, Sinha himself was a captive of American anthropological tradition, particularly of Chicago School, but at the later phase, he initiated an effort to develop an Indian Tradition in the discipline. His famous writing on "Is there any Indian Tradition in Social/Cultural Anthropology: Retrospect and Prospect" is eye-opening for anthropologists in India. In this article, he not only examined and the history of the growth and development of anthropology in India, but also expressed his agony about western domination and academic colonialism in the discipline of our country. He held the view that we must appreciate whatever best in western thoughts, ideas, and methods in anthropological studies, but at the same time, we must be very careful about the use and application of them in examining the socio-cultural issues and problems of India.

Sinha strongly believed that India is a land of plural and tolerant society. Both diversities and unity is its unique social flavour. Hence, the adoption of western concepts and methods that are mostly grown in the homogenous and uni-dimensional social context of the west may not be very helpful for understanding the multi-dimensional social-cultural realities of India. For him, the indigenisation of the discipline must require a deeper understanding of Indian history, societies, cultures, and their surroundings. (Chakraborty. 2012; Sinha, 1968).

Methodology and fieldwork

Sinha significantly contributed to evolving fresh methods and techniques of doing anthropological research. His framework of research consists of four major vantage points viz: (i) For good field research selection of research problem and formulation of theoretical and methodological framework of study are very important, (ii) Societies and cultures need to be examined for exploring both missing and existing links between different social categories living in the place, (iii) Learning from history is very necessary for understanding the present, (iv) Anthropological inquiries must focus on the problems as well as the desires of the people under study so that research findings to be used for social reconstruction and development.

According to him, contextual and historical perspectives must guide fieldwork. The most important lesson he left for us is the tridimensional approach to doing fieldwork. These are: (a) Temporal and Historical, (b) Spatial and contextual, (c) Ethnic and Cultural. His approach of the field study is popularly known as the spatial-temporal perspective of ethno-analysis. Sinha's emphasis was a holistic understanding of the research problem and which is only possible if it is backed by good research design based on an appropriate theoretical and methodological foundation. In his view, both research design (thinking) and research proposition (acting) are equally important for anthropological field studies. To him, a field worker in the field must be a good learner, listener, and observer. A field worker should note what people think. What do they act? Moreover, how they perceive the meaning of their act?

For fieldwork, Sinha was in favour of both extensive and intensive studies. He was very fond of the comparative methods and re-studies for understanding the social similarities, differences, and processes. He was a strong believer in "Cultural relativism" in field studies. He also emphasised the need for the selection of good informants as well as impress management and rapport establishment with the peoples for doing fieldwork among them. He was the man who advocated for ethics in doing fieldwork.

Repeatedly he pointed out that in all ethnographic writings the scholar should vividly describe his or her experiences of doing fieldwork, consisting of field strategies, problems, and procedures of management of conducting fieldwork. To him, a field diary is very essential for recording the events of data collection in a field situation. This he learned from his teacher Prof. T.C. Das and Prof. N.K. Bose (Sinha, 1978).

Studies on science and scientists

Sinha's anthropological studies were not only confined to the study of tribes, castes, peasants, and urban societies but also shifted to the arena of science and scientists of the Indian social-cultural milieu. He meticulously examined how traditional idioms played vital people in the pursuit of science and scientists of this country. In his view, science has also acquired some adaptive idioms in Indian socio-cultural and civilisational contexts (Sinha: n.d.).

[V]

Spotlight on the specifies

Being one of the great architects of Indian Anthropology, Sinha left behind a very rich tradition in the discipline. His contributions are very wide, ranging from theoretical to methodological and there to empirical dimensions. His concern for the future of the discipline in India is considered food for thought for the present generation of anthropologists. His empirical studies are varied in nature. He not only studied various social categories of India but also studied the science and scientists of the country. In all his studies, he has adopted the historical, structural, and organisational frame of Indian society, culture, and civilisation.

The conceptual frame that he developed through his empirical research is "tribe-caste-peasant continuum", "state formation" and "Rajputaisation" etc. are a clear indication of his civilisation mode of socio-cultural analysis of Indian society.

Sinha considered that the caste system in India to be examined from the perspectives of texts and contexts through the Varna-Jati model of social analysis. He held the view that the plights of weaker and marginal sections of the Indian society should be known meaningfully through the study of caste and caste-like systems prevalent in this country. He strongly believed that the classes and even the status groups in India have a deep relation with the traditional caste stratification of the country.

The perspectives and methods of field studies that Sinha was developed through his field research are still a reference to the field workers. His field strategy is still a matter of legacy in Indian anthropology.

American Cultural Anthropology undoubtedly influenced Sinha during his initial stage of professional life, but in later phases, he was successfully able to formulate his thoughts and ideas to examine the social reality of India and the civilisation of the country. His advocacy for an authentic identity of Indian anthropology has shown the new path of research for present generation Anthropologists.

His historical and contextual approach, evolutionary model, and structural – organisational perspective for examining Indian social categories are still a reference to many anthropologists.

Sinha's thoughts and ideas got the unique shape out of influences of both anthropologists and other scholars, including the social thinkers of India and abroad. It was not only his anthropology mentors but also the thinkers like Gandhi, Tagore, Ramakrishna, Vivekananda all have made significant impacts on his anthropological thinking and research.

References

Chakraborty, SB. 2012. 'Is there an Indian Tradition in Social-Cultural Anthropology. Retrospect and Prospect?' In S Chakrabarti and A Basu (Eds): *The Science of Man*, pp.598-607, Indian Anthropological Society, Calcutta.

NK Bose Memorial Foundation, 1978. *News Letter*, December.

Redfield, R., 1956. *The Peasant Society and Culture: An Anthropological Approach to Civilisation,* Chicago University Press, Chicago.

Sarkar, A and Dasgupta, S, 2019. *Doyens of Indian Anthropology,* Agam Kala Prakashan, New Delhi.

Sinha, SC. (n.d.). 'Indian scientists: The socio-cultural context of their professional environment', S.C. Sinha (Ed): *Science, Technology and Culture,* New Delhi.

Sinha, SC., 1955. 'Evolution reconsidered', *Man in India,* 35: 1-18.

Sinha, SC. 1957. 'Tribal cultures in peninsular India as a dimension of Little Tradition in the study of Indian civilisation: A preliminary statement', *Man in India,* 37: 31-118.

Sinha, SC. 1965. 'Tribe-caste and tribe-peasant continuum in Central India', *Man in India,* 45: 57-83.

Sinha, SC. 1966. 'Religion in an affluent society', *Current Anthropology,* 7, 2: 189-195.

Sinha, SC. 1967. 'Involvement in Social Change', *Economic and Political Weekly,* Sep.16, 1707-1710.

Sinha, SC. 1968. 'Is there any tradition in social/cultural anthropology: Retrospect and prospect?' *Conformance Proceeding on the Nature and Function of Anthropological Traditions,* Wenner-Grew-Foundation for Anthropological Research, New York.

Sinha, SC. and Bhattacharya, R. 1969a. 'Bhadralok and Chhotolok in rural areas of Bengal', *Sociological Bulletin,* 18, 1:50-66.

Sinha, SC., 1969b. *Urgent Problems for Research in Social and Cultural Anthropology in India,* Simla Indian Institute of Advanced Study, [Transaction No. 10, pp. 162-169].

Sinha, SC. 1974. Sociology of religion', *A Survey of Research in Sociology and Social Anthropology*, Vol. II, ICSSR, New Delhi.

Sinha, S.C., 1976. "Rabindranath Tagore's ideas about the structure and essence of Indian civilisation", *Presidential Address,* Indian Anthropological Society.

Sinha, SC. 1978a. 'Re-thinking about tribes and Indian civilisation', *Journal of the Indian Anthropological Society,* 18,2.

Sinha, SC.1978b. *Field Studies on the People of India,* Indian Anthropological Society, Calcutta.

Sinha, SC., and Saraswati, BN., 1978. *The Ascetics of Kashi,* N.K. Bose Memorial Foundation, Varanasi.

18

Indera Paul Singh

Gautam K. Kshatriya

Prof. (Dr.) Indera Paul Singh had an outstanding personality with an illustrious carrier. He did his I.Sc.(Medical) from Hindu College, Delhi, and completed his Bachelor's degree from Khalsa College, Amritsar in 1947. He then obtained a Master's degree in Anthropology from the University of Delhi in 1950. He was appointed as Lecturer in Anthropology at the University of Delhi on September 1, 1953. Professor Singh did his Ph.D. from the University of Delhi in 1959 on the inheritance of finger ball patterns on a human population, under the supervision of Prof. P.C. Biswas. He was the first student to obtain a doctorate from Delhi University in Anthropology.

It is maybe worth mentioning here that he took advanced training in Anthropology from Franz Weidenreich Anthropologiche Institut, University Frankfurt, Germany for two years from 1950 through 1952. He also obtained a certificate in the Russian language from Delhi University in 1950. Moreover, he also worked with the Ford Foundation as a Research Assistant for six months in the year 1952 through 1953. He also worked with USIS for six months in 1952. Prof. Singh became Reader in 1961 and eventually Professor of Anthropology in the year 1971. He retired in the year 1993 after serving for almost four decades.

Prof. Singh was also proficient in Punjabi, Urdu, Hindi, English, German, and Russian languages; which shows his amazing and towering personality.

Prof. Singh became the Head of the Department of Anthropology, University of Delhi, on June 16, 1968, and continued to be head of the Department till June 6, 1979. He again became the Head of the Department from April 4, 1981, through April 3, 1984. He has the Honour of being the longest-serving Head of the Department of Anthropology of the University of Delhi after Prof. P.C. Biswas.

It may be mentioned here that he was also In-Charge of Certificate Course in Forensic Science from 1968 through 1984. During his tenure as the Head of the department, he developed several laboratories in the department especially cytogenetics, biochemical genetics, molecular genetics, and human physiology. He also saw that a large number of foreign faculties and dignitaries of reputed background visit the department.

During his headship, the department had the privilege of a large number of visiting faculties from all over the world which helped the department to achieve as one of the best centers of Anthropological teaching and research. He was also responsible for many collaborative ventures, as a result, many of the faculty members got the opportunities to visit Germany and develop collaborative research.

Professor I.P. Singh was the Founder President of the Indian Society for Human Ecology; President, Indian Dermatographics Association; Vice-President, Ethnographic and Folk Culture Society; President of Indian Anthropological Association; Fellow of Indian Social Science Academy; Emeritus President, RUCHI, H.P.; Member of Asian Association of Bioethics, Tokyo. He was the Regional Commissioner for South Asia Regional Group of International Commission on Anthropology of Food and Food Problem. He was Associate Secretary-General, International Association of Anthropology Editors. He also served as a member of the Human Biological Council and International Commission of Urban anthropology. He was also a member of the International Commission on Documentation; a member of the Council of Nutritional Anthropology; a member of the American Anthropology Association; a member of the Indian Academy of Sciences and a member of the International Council for Scientific Development.

Professor Singh was Dean Faculty of Science from 1971 to 1973, 1973-1975, and 1983-1984. He was a Proctor of the University of

Delhi from 1973 to 1992, almost for 19 years and to date, he is the only faculty to have served for the longest period as a Proctor of the University of Delhi. Besides, he was also Chairman, of Delhi University Health Services Advisory Committee from 1983 to 1993, Chairman of Delhi University Sports Council from 1981 to 1993. He has also served as the Chairman, Gywar Hall Management Committee and Chairman, Board of Residence, Health and Discipline of the University of Delhi (1973-93).

His list of achievements is too long. He also served as the member of the Governing Bodies of many colleges and hostels of Delhi University, namely, Satyawati College, Hamdard College, Shyamlal College, Desh Bandhu College, St. Stephen College, Lady Irwin College, P.G. Hostel for Boys, P.G. Hostel for Girls, Gwyer Hall, Jubilee Hall among many.

Prof. Singh was the President of the Anthropology and Archaeological Section of the Indian Science Congress during 1968-69 sessions. He was Secretary-General of 10th ICAES, New Delhi, and was also General Secretary (Local) Indian Science Congress in 1976. He was also a member of the Executive Council of the University of Delhi from 1973 to 1992, of University Court from 1959 to 1993, and of Academic Council for 20 years. Prof. Singh was in the Special Assistance Programme, UGC Advisory Committee at the University of Calcutta, Gauhati, Ranchi, Chandigarh, and Tirupati for the UGC quality improvement programme. He was the Chairmen of the eleventh UNESCO conference of the International Voluntary Work Camp Organisation. Furthermore, he was a member of UGC (1989-92), Vice-Chairmen, Advisor Committee of Anthropological Survey of India (Department of Culture, Government of India), member National MAB Committee (Ministry of Environment, Government of India), member National Editorial Board (People of India Project). He was also editor-in-chief of various national Academic Journals.

In his long illustrious academic carrier, he guided at least 70 M.Sc. students for field dissertations and led M.Sc. students to numerous field areas namely; Manali, Chamba, Dharamshala, etc.

He did extensive fieldwork in North-western Himalayas (Bharmour Valley, Pangi Valley, Simla Hills, Kulu, Manali, Chamba, etc.) Jaunsar

Bawar, Punjab, U.P. and Delhi. He successfully guided thirty-three Ph.D. students and three M.Phil dissertations. He also completed eight research projects funded by various national and international agencies. He is well known all over the world in Anthropology. His ambition was to integrate various sub-disciplines of Anthropology which is why he supervised students in vastly varied areas of Anthropology.

His interest remained in applied Anthropology, Human Biology, and Village Studies. Prof. Singh was a keen field worker. He conducted fieldwork in the village of Daleke way back in the late nineteen fifties, in Taran-Taaran tehsil, of Amritsar district and Rani Kheda around Delhi. In his study in Daleke village in Punjab, he reported that the decline of Brahmins in the village began with the launching of reform movements i.e., around 1922-26. It was after these movements that a low caste Sikh was appointed as a priest in the local gurudwara who began to give equal treatment to members of all castes in the village. This process continued during the post-independence period as well. The introduction of a new Constitution strengthened those mobilising against caste. Reporting on his village, I.P. Singh wrote that what the new law demanded was just what the *gurus* had preached. It is in keeping with the percepts of Sikh religion i.e. equality.

There lies the major difference of caste structure between a Sikh village and a Hindu village. While in a Hindu village caste hierarchy and differences have religious sanction behind them, there are no such sanctions in the Sikh religion. Thus, it becomes easier to propagate and instill equality of caste relations in a Sikh village.

I.P. Singh restudied the community originally studied by him under the ICSSR funding in 2008 to understand and compare the contemporary peasant life in Punjab. The restudy used the findings of the original study as a baseline to assess social change over the years in Daleke. The study describes the changes in terms of population, literacy, several schools and health centers, infrastructure like roads and technical improvements, etc. to understand change and continuity. He was about to write a monograph on the study, but, his dream could not be fulfilled, because he left for a heavenly abode.

In his academic career, he published five books and more than two hundred research papers in National and International Journals.

Since he was so closely associated with all the Indian Anthropologists and UGC as a man of excellence, he was responsible for the opening of numerous anthropological departments in many States of the Country. The list of Conferences/ Seminars/Workshops he attended and presented papers and keynote addresses during his lifetime is beyond description.

It will not be less worth mentioning here that he wrote two laboratory manuals with Prof. M.K. Bhasin namely, *Anthropometry and A manual of biological anthropology*. These two laboratory manuals are extensively used in the Departments of Anthropology across India and indeed are very useful manuals for undergraduates, graduates and researchers too.

Prof. Singh was an epitome of both social and biological anthropology and taught each one of these subjects with comfortable ease. He was proficient in various sub-disciplines of biological anthropology and fieldwork too. He is an example of an outstanding anthropologist who was an architect of modern anthropology in India.

My heart is filled with a deep sense of gratitude when I recollect the humanistic qualities of Prof. Singh. A man with an all-embracing attitude, he would go out of the way to help whenever anyone needed, independent of students, teaching faculties, or administrative staff of the Department of Anthropology. His commitment to the ethic of equality and justice was the core of his humanitarian spirit. He excelled in executing his duties and loomed large, high above others as a role model. As an able administrator, he promoted a work culture that helped to instill values of love, care, and concern without letting the powers of his post overshadow human values.

I may add that he used to come to the Department during his late eighties and participate in seminars and conferences with meaningful inputs. His concerted efforts to expand the Ddepartment in different specialised areas have yielded extraordinary results. Prof. I. P. Singh left for heavenly abode on September 27, 2016, after completing a very successful and meritorious career in Anthropology.

19

Contribution of Professor Gopala Sarana to the Development of Anthropology

Geetika Ranjan

Introduction

Anthropology in India has traversed a long way. As the year 2020 marks 100 years of teaching of Anthropology in India, it is only befitting that the fraternity of Anthropologists in India celebrates this momentous journey by revisiting and deliberating upon the contribution of the stalwarts in the field. The name of one such stalwart, Late Professor Gopala Sarana shines bright on the canvas of these contributions.

Writing this chapter was nothing short of being a journey in nostalgia for me. Traveling back in time and reminiscing those days when I had just walked through the gates of the University of Lucknow to land at the department of Anthropology – the kaleidoscope of memories just kept rolling on. As a class 12 pass from the discipline personified school- Loreto Convent Lucknow, University of Lucknow appeared hugely cosmopolitan, crowded, and completely unrelatable to me. With great trepidation, I stood at the door of the Head of the Department of Anthropology, Professor Gopala Sarana's room and found him completely engrossed in reading a book. I politely asked – Sir please may I come in? Professor Sarana looked up with a start,

"Yes you may certainly come in *beta*", putting me instantly at ease. That first meeting with Professor Sarana is deeply etched in my mind.

I had the good fortune of being taught by Professor Sarana at both undergraduate and postgraduate levels. A truly committed teacher, he had the knack of explaining the most complex topics of the curriculum in a very simple and lucid way, making those appear to be the easiest and most interesting to learn about. Equally eloquent in both Hindi and English, his bilingual lecture was well understood by a whole lot of students, whatever be their medium of learning. His students were an integral part of his life. Citing anecdotes and interesting examples, his pedagogic style was rather unique, with a subtle dash of humor and jest. Needless to say, that as the Head of the Department, he had many responsibilities and tasks to address. Yet despite his hectic schedule, he always took his classes religiously. On account of the continuous running of late academic sessions over the years, the academic schedule of the University could not accommodate an adequate number of teaching days. However, this was never taken as an excuse by Professor Sarana to adopt any short cuts in teaching the course. He took several extra classes to complete the course which he did with infectious interest and focus.

Professor Gopala Sarana was born in a village in district Balia, Uttar Pradesh on January 2, 1935. A meritorious student, he achieved a first-class in both BA as well as MA in 1953 and 1955 respectively. A significant feather in his cap was his Doctoral Degree from the University of Harvard in 1966 under the supervision of Professor Cora du Bois.

Professor Sarana's journey in teaching and research can be traced from the days he started teaching at Lucknow University. For some time he taught at Punjab University before going to Harvard University in pursuit of his research towards a doctoral degree. He also taught at California University, Santa Barbara. He returned to India and joined the Karnataka University where he went on to become the Professor and Head of the Department of Anthropology. It was in this very capacity that he joined Lucknow University where he continued to work till his retirement. Life had come full circle. His homecoming back to Lucknow and his journey thereon forms one of the most vibrant chapters of his illustrious life. He retired from Lucknow University in the year 1995.

A social-cultural anthropologist by specialisation, he, like his *Guru* Professor D.N. Majumdar, persevered in seeking a sound knowledge of the other branches of Anthropology as he firmly believed in the integrated nature of the discipline of Anthropology. In his book *Anthropology and Sociology*, he brings out the element of 'unity and diversity of Anthropology'(2005:19). He writes, "Human beings share ideas, experiences, and biological endowments. The task of Anthropology is to understand human similarities and differences from biological and cultural angles and also how biology and culture interact. In this sense, the diversity of Anthropology is not at all a hindrance but paves the way for integration. Anthropology has a loose structure in which there is a lot of opportunity for the development of various fields. I want to state in no uncertain terms that when we talk of integration of anthropology, we do not at all mean that it should come in the way of specialised development of its sub-fields like biological (physical) anthropology, linguistics, etc. Please remember that the rationale for the integration of Anthropology lies at a deeper level than the level at which a particular subdivision deals with its specialised subject matter. It can be experienced in terms of the need to understand different kinds of human beings and the diversities as well as similarities of the patterns of human living. This is necessary to know what man has been, what he is today, and what he may become tomorrow so that efforts may be made to make human life better than what it has been up to date" (Sarana and Srivastava, 2005: 22).

As the editor of the journal *The Eastern Anthropologist*, Professor Sarana took the journal to a greater height. A well-acclaimed teacher and an outstanding scholar, Professor Gopala Sarana was a recipient of prestigious awards like the Asiatic Society, Calcutta Medal and, the Shikshak Sri Samman conferred upon him by the Government of Uttar Pradesh.

Professor Gopala Sarana: The scholar par excellence

Professor Sarana was a prolific scholar in the true sense of the word. Going deep into the area of concepts and methodology, his writings explain, challenge, and invite discourse to almost ubiquitously accepted and seldom challenged core concepts and methods of Anthropology. This rare attribute is aptly summarised by Professor Subba Reddy's remark, "Among the anthropologists in India and abroad, Dr. Sarana stands out as one among the rare few whose reach extends to the terse areas of methodological issues, philosophical problems, epistemological queries, logical procedures and scientific frames of analysis, applicable to social sciences in general and social anthropology in particular" (Sarana, 2010: p. xi).

Professor Vinay Srivastava rightly opines "Gopala Sarana is perhaps one of the few Indian anthropologists who has written on topics such as social structure and social organisation, functionalism, structuralism, the definition of marriage, comparative method."(www. India-seminar.com)

His masterpiece work, *The Methodology of Anthropological Comparison*, (1975) brought him international acclaim for meticulously and holistically bringing to the fore, the significance of one of the most powerful unique selling points of Anthropology- the essence of comparison in Anthropology. While discussing the relevance of the Comparative Method, Sarana elucidates, *what* should one compare, *why* should one compare, and *how* should one compare? He makes a distinction between three kinds of comparative methods: global-sample comparison, controlled comparison, and illustrative comparison. He systematically explains these under the categories of terms of reference, units of comparison, purposes of comparison, and techniques and methods. In an earlier publication, he made a detailed analysis of the use of the comparative method in Anthropology as well as in Linguistics (1965).

Professor Sarana's writings show a focussed inclination towards offering *the* correct explanation of such terms and concepts which are many a time used erroneously. In the *Methodology of Anthropological Comparisons* (1975), Professor Sarana makes a conscious and deliberate effort to explain the difference between technique, method, and methodology, between concept, conception and conceptualisation - terms which are very often used casually and incorrectly, and unfortunately, such usage is mostly acceptable as passe. The fact is that such errors in usage are inexcusable in scholarly endeavours. There is a pivotal need to clearly explain these terms with detailed clarity, something which Professor Sarana did painstakingly.

Following in the footsteps of his master, Professor D.N. Majumdar, who called for intensive research, Professor Gopala Sarana undertook a detailed study in various parts of South Asia like Israel, Japan, and Iran. He carried out fieldwork among the Khasa and the Oraon tribals. An American village, Groveport, in Ohio was also studied by Sarana.

There is no substitute for fieldwork if one wants to understand the reality of human life. Ethnographic research in Anthropology has time and again come under critical scrutiny which raises doubts over its efficacy. Sarana goes on to clear the doubts raised on traditional fieldwork procedures. He writes the "main complaints have been about the lack of quantification, objectivity, and replicability. Some of these critics have said that to the extent that anthropology does not conform to the social-science methodological norm, its procedure falls short of being scientific (1976:255). As a contributor to the important volume *The Personal Approach in Cultural Anthropological Research*, Sarana cites the researches of Honigman, Kroeber, Kluckhohn, to put these criticisms to rest and reinforce the strengths of ethnographic research while clearly emphasising Honigman's view that there is zero probability of testing the reliability of an ethnographic monograph, adding further, Kroeber's insightful remark that, "there are strictly speaking no proofs in this method" (1952:3).

Professor Sarana's devotion to Anthropology was inspiring. His life's trajectory was marked by several twists and turns, challenges, and changes. Yet these could never dampen his infectious enthusiasm to continue to retrospect, introspect and prospect about all that came within the anthropological gaze. His perennial desire to read, research, and 'do' Anthropology remained a constant all his life.

His seminal work towards the last years of his life *Explorations in Method and Theory in Anthropology* (2008) is a rare and valuable contribution to the field of Anthropological theories and concepts. Professor Nita Mathur befittingly captures the essence of the book as she writes, "What makes the book useful is not only a critical appraisal of the contribution of classical theorists to specific themes but also how the author churns each of them to surface core ideas and weave them together to develop fully-fledged theoretical premises. The strength of the book, as I see, lies in highlighting the nuanced connection between ideas, and, in doing so, providing a critique of each theoretical premise. This is certainly not a text for beginners in the discipline of anthropology but one for the matured, well-grounded students and academics engaged in the pursuit of anthropological knowledge in a particular sense and social sciences in a general sense" (2010: 430-432).

Through his various writings, Professor Sarana highlight's anthropology's forte in addressing the totality of human life. He also draws attention towards the allegations directed towards Anthropology such as Indian Anthropology readily conforming to the western molds of understanding the human and, Indian anthropologists applying simplistic formats to understand complex societies. That Indian Anthropology is failing to influence the administration at large, was yet another point of criticism of Anthropology which Sarana brings out (Sarana, 2007). This, I firmly believe is a focal area of concern and needs focussed attention. Anthropologists are hardcore fieldworkers, who toil at the grass-roots level and unearth the unseen reality, go deeper than the surface view, understand the felt-needs of the people, and hence, are best suited to suggest measures to the policymakers and administrative structures at large. The anthropologists need to hear out. The viability of a discipline requires revisiting its essence, again and again, to make it more practically important and action-oriented. It is this vein that Sarana calls upon the need to bring together the different voices such as those of the academia, the policymakers, and others in the large arena of administration for development, in a collaborative way, to address the new challenges to human life in this era of globalisation.

A teacher par excellence, Professor Sarana knew the imperativeness of drawing home to the students, the basics of Anthropology in the most student-friendly style. This is well reflected in his work *"Anthropology and Sociology"* (2005). It caters to the common curiosity of the students seeking answers to their quests around the 'human being'. This book (one section of which 'Physical Anthropology in India' is written by Professor R.P. Srivastava), brings out most simply the essentials of Anthropology as a discipline. Its first section, Invitation to Anthropology, is in every way a cordial invitation to all to visit the wonder that is Anthropology. Written as an engaging narrative, it makes for a very interesting and informative read.

A complete section of the book is devoted to the discussion on the relationship between Anthropology and Sociology. While practically every book dealing with the basics of Anthropology discusses the relationship between Anthropology and Sociology, but it is done in a rather customary and oversimplistic fashion, primarily to convey to the beginners in the discipline about the close relationship which the two disciplines share. Sarana, in the section, *Sociology, and Anthropology*, goes deeper to unravel, layer after layer the complexities in the relationship between Sociology and Anthropology (particularly social anthropology), and how, despite the ubiquitously agreed similarities between the two, the terms Social Anthropology and Sociology cannot be treated as interchangeable. He counters Andrei Beteille in particular. Sarana writes, "When we put sociology and anthropology side by side we are struck by the similarity between their general assumptions, their basic concepts, and 'theory'. But these two disciplines are very much dissimilar in their preoccupations and in what they do. Andre Beteille, who advocates that Sociology and social anthropology are identical,.......himself concedes that " sociologists and social anthropologists have often done very different kinds of work" (1974:4). In light of his admission, I am unable to understand Professor Beteille's argument that though "sociology and social anthropology have similar or even identical aims" (1974:4) (*ibid*, p.4), and have the same approach to the study of social life, (and) that their methods are similar" (Beteille, 1974:9) and yet the two disciplines do 'very different kinds of work'. (*ibid*, p.4). How can this be possible?

Professor Sarana spent long hours teaching and supervising students and this close interaction between him and his students helped him to get the feel of the curiosities of the students who wanted to know in rather simple terms the journey of humans from the past to the present. His book *Studies in Social and Physical Anthropology* (2012) (co-editor R.P. Srivastava) is written keeping this requirement of the students' in mind. Rather seamless integration of physical and social anthropology to holistically deliver, in simple words the significance of understanding the totality of human life is the characteristic feature of this book. While social and physical anthropology is dealt with in different sections in the book with their exclusive subject matter, the subtle message of seeing the two in a natural alliance, rather as unlinked watertight compartments, is smoothly conveyed to the reader of the book. The book brings in large areas of importance within its ambit. From a discussion on looking at the stages in human evolution from the palaeoanthropological dimension, to bringing out the pertinence of addressing diseases through the human genome, the volume sails through significant areas of knowledge.

The second section of the volume is a revisit to the institution of the family. It brings in debates around the family's basic characteristics and engages in discussion on the values it upholds particularly when seen in perspective. Discussion on the Indian diaspora, the aftermath of colonialism in India, and the role of the bureaucracy in that context are other pivotal areas covered in the volume.

In his book, *Studies in Indian Anthropology: Festschrift to Professor Gopala Sarana* (2004), Professor P.K. Misra gives a detailed account of Prof. Sarana's contribution to Anthropology which made him a renowned scholar, nationally and internationally. Misra makes a very comprehensive categorisation of the works of Professor Sarana. He writes, " He had written 76 articles, 7 reviews, and 6 books by 2004. Of these, 32 articles are on theoretical issues in anthropology, anthropological method, and the comparative method. 11 articles are on applications of anthropology in various areas. Two articles (one an obituary) are on D. N. Mazumdar. The others have been written on caste, the relation of anthropology with other disciplines, anthropology of Indian civilisation, change, development, physical anthropology, prehistory and archaeology" (Misra, 2004).

Conclusion

People do not remain forever but their works do. Professor Gopala Sarana's demise on 7th November 2010, has created a deep void in the field of Anthropology. His colossal contribution towards enriching the discipline is well etched in the history of the development of the subject.

As a researcher, he not only gave a fresh perspective to the established and ubiquitously accepted explanations of social structure, social organisation, and other concepts but also challenged these. Such was his devotion to making anthropology more and more popular that he offered to teach Anthropology for free wherever required. My mother, a Professor of Sanskrit started a Degree College in Lucknow way back in 1998 with Anthropology being one of the subjects offered. This was under the newly created self-finance scheme of the Government. The college which had newly started was going through some teething problems, such as those which came with fund crunch. Getting experienced, sincere teachers to teach was one of the challenges. When Professor Sarana, who had already retired by now, learned of this, he offered to teach Anthropology free of any charge to help the cause of the college and the cause of Anthropology. As the college administration could eventually recruit the teaching faculty as per the stated norms, Prof. Sarana did not have to do the needful. But his benevolent gesture came as a much-needed assurance and moral support for the college which had just started its journey of imparting education. Professor Sarana did not leave any stone unturned in lending his voice on the matter of opening Anthropology at the High School and Intermediate (11th and 12th) levels in Uttar Pradesh. His long tenure as the Head of the Department of Anthropology at Lucknow University saw the department flourishing in both quantity and quality. Anthropology was a much-coveted subject for the new students who took admission in the undergraduate programme at Lucknow University. Professor Sarana led by example. He regularly took classes. Such sincerity rubbed well on most of the other teachers in the Department who followed suit. He had his idiosyncrasies which many a time irked people in the field and did not leave them with a *feel-good* factor and naturally so. Yet for me and many like me who were taught by him, he epitomised all the virtues that one looks for in a teacher – sincerity, dedication, clarity, along with compassion and paternal love.

References

Beteille, Andre. 1974. 'Six essays'. In *Comparative Sociology*. Oxford University Press, Delhi.

Honigmann, JJ, Caulfield MD, Chilungu SW, Eches R, Wald P, Hellbon AB, Keil C, Kuper H, Langness LL, Maquet J, Nash D, Pelto PJ, Pelto GH,

Sarana G, Siegel CL, Whittaker E and Wirsing R. 1976. 'The personal approach in cultural anthropological research [and Comments and Reply]'. *Current Anthropology*, 17,2: 243-261.

Kroeber, AL. 1952. *The Nature of Culture*. The University of Chicago Press, Chicago.

Mathur, Nita. 2010. 'Review of explorations in method and theory in anthropology by Gopal Sarana'. *Sociological Bulletin*, 59, 3: 430-432.

Misra, PK. 2004. *Studies in Indian Anthropology: Festschrift to Professor Gopala Sarana*. Rawat Publications, New Delhi.

Sarana, Gopala, and Srivastava, RP., 2005. *Anthropology and Sociology*. New Royal Book Co, Lucknow.

Sarana, Gopala, and Srivastava, RP., 2012. *Studies in Social and Physical Anthropology* (Eds.). Rawat Publications, New Delhi.

Sarana, Gopala. 1965. 'On comparative methods in social-cultural anthropology and linguistics'. *The Eastern Anthropologist* 60,3 & 4:307- 25.

Sarana, Gopala.1975. *The Methodology of Anthropological Comparisons: An Analysis of Comparative Methods in Social and Cultural Anthropology*. The University of Arizona Press, Arizona.

Sarana, Gopala. 2008. *Explorations in Method and Theory in Anthropology*. Rawat Publications, Jaipur.

Srivastava, Vinay. *Teaching Anthropology*. Indiaseminar.com/2000/495/ 495%20vinay%20kumar%20srivatava.htm

20

K.S. Singh: Anthropologist and Tribal Historian

N.K. Das

Kumar Suresh Singh (1935–2006) was a renowned anthropologist who had combined anthropological and historical methodologies in studying the transformation of society. This article pays homage to K.S. Singh by illuminating some of his major contributions in the fields of anthropology and tribal history.[1] Most of the anthropological contributions of Singh were made during his tenure as fellows of various research organisations and as the head of the Anthropological Survey of India (AnSI). He was the recipient of the Jawaharlal Nehru Fellowship as well as a post-doctoral fellowship at Chicago University. He joined the Indian Administrative Service in 1958. One of his early tasks was to survey 100 Ho villages. He was Director of the Anthropological Survey of India (AnSI) during 1976-77. In 1984, he joined the AnSI and National Museum of Man (now Indira Gandhi Rashtriya Manav Sangrahalaya) as the first Director-General. He was with the AnSI till his superannuation in 1993. He later held the chair of Rajiv Gandhi Professor at the North-Eastern Hill University, Shillong. He was a National Fellow of ICHR before his death.

Singh's first book was on the Birsa Munda movement. His book '*The Indian Famine 1967: A Study in Crisis and Change*' (1974) may be described as an early anthropological study of famine. His other books include *Tribal Situation in India*, 1971; *Tribal Society in India: An Anthropo-Historical Perspective*, 1985, and *Tribal Movements in India*, Vol. I & II, 1982-83. Singh has edited several books on tribal economy, customary law, and other themes such as visual anthropology. Singh's '*People of India –An Introduction*' (1992 and 2002) is part of his magnum opus, the 43 volume People of India project, based on a pan-Indian survey of all communities of India, which he conceptualised, spearheaded, and edited as Director-General of the AnSI (1984-1993). Singh's volume, '*Diversity, Identity and Linkages: Explorations in Historical Ethnography*', published by Oxford University Press on behalf of ICHR in 2012, contains essays on the indigenous traditions of ethnography.

Anthropological and historical explorations

Kumar Suresh Singh was posted in Palamau in 1965 where he witnessed the terrible famine of 1967. According to Walter Hauser (2006), Suresh Singh could gather relevant anthropological data about the impact of famine in that region as he was directly involved with the administration of famine relief. Singh's works are seen as a manifestation of the intellectual legacy of S.C. Roy and the emotional engagement of Verrier Elwin (Singh, D.K., 2006). He entered anthropology through folklore. The folkloric interest of Singh continued and thus he later brought out edited volumes on 'tribal versions' of Ramayana and Mahabharata as spread throughout India and beyond. He learned several tribal languages and he also passed departmental examinations in Mundari and Oraon. He also compiled a book on Mundari poems.

Birsa uprising, subaltern studies, and K.S. Singh

K.S. Singh had contributed to the development of what he coined as the "combined methodology" for the study of tribal society. Writing in Tehalka Magazine, Uday Prakash (2006) eloquently observed that,

'Kumar Suresh Singh was one of the very few Indian scholars to have received a UN award for field research, in Geneva. Filmmaker Mrinal Sen compared him with any of the "five great sons of Bengal", though Singh was from Bihar; and Mahasweta Devi was deeply indebted to him while writing one of her best novels *Aranyer Adhikar*

(Owners of Forests). Dedicating her novel to Suresh Singh, Mahasweta Devi wrote,

> "If Birsa Munda today has become a symbol of 'Adivasi desires' — for freedom, justice, and rights — and has turned into a long awaited hero of tribals in India, the credit must go to Kumar Suresh Singh and his path-breaking research and discovery of this hidden saga of a great tribal upsurge in British India."

"Singh's *Dust Storm and the Rising Mist* created ripples as it was the first subaltern quest in mainstream Indian historiography. Singh was criticized, eyebrows were raised and his work was dubbed 'non-scholastic' as it had used tools and methods alien to the writing of history. But the book's impact was enormous. In the central hall of Parliament, if we see a portrait of a young tribal, an icon of self-esteem for Dalits and tribals as Gandhi, Nehru, Tilak, and Shastri, some credit must go to the storyteller. He was a Homer who scripted 'Ulgulan', an Iliad for Indian Adivasis. Birsa now is undoubtedly a Gilgamesh to them" (Uday Prakash, 2006).

The Chotanagpur Plateau, Jharkhand, is famous for tribal rebellions against the state. Ranajit Guha's (1983) *Elementary Aspects of a Peasant Insurgency* – which gave birth to the subaltern studies, is situated around the Birsa movement. Guha and his collaborators however have been charged with presenting a false divide between the elite and the subaltern (Bayly, 1988; Sivaramakrishnan, 1995). A critical reappraisal of Guha's analysis of the Birsa movement reveals that Guha's analysis (1983) of the movement relied not on official records but narratives provided in a 1966 book authored by K.S. Singh which is based on his doctoral thesis (Shah, 2014). In the 2002 edition of his Birsa book, Singh wrote that "When about forty years ago I wrote the story of Birsa– little did I realise that it would have such a far-reaching impact on subaltern studies (Singh, 2002). Singh's book had established Birsa as a cult, inspired folk and regional literature, poetry, and songs, and most significantly, formed the basis of Elementary Aspects and thus the foundation for subaltern studies (Shah, 2014).

Colonial and postcolonial People of India study

The People of India study launched by the AnSI on 2nd October 1985, was the brainchild of K.S. Singh, who designed and implemented this project. Singh made this study a collaborative exercise and involved as many as 26 universities and research institutes for the collection of data and preparing reports. In all, about 600 scholars participated in this project. At the compilation and publication stage, local university scholars were involved. Thus, in most of the state volumes, the university scholars are the main editors (Das, 2018).

M.N. Srinivas has compared the People of India project with human relation area files of Yale University, USA.

The PoI project was planned on a breathtaking scale and it had identified mainly '2753 communities' distributed over 32 states/Union territories. They made up for 4653 elements when a community population is counted in each state/union territory as a separate element. A team headed by the renowned socio-biologist Madhav Gadgil studied the PoI findings at the National Informatics Centre and Centre for Ecological Science, Bangalore. The team, which included an AnSI anthropologist and a linguist, examined the demographic history of India based on fresh insights into linguistic and anthropological patterns based on the People of India data (Gadgil *et al,* 1997). The team published three articles (vide Joshi, *et al.*, 1993a, 1993b, and Gadgil *et al.,* 1997).

There is no doubt that the value-loaded narratives and 'racial' prejudices were replete in colonial ethnographies. Yet, some Indian scholars and a European scholar Jenkins (2003) claimed that the "AnSI's postcolonial study of People of India is an ethnographic account carried out in the manner done by H. H. Risley". In reality, the AnSI ethnographic reports are more comprehensive empirically than the ethnological reports of the British Raj, which laid much emphasis on 'anthropometry'. H.H. Risley's (1908) 'People of India' volume was a rehash of the census report of 1901, in which the long chapter '*Caste, Tribe and Race*' was written by Risley earlier for the 1901 census (co-authored with Edward Gait). Other chapters (including 'animism' and language) were written by Gait and George Grierson. Risley's *People of India* was first published in 1908 and reissued as a 'memorial' edition in 1915. Risley's '*People of India*' had highlighted the race basis of Indian society, and the physical characters of Indian people with a focus on anthropometry. In this and other works, Risley hypothesised and constructed an idealised 'Aryan race' through a distorted reading of Indian scriptures (https://hinduism.stackexchange.com/questions/11511/how-castes-were-produced-in-india). Jenkins (2003) and others did not consider these racialised features of colonial writing. There are other versions of People of India publications issued in colonial India, such as Anderson's summarised People of India and John Forbes Watson and John William Kaye compiled eight-volume pictographic '*People of India*' (1868 -1875), which contained 468 annotated photographs of the native 'castes and tribes' (Das, 2018).

Walter Hauser (2006) and Christopher Pinney have examined the People of India study of AnSI. Referring to huge volumes of PoI study, Pinney says,

> "These volumes are assembled by an extraordinary man as part of a remarkable project. The circumstances of the project's inception help make sense of these volumes' peculiar qualities– social idealism mixed with an uneasy legacy of Victorian social science against the background of statistical giganticism' (Pinney, 1994).

The PoI project has been criticised for relying too heavily on colonial categories, as Pinney does while referring to a 'legacy of Victorian social science'. This is a major misconception since the PoI project constantly used the term 'community' to describe the castes, tribes, and minorities in entire India (Hauser, 2006; Das, 2006b). Ethnonyms and the historical growth of identities were critically investigated and reports were prepared accordingly, without adhering to administrative categories such as scheduled castes and tribes.[2] Indeed, an 'ethnographic report' prepared 'exclusively' on the Pochury community in Nagaland had helped this community to be recognised later as an 'independent Naga tribe' (Das, 1994). The use of the term 'community' in the whole country helped to study minority groupings based on language and religion in different regions. Ultimately, therefore, the colonial ethnography and postcolonial ethnography of India need to be distinguished, from theoretical-methodological perspectives.

PoI study: Beyond communities and regions

K.S. Singh had not concentrated only on the 'communities'. He aimed to locate and identify communities in terms of their cultural regions as also linguistic, biological, ecological, and cultural traits. Thus, India was divided into 91 cultural regions, not as static units but in a state of continuous flux. Within these regions, as many as 775 traits were identified, relating to ecology, settlement, identity, food habits, social organisations, economy, and occupation, including linkages and impact of change and development. It was revealed that 55 percent of the communities derived their names from the traditional occupations (Singh, 1994, 1996). In terms of religious affiliation, Andhra Pradesh recorded the largest Hindu communities (340), Gujarat recorded the largest number of Muslim communities (87) while Tamil Nadu showed 65 Christian communities. The People of India (AnSI) study has been described as an exploration of diversities and affinities among the people of India. Unlike the colonial-era people of India study, this postcolonial people of India study did not treat communities as disparate islands but as part of a "vibrant interaction" (Das, 2006a).

People of India data reveal that there are communities that simultaneously identity themselves as Hindu-Sikh, Hindu-Muslim, and Hindu-Buddhist (Singh, 1996, 1998). There is a high percentage of trait-sharing among Muslims, Sikhs, Buddhists, and Jains. Even though PoI has revealed the existence of greater adherents of 'tribal religions' in east India, in other parts of India too there are followers of 'tribal religions' often fused under major locally prevailing religions. Several communities have segments, which follow different religions (Singh, 1998). This author has reported elsewhere that Indian communities do not erect rigid boundaries between themselves and often discard religious and cultural borders and do not hesitate to intermingle. A broad rationale and explanation are that most of the communities have emerged from the same ecological, ethnic, and socio-cultural background, even though they later embraced 'other' religions, they never severed pre-change cultural-religious traits (Das, 2006b, 2009). The PoI data revealed that one-eighth of the communities have been affected by socio-religious movements, which included conversion from one religion to another. About two-thirds of the communities engage sacred specialists from other communities, such as Brahmans of all grades, as also the Deori, Baiga, and Paharia who serve tribes and peasant/caste communities by performing rituals. There are about one thousand communities, which avail of priests from dual religious orders.[3]

People of India: Cultural and biological elements and anthropological atlas

There was a fear that the PoI study will further contribute towards the substantialisation of caste. This proved to be ill-founded because caste or jati was not the focus of the study. The basic unit of study was 'community', as perceived and acknowledged by people. Moreover, under the category 'community' non-caste structures, language, and religion-based identities including the minorities as well as those social formations, which stood beyond the jati framework were subsumed. Indeed the preferred category of 'community' carried a value-free connotation (Singh, 1996, 1998).

There is an appropriate use of biological anthropological data in the analysis of PoI data, particularly by incorporating the earlier Anthropometrics Survey (1961-1969) and the Bio anthropological Survey (1972-1980) projects of AnSI. This analysis revealed that the genetic and morphological traits within some communities vary more than those between communities. Homogeneity is along the lines of the region, not caste or religion (Singh, 1994, 1996). Singh also brought out an Anthropological Atlas providing cartographic representation of the distribution of cultural traits and languages, linguistic traits, anthropometry, demographic dimensions of population, ecological features, and biological traits (Singh, 1994).

Tribal study/ Adivasi study redefined: Studies of tribal movements, religions, and other themes

K. S. Singh had joined the AnSI as a Director in 1976. He found that most works focused on regional ethnographies. They did not provide an all-India picture. He, therefore, planned a series of studies and presented such materials in thematic seminars. This exercise led to three pioneering publications (*Tribal Movements*, 1982-1983, *Economies of the Tribes*, 1982 and *Customary Law*, 1993). Two of these works became landmark studies. They continue to remain part of university syllabuses in the entire India. These volumes filled crucial gaps in the arena of tribal-Adivasi studies. Robert Hitchcock included these books in the bibliography on "Indigenous Peoples and Environmental Issues" on behalf of the American Anthropological Association.

Singh's *Tribal Movements in India*, I, and II are reviewed by K L Sharma. He says,

> "These volumes have positively enriched our information and understanding of the tribal movements. 36 movements are located in a unique geopolitical setup and discussed from a historical perspective. Questions of exploitation of the Adivasis by 'outsiders', non-Adivasis, and dominant elements among the tribes are duly attended. The credit for this mainly goes to the editor, but the contributors certainly deserve their share of praise. The authors have not entangled themselves in conceptual jargon and hence have eschewed the corrupting influence of Western social sciences. These two volumes are landmark studies on social change among the tribes of India" (Sharma, 1985).

Many scholars treat tribal movements as peasant movements (Guha, 1983). K. S. Singh argues that 'such an approach tends to gloss over the diversities of the tribal social formation of which tribal movements are a part, they being structurally related' (1985: 119, 1986). Singh has divided earlier tribal movements between India into three phases: first phase (1795 and 1860) coinciding with the rise, expansion, and establishment of the British Empire; second phase (1860 and 1920) coincided with the intensive phase of colonialism, and the third phase, from 1920 till 1947, saw tribes launching 'pro-self-rule' movements (Singh, 1985). During the nineteenth century, messianic movements were also launched by 'rebellious prophets' who promised their followers that they would bring back the golden age of the past (Singh, 1966). Singh (1985, 1986) called them the 'millenarian' movements. By the turn of the twentieth century, when the global indigenous people's movement was intensifying, Singh observed that in recent years, with the rise of the international movement of indigenous people in the post-modernist phase, the focus has shifted to self-determination or self-management of the resources, identity, and ethnicity. The environmental movement has focused on communities in situ, their relationship to resources, their rapport with nature, their worldview (Singh, 1998: 9-10).

Following the colonial-era tendency, anthropologists in the post-independence era remained reprehensively passionate about the phenomenon of the 'Hinduisation' of tribes. Thus, N. K. Bose (1941) pointed to tribes being absorbed into Hindu society and Ghurye (1963:205) described tribes as 'backward Hindus'. Earlier, Singer (1972: 45) had positioned Sanskritisation at par with the "Hindu method of tribal absorption" proposed by Bose. Surajit Sinha saw tribal culture as a "folk" dimension of the Little Tradition of Hindu civilisation (Sinha, 1958). Denial of the autonomous existence of tribal religion, which is even revived often, was advanced under the influence of irrational theories of acculturation and great /little traditions, which were employed unreasonably. Cultural change among tribes was wrongly viewed as a one-way 'fixed' trajectory and the duality in the religious sphere and religious syncretism being a central feature of 'tribal religion' of India was ignored (Das, 2003, 2009).

Singh had visualised tribal religion as an autonomous phenomenon. In his article titled '*Tribal Religion and Hinduism*', included in this author's edited volume (Das, 2003), Singh observed that,

> "Tribal religion is no longer identified with animism but is seen as part of the culture and society of the tribal people which is rich, positive, harmonious and autonomous, with a very healthy set of relationships with the natural environment. Many elements of tribal religion are as alive, even as vibrant as ever. - - - tribal religion has not lost its distinct identity despite its long years of interaction with Hinduism and Christianity." (Singh, 2003).

Stratification and post-colonial transformation in tribal society

K.S.Singh had identified various stages and causative factors in the process of tribal-state formation. Such stages included peasantisation of the tribes, transformation of the tribal economy, surplus generation through technological advancement, and building trading networks, etcetera (Singh, 1971). Regarding medieval Assam and middle India, Singh wrote:

> "The crucial factors of economic changes in the tribal regions were the formation of the state in the later medieval period and migration of peasant castes. The first phenomenon is witnessed all over the tribal territory extending from the Brahmaputra Valley to the Satpuras and the Godavari. — The Ahoms encouraged the

extension of the *Sali* (wetland) cultivation, and 'new' transplantation techniques. They built up a communal labour based system of massive dykes and embankments. Lands were improved and *Ahu* (upland) and *Bao* (broadcast rice) lands were transformed into lands suitable for the cultivation of the *Sali* crops in upper Assam, the cradle of Ahom culture. — The Gond Rajas in middle India reclaimed and peopled their wild forests and dotted their kingdoms with embankments and other irrigation schemes. As surpluses emerged economic differentiation and social stratification developed in tribal society" (Singh, 1982b: viii-ix).

Singh had encouraged this author to scrutinise and compile materials on pre-colonial social formation, colonialism, and post-colonial transformation of tribal society in northeast India. This advice led to the publication of the author's book, '*Ethnic Identity, Ethnicity, and Social Stratification in Northeast India*' (Das, 1989). In his Foreword to this volume K.S. Singh wrote that,

> "In recent years the process of state formation in North-East India has been critically analyzed. State formation was a multi-pronged process here. It involved experiments with a new organisation and technology of production, a new set of social relations. It resulted in the rise of multi-community or multi-ethnic formations in the Brahmaputra valley and beyond. Even those communities which were not brought within the state system had a well-integrated, cohesive pre-state system of authority based on a sharing of power. The pre-state system did not exist in a vacuum and did not necessarily imply a situation of chaos. The author's study of the segmentary social system among the Zounuo-Key-honuo (Southern Angami Naga) throws an interesting light on how such a pre-state system worked until it was peripherally integrated with the colonial system and the post-colonial state. We require today a conceptual framework for the study of the North-East that partakes of both historical perspective and anthropological insight. I am glad to note the application of the combined methodology in the exploration of North-East situation in this book" (Singh, 1989).

Decolonisation of Indian anthropology and K.S. Singh

In India, anthropologists/sociologists had articulated concern for 'indigenisation' (Dube, 1973), questioning 'academic colonialism' (Singh, 1984); seeking 'swaraj' ('self-rule') in Indian social sciences (Uberoi, 1968) as also 'decolonisation' of anthropology in India (Sinha, 1971). In a postcolonial context, AnSI's PoI study emerges as a major study contesting the Orientalist and Indological image of India, by highlighting India's cultural, ecological, socio-economic, and religious harmony, thereby discarding the British narrative of India as a monolith. Long before K.S. Singh conceived and launched the modern postcolonial brand of people of India study, N. K. Bose had launched through a major academic innovation in the 1960s, the all India material traits survey, by conceiving Indian Civilisation in terms of 'culture zones' which he argued did not coincide with fixed linguistic zones, created in the colonial era. N K Bose and Surajit Sinha both coordinated the project in which data were collected from 313 districts, to map the distribution of material traits. The summarised result of this national survey was published in '*Peasant Life in India: A Study in Indian Unity and Diversity*' by Bose (1961).[4]

Bose's study proved to be a major departure within the Indian ethnographic realm and it facilitated the nascent indigenisation of Indian anthropology. This effort of indigenisation was further pursued by K.S. Singh in PoI study of the 1990s. He (2000) wrote that the decolonisation of the AnSI was speeded up in the 1960s with the launch of the first study of Material Traits. Much of Material Traits data remained unpublished, hence K.S. Singh had retrieved and brought out several publications about that project such as '*Basketry in India: Material Traits Survey Additional Data*' (1993).[4] In his introductory volume of PoI Study, K.S. Singh made suitable use of material traits data of earlier surveys to compare with the PoI data set. The data generated by PoI suggests that contrary to the general impression and despite the higher value attached to vegetarianism, only about 20 percent of Indian communities emerged as a vegetarian (1998).[5]

People of India study-An indigenous mission

The People of India study conducted by K.S. Singh was entirely *swadeshi*. This presented a breakthrough not only in terms of the conceptual framework but also in methodology. The PoI project sought to assemble people's knowledge about culture and environment, and explore the idioms, the structures, and the cognitive processes reflected in the understanding and perception of people about themselves, and their relationship to one another and with the environment. Generating ethnographic accounts of 4,694 communities (main communities being 2,205, major segments being 589, and territorial units being 1,900) was not an easy task. Even more complicated was gathering nomenclatures of communities, a range of synonyms, surnames, and titles and investing their vibrant involvement in space, ethos, and cultural traits. PoI study never ignored the basic identities of the communities, which have many segments/layers tied with regional cultural/linguistic, and ecological patterns. Thus, the project explored the various ways in which people interact, integrate, enmesh, share traits and space, and also discover the processes that bring them together. This view of Indian society, to use K.S. Singh's evocative metaphor is a 'honeycomb' in which communities are engaged in vibrant interaction sharing space, ethos, and cultural traits (Singh, 1992, 2002, 2012). Asghar Ali Engineer called it an eye-opening study. It is this home-grown approach to visualise Indian society in terms of native paradigms that made the PoI project an essentially Swadeshi Mission, designed in terms of indigenous prerequisites and the ethos of people. It was meant to situate the people in diverse cultural zones that were not bounded but porous. The 'People of India' study has indeed proved to be a milestone in post-colonial ethnography, with emphasis on the Indian ideal of cultural pluralism.

A concluding tribute

The author would like to cite and reiterate below a few lines from his tribute to K.S. Singh published earlier:

> 'Singh was a scholar of Indian society. His exceptional ability, fertile imagination, and the courage to go against prevailing opinion and to bear sometimes vicious attacks had marked his distinguished style and explain his enormous and varied contributions. With the passing away of K S Singh, a glorious era of anthropological-historical research has ended. His scholarly output and his example will continue to influence and inspire future generations of scholars in India and abroad' (Das, 2006b).

Endnotes

1. This article is a part of a larger ICSSR project on 'Social Theorising in Contemporary India' organised by Ananta Kumar Giri (Madras Institute of Development Studies, Chennai). Hence, no part of this article may be republished or reproduced elsewhere in any manner without the consent of the author.
2. The term community was retained throughout national and state volumes of PoI and all national volumes are titled as 'communities' and 'segments'. However, as per the needs of the government following parliamentary intervention, there was a demand which led to the retrieval of data on the SCs and STs, and such materials formed two national volumes devoted to scheduled castes and scheduled tribes.
3. Elsewhere this author, who was a national coordinator and in charge of the publication programme of the PoI Project, had stated that one of the objectives of the project, was to examine the economic and cultural linkages between the communities and to identify the basic character of inter-cultural and inter-religious alteration. This author has reinterpreted and thereby highlighted the syncretistic religious character of the people of India by using the data-sets of the PoI project (Das, 2003, 2006a & b, 2009), even though K.S. Singh has used terms like synthesis and metaphor like 'honeycomb' to describe the pluralistic traditions of the people of India.
4. N.K. Das with the help of Santanu Mitra and through sponsorship of AnSI had translated 'Peasant Life in India' and published '*Bharat ka Gramin Jivan: Ekta avam Vividhata*' (Hindi Translation of *Peasant Life in India* by Nirmal Kumar Bose). 2013. Jaipur: Rawat Publishers.
5. Incidentally, K.S. Singh had also retrieved the unpublished material of another AnSI project *'Study of Indian Weaker Sections'*, which was supervised by Surajit Sinha earlier. K.S. Singh had entrusted N.K. Das to organize and re-edit the reports and write a concluding chapter for the project (vide Surajit Sinha, R. Bhattacharya, and N.K. Das, 1993). Surajit Sinha wrote the preface and K.S. Singh wrote a critical introductory chapter in this volume.

References

Bayly, C. 1988. 'Rallying around the subaltern'. *Journal of Peasant Studies*, 11, 1: 110-120.

Bose, NK 1941. 'The Hindu method of tribal absorption', *Science and Culture* (7).

Bose, NK 1961 *Peasant Life in India: A Study in Indian Unity and Diversity*, Anthropological Survey of India, Calcutta.

Das, NK. 1989. *Ethnic Identity, Ethnicity, and Social Stratification in Northeast India*. Foreword by K.S. Singh. Inter-India Publications, New Delhi.

Das, NK. 1994. ' Pochury', In NK Das, and CL. Imchen, Editors. General Editor: K.S. Singh: *People of India, Nagaland Volume*, Anthropological Survey of India & Seagull Books. Calcutta.

Das, NK. 2003. *An Outline of Syncretism: Culture, Religion, and Philosophy: Critical Studies in Syncretism and Inter-Faith Harmony*. Rawat Publishers, Jaipur.

Das, NK. 2006a. 'Cultural diversity, religious syncretism, and people of India: An anthropological interpretation'. *Bangladesh e-Journal of Sociology*. 3, 2. July 2006.

Das, NK. 2006b. 'People of India and Indian anthropology: K.S.Singh: A tribute'. *Economic and Political Weekly.* July 22, 2006, pp. 3156-3158.

Das, NK. 2009. 'Identity politics, cultural pluralism and the state in South Asia: An anthropological reappraisal', In NK.Das and VR.Rao (Eds): *Identity, Cultural Pluralism, and State: South AnSIa in Perspective* Macmillan India, New Delhi.

Das, NK. 2018. 'Indian anthropology: A plea for pragmatic appraisal'. *Bangladesh e-Journal of Sociology*.Volume 15, No. 1. 11-29. January 2018.

Dube, SC. 1973. *Social Sciences in Changing Society*, Ethnographic and Folk Culture Society of India, Lucknow.

Gadgil, M., Joshi NV, Shambu Prasad UV., Manoharan S, and Patil Suresh,1997. 'Peopling of India'. In D. Balasubramanian and N. Appaji Rao (Eds): *The Indian Human Heritage*, pp.100-129. Universities Press, Hyderabad.

Ghurye, GS. 1963. *The Scheduled Tribes* 3rd edition (first published as *The Aborigines so-called and their Future* 1943). Popular Press, Bombay.

Guha, Ranajit. 1983. *Elementary Aspects of Peasant Insurgency in Colonial India*. New Oxford University Press, Delhi.

Hauser, Walter 2006. 'Remembering Kumar Suresh Singh: Scholar, administrator, and friend'. *Seminar*. #566. October 2006.

Jenkins, LD 2003. "Another 'People of India' project: Colonial and national anthropology', *Journal of Asian Studies*, 62, 4: 1143–1170.

Joshi, NV., Gadgil M, and Patil S. 1993a. 'Exploring cultural diversity of the people of India'. *Current Science*. 64, 1: 10-17.

Joshi, NV, Gadgil M., and Patil S. 1993b. 'Exploring cultural diversity of the people of India', in SB Roy and AK Ghosh (Eds): *People of India: Bio-cultural Dimensions,* Inter India Publications, New Delhi.

Pinney, Christopher, 1994. 'Review of People of India'. *The Times Higher Education Supplement,* 2 September 1994

Risley, HH. 1915. *The People of India*. Thacker, Spink & Co Calcutta, W. Thacker & Co, London.

Shah, Alpa. 2014. 'Religion and the Secular Left: Subaltern Studies, Birsa Munda and Maoists'. *Anthropology of this Century*. Issue 9. January 2014;

http://aotcpress.com/articles/religion-secular-left-subaltern-studies-birsa-munda-maoists/

Sharma, KL 1985. 'Social change in tribal India, Review of tribal movements in India', Volumes I and II, edited by KS Singh. *Economic and Political Weekly*, October 12, 1985.

Singh, DK 2006. 'K.S.Singh –A tribute'. *Liberation*. Central Organ of the Communist Party of India (Marxist –Leninist). July 2006; http://archive.cpiml.org/liberation/year_2006/July/rememberance.htm/

Singh, KS. 1966. *Dust-Storm and Changing Mist: Story of Birsa Munda and His Movement in Chotanagpur*, Firma KL Mukhopadhyay, Calcutta.

Singh, KS. 1971. *Tribal Situation in India*. Indian Institute of Advanced Studies, Shimla.

Singh, K.S.1971. 'State-formation in tribal Society: Some preliminary observations', *Journal of Indian Anthropological Society*, 6, 161-181.

Singh, KS. 1975. *The Indian Famine, 1967: A Study in Crisis and Change*. People's Publishing House, New Delhi.

Singh, KS. 1982. *Tribal Movements in India*, Vols. I. Manohar Publishers, New Delhi.

Singh, KS. 1982b. *Economies of the Tribes and Their Transformation*, Concept Publishing, New Delhi.

Singh, KS. 1983. *Tribal Movements in India*, Vols. II, Manohar Publishers, New Delhi.

Singh, KS. 1984. 'Colonialism, anthropology and primitive society: the Indian scenario (1928-47)', *Man in India*, 64, 4: 400-11.

Singh, KS. 1985. *Tribal Society in India: An Anthropo-Historical Perspective*. Manohar Publications, New Delhi.

Singh, KS. 1986. 'Agrarian dimension of tribal movements' In AR. Desai (Ed): *Agrarian Struggles in India after Independence*, Oxford University Press, Delhi.

Singh, KS. 1989. Foreword. In *Ethnic Identity, Ethnicity, and Social Stratification in Northeast India* by N K Das. Inter-India Publications, New Delhi.

Singh, KS. 1992. *People of India: An Introduction*. Vol. 1 *National Series*. Anthropological Survey of India, Calcutta.

Singh, KS. 1993. *Tribal Ethnography, Customary Law, and Change*. Concept, New Delhi.

Singh, KS 1994. *People of India: An Anthropological Atlas: Ecology and Cultural Traits, Languages and Linguistic Traits, Demographic and Biological Traits*. Oxford University Press, New Delhi.

Singh, KS. 1996. *Communities, Segments, Synonyms, Surnames, and Titles* (People of India, National Series, Vol. VIII). Oxford University Press, New Delhi.

Singh, KS. 1998. *People of India: India's Communities*. Oxford University Press, New Delhi.

Singh, KS.2000. 'A perspective on the Anthropological Survey of India' *Seminar* 495: 40–44.

Singh, KS.2002. *People of India: An Introduction* (revised edition) People of India: National series. Oxford University Press, New Delhi.

Singh, KS. 2002. *Birsa Munda: A Centennial Edition*. Seagull Press, Calcutta.

Singh, KS. 2003. 'Hinduism and tribal religion: an anthropological perspective on interaction'. In N.K. Das (Ed.): *Culture, Religion, and Philosophy: Critical Studies in Syncretism and Inter-Faith Harmony*. Rawat Publications, Jaipur.

Singh, KS. 2012. *Diversity, Identity, and Linkages: Explorations in Historical Ethnography*, Oxford University Press, New Delhi.

Singh, KS., and Manoharan S. 1994. *People of India: Languages and Scripts* Oxford University Press, New Delhi.

Sinha, Surajit 1958. 'Tribal culture of peninsular India as a dimension of little tradition in the study of Indian civilisation', *Journal of American Folklore* (71).

Sinha, Surajit 1971. Is there an Indian trend in social-cultural anthropology? *Journal of Indian Anthropol. Society.* 6:1-14.

Sinha, Surajit, Bhattacharya R., and Das NK. 1993. *Anthropology of Weaker Sections*. Concept and Anthropological Survey of India, New Delhi.

Sivaramakrishnan, K. 1995. 'Situating the subaltern: history and anthropology in the subaltern studies project'. *Journal of Historical Sociology*, 8, 4: 395-429.

Uberoi, JS. 1968. 'Science and swaraj'. *Contributions to Indian Sociology*. 2: 119-124.

Uday Prakash, 2006. 'The one from the tribe' *Tehelka Magazine* Jun 17, 2006, https://hinduism.stackexchange.com/questions/11511/how-castes were-produced-in-India

21

Life and Works of Satadal Dasgupta Towards Anthropological Studies in India

Rajatsubhra Mukhopadhyay

Satadal Dasgupta, Professor Emeritus of Anthropology at the University of Prince Edward Island (UPEI), Canada was an alumnus of the Department of Anthropology, Calcutta University. He was born in Calcutta (now Kolkata) on September 25, 1937; and breathed his last on May 27, 2018, in Halifax, Canada. Satadal Dasgupta by name is not all that familiar to the circle of the present generation of anthropologists in India. The possible reason for which maybe, he had spent a major part of his life teaching in the USA and Canada, and in pursuing research in the field of 'diffusion of agricultural innovations' that does not fit well in the domain of mainstream anthropology in India. He was, however, known to many others as the elder brother of Prof. Biplab Dasgupta, a noted economist and Marxist leader in India.

At the Prince Edward Island (PEI) Prof. Dasgupta had shaped the Sociology and Anthropology department and spent his life as a devoted professor and passionate researcher. As an anthropologist, his professional career began along with his appointment as a Research Officer in the Socio-Agro-Economic Research unit of the Department of Agriculture, Govt. of West Bengal in 1962. Later he served as a

Lecturer in Rural Sociology at Kalyani University, West Bengal for the period 1963 – 65. He was in faculty as Assistant Professor in Anthropology at Mississippi State University, USA (1965 – 69). Afterward, he was appointed as Professor in the Department of Sociology and Anthropology at UPEI in Canada in 1969, and where he had spent the best and the most productive years of his life spanning almost 50 years. He was in the chair of the PEI Museum and Heritage Foundation for some period.

Prof. Dasgupta's interest in the diffusion studies concerning agricultural innovations in India began when he came in contact with Mr. Santi Priya Bose, the then Joint Director of Agriculture, Govt. of West Bengal, and who was his immediate supervisor. Prof. Dasgupta is also known for his work on peasant societies, rural social change, community sociology, and family and kinship studies. Dasgupta's anthropological works and writings on India fall broadly into four major groups. They are (i) Diffusion of Agricultural Innovations, (ii) Family and Kinship Studies, (iii) Caste and Agrarian Class Structure, and (iv) Conflict and Rural Social Change. These groupings are, however, not exclusive. This essay purposefully does not make any attempt to review Dasgupta's publications on several other topics, having considerable anthropological relevance, and written in the particular context of the USA and Canada. That does not mean that we could ignore his other valuable contributions in anthropological/ sociological studies in the context of countries other than India. However, as our focus is mainly laid down on Indian anthropology, we should pay our attention to his studies in India only.

On diffusion of agricultural innovations

Professor Satadal Dasgupta is mainly noted for his research and publications in the transformation of agricultural practices and community organisations done in India. He has been internationally recognised as one of the front rank scholars devoted to the study of diffusion and adoption of modern agricultural technology by Indian farmers. He had a modest beginning in diffusion studies in the early 1960s and his research outputs grew rapidly in the 1970s. His compilation titled *Diffusion of Agricultural Innovations in Village India* (1989) highlights the distinctive elements of the diffusion process in agricultural innovations in Indian villages. Besides, it contains a comprehensive bibliography on diffusion studies.

Historically, Anthropology has the longest tradition in diffusion research and has been primarily responsible for the development of its basic theoretical and methodological conceptualisations. One may note that the 'diffusionist schools' continued to play an important role in anthropological theories of social and cultural change. But unfortunately, diffusion as a topic of research failed to have any significant influence in Indian anthropology excepting a few sporadic attempts by scholars.

On the question of the adoption behaviour of cultivators in favour of or against modern practices, Dasgupta had a perceptive argument. He was in view that economic gain is not always a sufficient incentive for farmers to adopt a new practice. Social and cultural considerations frequently take precedence over the economic advantage of adopting a new agricultural practice. This socio-cultural 'embeddedness' of economic activities is especially pronounced in traditional societies such as India, where activities in the economic sphere are closely interlinked with those in the social, cultural, and ritual domains, and with the existing structure of social relationships, local norms, habits or values. And at the same time often influenced by other factors that are purely personal and situational. Thus, Dasgupta's major contributions in the area dealing with the problem of differential acceptance of farmer practices as a function of the socio-cultural system have an important bearing on his anthropological understanding and imagination.

As an anthropologist, he has not only been interested in the study of inter-sectoral diffusion of cultural traits and complexes but also in the process by which such traits and complexes diffuse within a social system. From the said perspective, Dasgupta's several studies (1975, 1978) indicate the types of community structures that are conducive to technological development, as the technological development is expressed and carried by the social structures. According to Dasgupta, agricultural development in a village could hardly take place in isolation from other structures for there are important linkages among structural unity of a village society which has an organic unity of its own as a social system. Therefore, the village differences in agricultural development are strongly influenced by structural configurations which are variably related to levels of agricultural development. His study (Bose, 1963) reveals that the caste and leadership structures had a lot to do with its agricultural modernisation and productivity. To put it more explicitly – a village dominated numerically and/ or economically by a traditional agricultural caste tends to have a higher level of agricultural development as that caste by orientation tends to maximize skill inputs and importance attached to agriculture.

Family and kinship studies

The core area of research of Dasgupta was on family and kinship. His doctoral thesis in Anthropology was on 'Social organisation of the Dule Bagdi, a backward caste in the Jaynagar region of West Bengal, India'. For that study, he made intensive fieldwork in 1960-61 followed by a revisit in 1978-79. The findings of which he later published as a monograph titled *Caste, Kinship, and Community: Social System of a Bengal Caste* (1986). In this study, the kinship structure of the Dule Bagdi has been examined at five levels: (a) *Sansar* – independent nuclear family, (b) *Paribar* – extended family, (c) *Goosthi* – localised lineage, (d) *Bansa* – dispersed lineage, and (e) *Gotra* – common ancestry.

This monograph of Dasgupta meticulously analyzes the structures of internal and external relations of the localised Dule-Bagdi's in the famous functional model of Talcott Parsons popularly called the AGIL scheme. The three differentiated structural units of the Dule Bagdi social system, according to Dasgupta, are intimately related to its four functional needs and where the caste system deals with the 'goal attainment' and 'integration', the kinship with 'pattern maintenance' and 'tension management', and the community with 'adaptation'. In Indian anthropology, this particular approach was certainly a significant departure from the study of a caste/ community in a traditional ethnographic model to a more analytical and advanced theoretical frame of reference. The unique feature of this classic study is – there is a difference of approach as well as differences in analytical treatment. The strength of this monograph lies in its being firmly grounded in a clearly defined theoretical frame.

Prof. Dasgupta's interest in family and kinship studies continued throughout his life. That was the most favoured area of his research and writings. In the very formative phase of his professional life, during 1963-64, he published several important articles in the *Bulletin of the Cultural Research Institute*, Calcutta on the kinship structure, marriage, and locality groups among the Dule Bagdis.

On the persistence of joint family system

Based on his latest data on Hooghly villages in West Bengal (1993), Dasgupta concluded that a joint family household is not the typical household in rural West Bengal either in terms of its proportion to total households or in terms of people belonging to it. However, he observes that the incidence of joint family households is more among 'owner-cultivators' as among tenants, agricultural labourers, and people engaged in non-agricultural occupations. This remarkable stability of the joint family households in West Bengal villages support the cyclical view that emphasises the stability of the incidence of joint family households and views nuclear family households as transitional forms in the normal functioning in the development cycle of joint family households.

Dasgupta further opined that a major factor that contributes to the survival of the joint family households in the West Bengal villages, albeit at a rather low level of incidence, is that it continues to be idealised as a preferred household type in the villages although they vary in their ability to attain and maintain it. The persistence of a joint family thus formed or the immediacy of its dissolution, however, depends on its status of land ownership, occupation, and literacy.

Caste, class, and family structure

Another important contribution of Dasgupta to family studies in India relates to the question of an association between caste, class, and family structure in West Bengal villages (1999). He observes that although caste status is significantly related to the family structure, class status, whether based on occupation or landownership, also has a strong relationship with the family structure. Classes based on land ownership, however, appear to be more predictive of the variation in family types than occupational classes. To Dasgupta, the influence of caste status on the family structure is there because of the innate relationship of caste with landownership. So the variation in the family type cannot be comprehended properly ignoring the inherent congruence between caste and agrarian hierarchy.

Caste and agrarian class structure

Dasgupta in some of his recent studies (2000a and 2000b) examines the influence of caste on land ownership, tenancy/ sharecropping, and labour employment in agriculture. He identifies a strong association between caste and land ownership. The cultivating middle castes not only own land but also participates in its management and operation mostly as 'owner-cultivators', who primarily use family labour, and hired labourers when additional hands are required. Among them, the proportion of 'supervisory-cultivators' is not all that significant. In contrast, the landowning high caste households in the region have traditionally 'non-cultivating owners', leasing out all or most of their land and thus avoiding direct participation in agricultural operations. In recent years, however, out of the fear of 'Operation Barga', and to counter the legal measures adopted by the government in favour of tenants/ share-croppers, they have mostly stopped further leasing out of their land or take back their land out of tenancy, and get them cultivated themselves as 'supervisory cultivators' by appointing hired agricultural labourers.

In the agrarian social structure, the caste plays an important role in tenancy arrangements. The high and particularly middle-class landowners normally prefer to lease out the land (if they so desire at all) to their caste or lower caste tenants. On the other hand, agricultural labourers almost come from low caste or tribal households. High and middle caste members tend to avoid the rather demeaning status of working as hired agricultural labourers, unless forced by economic exigencies. This increasing degree of correspondence between the higher/ middle castes and the landed, and the lower caste and the landless, thus, according to Dasgupta, has not only contributed to the polarisation of the two groups but increased awareness of the opposition of their interests has led to overt conflicts between them. Whether or not such conflicts will necessarily lead to any significant social change and development in rural West Bengal is, therefore, a moot question at present.

On conflict and rural social change

Despite his stay in Canada, Dasgupta continued to pursue his research interest in India and spent a year (1985-86) in West Bengal conducting an empirical study on his project 'Conflict and Social Change in West Bengal Villages'. It has been my privilege to be associated with that project in different capacities. Dasgupta's study on conflict and rural social change is altogether a different attempt to empirically address the problem from a 'conflict' perspective. In his view (1988:147) the social anthropological 'consensus' or 'harmonic' perspective of the Indian village presents a rather static view of the rural social structure. The 'conflict' perspective, in contrast, provides a more dynamic view, and where it locates the 'conflict' as a potent source of social change and which is a product of the existing inequality structure of the society. The 'conflict' perspective, according to Dasgupta, is, therefore, a more appropriate theoretical frame of reference and befitting in comprehending the political conflict and social change in West Bengal villages.

In his 'Panchanan Mitra' lecture in the Asiatic Society, Calcutta, Dasgupta (2001) presented some findings of the said research project. All they have much social anthropological and sociological importance. He had observed that the political conflict brought about by the reform measures and their manner of implementation by the CPI (M) led 'Left Front Government' have contributed to an overt structural rift in West Bengal villages polarising the landowning high/ middle castes and the predominantly landless and near landless lower castes into two groups with opposite interest and views regarding the effect of the resulting conflict on the unity and integrity of the village society.

The landowning high and middle castes claimed that party politics had permanently divided the village as a community and did not see any hope for reconciliation soon. They were unhappy for losing economic control over the lower castes/ class and for being displaced from the position of authority and power in the political and ceremonial spheres of the village life. The people of the opposing camp belonging to the low castes were not all that pessimistic and believed that the present conflict in the village was temporary, and there was still some unity among the villagers. However, the low castes are now socio-politically more united than before. This perceptual rift between the people of two contending groups was certainly a reflection of a kind of discord that prevails in rural West Bengal. Earlier also from the findings of another field study (1989), Dasgupta came to a similar conclusion that has immense contemporary relevance.

Concluding observations

In his long professional life, Prof. Satadal Dasgupta was a passionate researcher. His writings on human factors in technological development in agriculture; family, caste, kinship, and community; and changes in India's villages, though diverse, are nonetheless important contributions to Indian anthropology. Most of them are well-researched publications based on concrete empirical data collected through intensive fieldwork. His writings especially on 'diffusion studies' are read by students in many Agricultural Universities in India and abroad in their curricula on 'agricultural extension' and 'rural community development'. His works on the process of diffusion of agricultural innovations are quite significant, empirically sound, and theoretically oriented contributions to Indian anthropology particularly having considerable bearing with applied anthropology.

His research on the social organisation of the Dule Bagdis, a backward caste in West Bengal marked a sharp departure from descriptive ethnography to an analytical one based on substantive theoretical formulations. Significant empirical research on family and class has been done by Dasgupta in the context of rural West Bengal. Dasgupta's explorations on how far the rural family structure is still influenced by caste and class provide valuable empirical insights about the nature and extent of their association in the recent past. On the question of the persistence of the joint family system in rural areas, Dasgupta observes that the relative proportion of the joint family households has remained remarkably stable and it does not face an imminent threat of extinction. Dasgupta's study on 'conflict and social change' in West Bengal villages attempts to address this particular problem from a conflict perspective discarding the 'consensus'/

'harmonic' perspective with which the anthropologists are mostly familiar. Despite all his aforesaid valuable researches, our scholars are somewhat not all that familiar with such works of Dasgupta. We are yet to seriously assess the value of his works towards Anthropological studies in India.

References

Bose, Santi Priya. 1963. *Eadpur: A Study into rice yields of a Bengal Village*. Govt. of West Bengal: Department of Agriculture, Calcutta.

Dasgupta, Satadal. 1986. *Caste, Kinship, and Community: Social System of a Bengal Caste*. University Press Ltd, Hyderabad.

Dasgupta, Satadal. 1988. 'Agrarian crisis and social change in West Bengal villages'. In Madhu S. Mishra (Ed.): *Rural Development in Eastern and North-Eastern India*, pp. 146–174, Indian Institute of Management, Calcutta.

Dasgupta, Satadal. 1989. *Diffusion of Agricultural Innovations in Village India*. Wiley Eastern Ltd, New Delhi.

Dasgupta, Satadal. 2001. 'Caste, class, and political conflict: perception of social change in West Bengal villages', *Journal of Asiatic Society*. 53,1: 48–76.

Dasgupta, Satadal, and Madan GR. 1978. *Community and Agriculture in Two Indian Villages*. Editions India, Calcutta.

Dasgupta, Satadal, and Mukhopadhyay Rajat Subhra. 1989. 'Party politics, panchayat, and conflict in a West Bengal village', *Man in India*, 69, 1: 24–41.

Dasgupta, Satadal, Weatherbie Christine, and Mukhopadhyay Rajat Subhra. 1993. 'Nuclear and joint family households in West Bengal villages', *Ethnology*, 32,4: 339–358.

Dasgupta, Satadal, Hennessy Seana, and Mukhopadhyay Rajat Subhra. 1999. 'Caste, class and family structure in West Bengal villages', *Journal of Comparative Family Studies*, 30, 4: 561–577.

Dasgupta, Satadal, Hennessy Seana, and Mukhopadhyay Rajat Subhra. 2000a. 'Caste and agrarian structure in West Bengal', *Man in India*, 80,1-2: 31–55.

Dasgupta, Satadal, Hennessy Seana, and Mukhopadhyay Rajat Subhra. 2000b. 'Caste and agrarian structure in West Bengal: implications for rural development', *Man and Development*, 22,2: 45–62.

Kaufman, Harold F., Singh Avtar, and Dasgupta Satadal. 1975. *Villages Upward Bound: Community Structure and Technological Development in Selected Indian Villages*. Editions India, Calcutta.

22

Life and Works of Amitabha Basu: A Tribute

Subho Roy

I

It is always a great honour and privilege for a student to make an appraisal of the scholarship of his/her teacher, especially of an illustrious person like Amitabha Basu. Every individual grows up with a worldview, i.e. the fundamental cognitive orientation of an individual encompassing the whole of the individual's knowledge and point of view, including natural philosophy; fundamental, existential, and normative postulates; or themes, values, emotions, and ethics. And perhaps, this remains in the individual's conscious or subconscious mind and eventually gets reflected in his/her life and works.

If one reads "Anthropologist in Search of a Purpose: The test case of the Pahira of Manbhum", published in Indian Museum Bulletin (Basu, 1974), one can understand the turmoil and tribulations of a restless researcher (here Amitabha Basu) drifting between its act and conscious mind. The title itself is interesting; two contrasting topics have been dealt with in a single article. In the first section of this article, Basu presented his doctoral research on the population genetics of the Pahira community following the post-1950s tradition of anthropological genetics. In the midway of this write-up (the second section) he drifted and questioned the relevance of his research. I quote from his statement "I would now like to raise a nasty question: Is this kind of research worthwhile? ...He continues "Is it to gather knowledge of any kind, for the fun of it? How does it matter whether the Pahira subgroups differed concerning certain blood groups, or taste blindness or anthropometrics?" The second section of this article reveals the reflexivity of Basu towards Anthropological research in general and to his research in particular. In the third section, finally, Basu wrapped up the findings of the population genetic study of the Pahiras.

The end of World War II saw the beginning of a wave of popular protests in Bengal. One such protest was *Khaddo Andolon* (Protest for Food) that took place in the year 1959. The Protest for Food movement took a 'spontaneous' shape, as common masses, without party affiliations or discipline joined the movement. Basu, a college-going student at that time, took an active part in this movement. As a part of the protest, rallies were organised, and in one such protest rallies, he became a victim of police atrocity. Perhaps Basu was a born rebel. There are many other instances, where Basu inked his protest or physically came forward for the cause of the society. Let me remind you, Basu hails from the lineage of Subhas Chandra Bose.

From the above two examples, one can figure out how Basu, since his early life was receptive to social issues.

II

Since the late 1950's and early 1960's emphasis in physical anthropology gradually shifted from classifying human variation into discrete taxonomic categories to understanding the process responsible for human variation and evolution at a micro-level. And population genetics became an important tool in such endeavour. Like many scholars, Basu also became a part of the dominant discourse. He chose to work on the population genetics of the Pahira, a small food gathering community that lived in the Ajodhya and Dalma Hills of the Purulia district of West Bengal for his doctoral programme. The Pahiras are divided into three subpopulations based on culturally and territorially defined groups, Northern Pahira (NP) and Southern Pahira I and II (SP I and SP II). The objectives of his study were to describe the biological characteristics of the population; to investigate how far marital isolation led to genetically different subpopulations within the population; and to discuss the implications of such subpopulations and to examine the common assumption that allele frequencies throughout a population (i.e., among its several subpopulations) are homogeneous. This study fetched him a direct D.Sc. degree from Calcutta University.

The results of his study revealed that the subpopulations are different concerning several genetic traits ranging from blood groups, PTC taste blindness, digital anomaly, and anthropometric measurements and demographic trait; the variations in the trait show a clinal trend; that N.P. and S.P.I. are closer to each other than either of them to S.P.II. The study also revealed how this type of breeding structure and genetic composition has important evolutionary implications, about the importance of demographic information in population genetics; and, that the common assumption that allele frequencies throughout a population are homogeneous may not be valid. He further derived how breeding structure affects not only the genetic traits but also anthropometric variables.

He concluded from the study that the Pahira community is divided into three martially isolated and genetically distinct subgroups with a limited amount of gene flow among them corroborating the concept of Wright's 'Island Model'. On closer scrutiny, he observed that the variation in younger and older age groups is six times the standard deviation of the variation expected in terms of the given effective population size, admixture rate, and initial allele frequency. Basu was ahead of his times and published articles based on this research in the American Journal of Physical Anthropology (1969), Man (1969) (a publication of Royal Anthropological Institute), and Journal of Social Biology (1971).

Here, let me refer to a very interesting incident. When Basu submitted the manuscript of his thesis to Dr. S.S. Sarkar (his supervisor), he received a rebuttal from his supervisor. Sarkar asked Basu to give up his research and open a *pan* shop for livelihood. But Basu was confident in his work. He mustered the courage to request Sarkar to give a relook on the manuscript. After a few days, Sarkar called Basu in his chamber and asked to finalise the manuscript of the thesis for submission of a D.Sc. degree. The doctoral work of Professor Basu was extremely appreciated by Curt Stern, and the rest is history.

III

Shortly after the submission of the thesis, Basu got an opportunity to work on an international project, headed by S.L. Shapiro which aimed to measure the stress of slum dwellers of Kolkata city. But Basu could not continue with this project. He left for the US with a Fulbright post-doctoral fellowship and worked in the Department of Anthropology, the University of North Carolina at the Chappel-Hill, the USA during 1967-1969. There, he received intellectual stimulation and academic adoration from Professor William Pollitzer. Pollitzer during that time was the Editor of the American Journal of Physical Anthropology. His post-doctoral work was on demographic-genetic aspects of the Haitian populations.

Haiti is a small Caribbean country. During the time 1968-69, nearly all of Haiti's population was of African origin (termed blacks). A small minority of people were of mixed European and African descent (called mulattoes) who constituted a wealthier elite and account for most of the remainder. There were also a small number of people of European descent. Haiti differentiated itself ethnically, linguistically, and culturally from the other Caribbean and Latin American countries, notably the Spanish-speaking and the English-speaking countries of the region. The project (which Basu took for his Full Bright Programme) aimed to examine the biosocial interrelations in the rural Haitian population at micro and macro levels. This study was based on four villages on the island of Grand Cayemite, and the town of Pestel, in Haiti, West Indies. He wanted to examine the genetic contribution to the rural Haitian population of three supposed ancestral populations namely, central and western African Negros, French White, and American Indian. Precisely, it was an effort to estimate the effect of social factors on the biological characteristics based on social-historical information. He hypothesised that among the three ancestral populations, the contribution of the western and central African Negro to the genetic makeup of the pooled Grand Cayemite population was maximum, of the French White and American Indian was small. He further hypothesised that the four villages of Grand Cayemite, which were non-marrying, would be biologically more distant than the village of Pointe Sable (on the island) and the town of Pestel (on the mainland) from each other. He used demographic information, anthropometric measurements, dermatoglyphic and serological traits in this study. The data were analyzed to study the gene distribution in terms of racial admixture from probable ancestral populations and to examine the genetic micro differentiation among the different villages through drift, migration, etc. Basu used Hiernaux's (1965) method of 'distance' analysis of dermatoglyphic traits and found his hypothesis stands (Basu and Namboodiri, 1975). Later, Basu and his collaborator (Namboodri) established a mathematical relationship between total ridge count (TRC) and pattern intensity index (PII) using data from males and females of Negroid origin from southwestern Haiti, West Indies. Predictions of TRC from PII based on regression estimates from Haitian data gave satisfactory results for Negroid and some Caucasoid populations but, less satisfactory results for Mongoloid groups, suggesting that the relationship might be different in different ethnic groups. These findings got published in the American Journal of Physical Anthropology (Basu and Namboodri, 1971).

Biological distances among the four island villages reflect their geographical distance. While showing little migration among them, two of the island villages showed considerable in-migration from Pestel on the mainland. The villages probably originated from a homogeneous population with varying degrees of differentiation following marital isolation. Migration and admixture appeared to be the major evolutionary factors responsible for the general genetic pattern in the rural Haiti populations.

Basu replicated the same study design on a small coastal village, namely Mirpur of erstwhile Medinipur District, West Bengal. The population of this village claimed partial Portuguese ancestry (Basu *et al.* 1980).

IV

After the completion of postdoctoral work, Basu returned to India and joined the Indian Statistical Institute (ISI). But within a short period, Baus again left for the UK to visit the Department of Human Genetics,

University of New Castle-upon-Tyne, in 1974 as WHO fellow. This visit provided him the opportunity for academic interaction with Professor D. F. Roberts. There he received training on human chromosome techniques. Upon his return to India and his rejoining the ISI in its Research and Training School as the Senior Lecturer, he established a Human Chromosome Research Laboratory. However, around 1976, a shift in his research focus was visible for two reasons. He understood that setting up a human chromosome laboratory will take a lot of time and he may not catch up with the advancement in technology. Simultaneously, and more importantly, he didn't want to remain a physical anthropologist any more describing only the nature and extent of genetic variation among groups and sub-groups of populations for determining population micro-evolution, or determining genetic abnormalities.

He wanted to study biocultural adaptation in man, the initiation of which was noticed in his first work in the ISI among the Calcutta population. He searched for opportunities to undertake studies on human biocultural adaptation with a multidisciplinary approach. His overarching research goal was to study different dimensions of the same including the limits to adaptability. Later, he was interested to investigate the survival strategies and coping mechanisms of the impoverished populations. He, furthermore, wanted to pursue a socially relevant biocultural anthropology that does have academic challenge and necessity on one hand, and practical value in terms of human welfare on the other (Mukhopadhyay, 2010).

In looking at the research trends during the middle of the 1970s, when the physical anthropological scholarship was still centering on ethnic diversity using various types of biomarkers, Basu actively campaigned for Anthropological research that will benefit human society. We find this reflection in his article entitled "Is Anthropology dead/dying (Basu and Biswas, 1980). He questioned (a) is there a central theme in anthropology? (b) is there an internal cohesion among subdisciplines/topics in the context of the central theme of the discipline? (c) is the central theme socially relevant? He concluded by saying "Overall, then, Anthropology in India/Indian Anthropology is not dead yet; it grasps and drudges (through the grotesquely perverted existence of a lumpen and a prostitute). Its total alienation to the masses condemning it to the quiet retreat of the grave in a not too distant future. The sooner the better." This article received a mixed response among the scholars and many of them disagreed with Basu and Biswas. But to me, it reveals how passionate Basu was for the cause of Anthropology and its future. Moreover, the article reflects his concern for humanity and society; his reflexivity toward anthropological studies; his philosophy of life. In a much later article, Basu (2009) perhaps showed regret for this writing and described his act as intemperate and rude. Thirty years later, I attended a colloquium on "Future of Anthropology" organised by the Department of Anthropology, Lucknow University. I picked up this article as the starting point of my lecture and finally got the article published in The Eastern Anthropologists (Ray, 2012).

V

Basu started his second innings, on the topic of the Human Adaptability programme, afresh with a group of young bright researchers. He used a combination of health-related traits ranging from demographic traits, haematological traits, anthropometry, body dimension, dietary intake, clinical, presence of intestinal parasite to self-reported morbidity as indicators of various health-related traits of people living in a different ecological setting. His initial studies were focused on high, middle, and low-level altitude dwellers and also among the subgroups within each of these ecological settings. The impetus in researching high altitude dwellers came from the work of Paul T. Baker on Andean high altitude dwellers. Baker (1989) compared high altitude residents with low altitude residents and found the following:

"1. lower fecundity and fertility as a consequence of poor gonadal function and reduced oxygen profusion of the placenta;
2. a higher neonatal death rate as a consequence of low birth weights and higher frequencies of *patent ductus arteriosus*;
3. infants and adolescents grow more slowly in general body size (particularly weight) but develop large chests and lung volumes at all ages;" etc.

Based on this study, Basu questioned (a) What are the effects of high altitude on human populations? Are these effects universal?

(b) If not, what could be the possible reason for the non-universality? (c) Could the non-universality of environmental effects operate at lower altitudes, within the same region but between populations, and if so, what could be the possible reasons?

Basu and Gupta used data on fertility, mortality, the physical growth of children, adult body dimensions, and hemoglobin level from the Sherpas of high altitude (3500-4500 m.) in northeastern Nepal, and the Sherpas of moderate (1000-1500 m.) altitude in Kalimpong subdivision, Darjeeling district, West Bengal, India. The high altitude Sherpa sample was subdivided into two socio-cultural subgroups namely 'more urbanised' and 'less urbanised', and the moderate altitude sample into several occupational subgroups. Their study showed completed family size was not that different between less urbanised and more urbanised Sherpas of high altitude as well as among the spatial and/or occupational subgroups of moderate altitude Sherpas. Infant mortality hardly differed between high and middle altitude Sherpas, unlike in the Andes; but sharply differed between 'more urbanised' and 'less urbanised' Sherpas. Again, compared to the Lepchas (residing in middle range altitude), the Sherpas have higher completed fertility and lower infant mortality. Physical growth of children was slower in high and medium altitude Sherpas, as found among the Andeans, but protracted; so that the adult body dimensions were larger in high altitude Sherpas than the Andeans. Interestingly, their study found haemoglobin levels higher in moderate altitude Sherpas like the Andeans; but it was less in high altitude Sherpas than high altitude Andeans. They concluded from the study that sociocultural factors may contribute more to the basic demographic traits than the physical environment; and different ethnic groups sharing the same micro-environmental stress or macro-environmental stress (like hypoxia) may act differentially in a similar environment.

This study raised further questions like, what could such a lack of universality in the responses of human populations to the stresses be associated with the high altitude? Is it because of the different genetic endowment? Or is it perhaps the Sherpas have prolonged exposure to high altitude than the Lepchas? Or is it a universal phenomenon that differential socio-cultural factors act differently on populations living in high altitudes?

This research programme was perhaps one of the landmark research endeavour in India from the bio-cultural approach.

Later, Basu studied with almost the same set of health-related traits on Lepchas of Sikkim (Basu *et al.* 1984) and a later group of caste population living in the plains (Bharati and Basu, 1990) and the subgroups based on socioeconomic condition.

VI

Basu received training from Igor De Garine of France on nutritional evaluation and intervention and initiated research in West Bengal. He studied sex bias in intra-household food distribution of traditional rural Hindu group, tribal populations, among economic, occupational, rural/urban, and religious groups. The idea was to examine whether male bias in food distribution exists only in Hindu tradition or in tribal tradition also; and does this bias exist across the various tiers of socioeconomic groups? This was a very interesting turn in his research career, relating to society, culture, and health.

Later Basu and his colleagues studied intra-household food distribution among the Lepchas, Sherpas, Oraons, and Mahishya caste groups. Their study concluded that the traditional Hindu system of male dominance and the consequent male bias in intrahousehold food distribution does not seem to operate in tribal populations; economic, occupational, rural/urban, and religious groups do not seem to affect this trait; higher microeconomic status and consequently increased capacity to obtain food do not automatically improve the chances of egalitarian intra-household food distribution or even cause or enhance sex discrimination; and perhaps this is determined by complex ethnic/socio-cultural than by simple economic factors (Basu *et al.,* 1986).

In a further study on the Mahishya caste group (an agrarian caste), Basu compared the food distribution in middle and low economic subgroups and found no inequality in food sharing patterns among the household members in terms of the standard recommended dietary allowance based on sex and age. But male bias exists in the higher economic group. When compared with Lepchas, as to the nature of inequitable household food distribution, the females occupy three of the upper four and males, three of the lower four intake ranks, irrespective of rural/urban residential status; this indicates a female bias, unlike the Mahishiyas (Basu *et al.,* 1987).

This study made a significant contribution to the field of Anthropology of Food and Nutrition. It examined micro-level differences in the food intakes within ecological, regional, and ethnic groups, and has implications in community health and nutritional intervention programme. Or, in raising a more précised question about cooping and survival strategy of different groups.

Perhaps, with this research, Basu made a solid grounding in Indian Anthropology as a bio-cultural anthropologist and as a scholar who is connected with the social reality.

VII

During the late 1980s, Basu shifted his interest in research on the health and well being of the urban population. I consider this as a departure from what he and other fellow anthropologists had been doing for decades; a shift of field from rural and/or indigenous population to urban city dwellers. He studied how stress factors affect differentially among urban working and nonworking women and coping strategies of squatter dwellers.

The questionnaire always remained a very important tool in all of his research. He used to say that designing a questionnaire is a very useful tool and requires a good deal of intellectual exercise. In my research career, I also use questionnaires for data collection and believe that *a good questionnaire is difficult to prepare and a bad questionnaire is difficult to analyze*. In fact, for the last couple of years, I am delivering lectures in different Research Methodology courses on "How to design a good questionnaire?"

Now, let me come back to his urban-based research. An increase in the proportion of female participation in the workforce in urban areas, sometimes during the 1980s, prompted Basu to think of a research problem on the stress level of working females. A working woman may face difficulties in attempting to fulfill the demands of both worlds, at home and outside, while a housewife may feel tired and irritated with her household chores and financial dependence. All these may cause stress for these groups of women. The study compared a group of working mothers with their non-working counterparts concerning: (a) stress level, measured in terms of their anxiety score; and (b) certain general indicators of health including a broad measure of stress. The results showed that the anxiety and health scores of the two groups of women are similar. Further, the health score and anxiety score seem to be correlated, more clearly among the working mothers. Further analyses of this research showed a possible relationship between anxiety score and the age of these mothers as well as their children. Non-working mothers showed higher anxiety levels than their working counterparts concerning the total anxiety score as well as its components, although the differences were statistically non-significant. The anxiety scores of non-working mothers showed increasing values with the increasing age of children. This trend was absent among the working mothers. The age of these mothers was not related to their anxiety level.

How people living in impoverished conditions survive remained a long-standing research interest in Basu. One of the scholars from the United Kingdom wanted to pursue this research under the joint supervision of Basu and Catherine Panter-Brick. But, this project did not materialise for some reason.

Later, in the early 1990s, in my Ph.D. research, I pursued this project. I chose to compare the health and well being of two social groups (namely, Hindu and Muslim), who lived in adjacent clusters in a squatter settlement in Kolkata. I used demographic, haematological, anthropometric, and clinical traits, and magnitude of intestinal parasitic infestation and self-reported morbidity to understand the differential health status of mother and child health of Hindu and Muslim groups. The study further compared the mother and child health of a subgroup of Hindus- one who were working as domestic help in middle-class households and the ones who do not. We hypothesised a difference between Hindu and Muslim health-related traits owing to their differential behaviour related to religion. A section of the Hindu participants used to work in the neighbouring middle-class household as domestic help. We further hypothesised that this working Hindu subgroup was likely to get exposure to middle-class household health-related behaviour compared to their non-working counterpart. There were two novelties in this research- the use of a case study in understanding health-seeking behaviour and a one-year longitudinal growth study on children. Perhaps this was the first study in which Basu advised a student to use a mixed-method approach (qualitative and quantitative) and restrained from using sophisticated multivariate statistical analyses, rather than stick on descriptive statistics. While supervising my study, Basu used to say that statistics cannot be the last word of any scientific research. He was also of the opinion that studying the trend in research is more relevant rather than concluding statistical significance. Later, I realised that research-based on quantitative data, calls for sophisticated statistical analyses for drawing a precise inference of the research problem. But this mixed-method approach is very exciting and I use this method in my ongoing research. It helps in understanding the underlying truth of a research problem.

Many of you will agree that Basu was not stereotyped in his research thoughts. He had flexibility in research approaches and was ready to listen to new ideas. He also gave enough space to his scholars in framing research proposals, designing a study, analysis, and preparing the write-up. This is perhaps very important for any scholar to grow as an independent researcher.

VIII

In the later part of his academics, especially after retirement, Basu (1996) became interested in writing articles on anthropological methodology ("Formulating 'good questions' is half the work done: Qualitative data and the anthropological approach in nutritional and health research") covering a wider canvas. He argued how important it is to ask a good question in research. For example, on the perspective of 'uncertainty in the food supply,' he raised questions like 'How to measure uncertainty?' 'Is this uncertainty predictable?' 'What do people do to cope with uncertainty?' 'Is the coping strategy successful in terms of the chances of survival of the populations?' 'Is this apparent equilibrium (if any) with the uncertainty in food supply related to demographic survival?' 'Can this demographic survival be achieved by sacrificing the state of well being of the population concerned?' He argued that these questions are 'good' because the questions are intrinsically interesting and have practical importance and are concerned with the occupation practiced by a large majority of the Indian population. Citing examples from rural India, where a large number of households are unable to produce enough food throughout the year, Basu questioned how do these households manage/cope during the months of the shortfall in food production? Can this be an indicator of 'uncertainty'? He took into account under-eating, amount of land holding, use of child labour, savings, loan, and household size. Except for household size, most of the data were qualitative.

I consider this article an important reading for contemporary scholars. The article provides a clear idea about how to problematise a research problem taking a critical perspective.

Basu (2003), while depicting his thoughts through the article entitled 'The Trends in Biological Anthropology in India', tried to draw a framework of research trends in Biological Anthropological in India, based on the existing research. He campaigned that Anthropologists should thrust in intensive data collection and explanation at the grass-root level, in small scale situations, and more so on the 'disadvantaged groups'. He talked about the practical utility of Anthropology in an understanding of real-life situations. In the subsequent year, Basu (2004) wrote another article "Popularising Anthropology: Do we have enough "popular eggs" in our basket?" The subtitle of the article is self-explanatory. He questioned, does Anthropology in India have enough materials that are likely to be meaningful, given the overall social scenario. This article was drafted based on the ongoing research projects, M.Sc./M.Phil/Ph.D. dissertation topics are undertaken by the Anthropology departments of this country.

These two articles reiterate his reflexivity towards Anthropological studies in India.

The political situation of West Bengal from 2007 onward was changing very fast. The ruling party of West Bengal, i.e. the left was reeling with problems of land acquisition and displacement for setting up industrial hubs at different places of the state. The intellectuals and the common men came down the street to protest. There were few, like Basu who not only joined the people's rally but took up the pen to protest. The last write-up of Basu, before his demise, came out in the year 2009 addressing this issue in a commemorative volume (The World of B.M. Das: A tribute). In this article Basu was still searching for an answer to the question raised in his 1980s article 'Is Anthropology Dead or Dying?' he questioned: 'Is it necessary for discipline to have social relevance'? 'Can a search for knowledge be value-free'? 'If social relevance is preferred, then which stratum of a given society has to be addressed'? And 'which aspects of the life of the given stratum need to be addressed'?

In this article, while writing against the decision of establishment of a Nano motor factory by the Tata Company in Singur, Basu argued that the self-sufficient Singur people upon losing their land will become a pauper. He was also concerned that without any gainful occupation, these land losers will quickly spend the compensation money, women will become maidservants in more prosperous cities and towns or around or join up the world's oldest profession and the children would take up criminal activities in the absence of their parent's inability to send them to school. And finally, the cultural content of a traditional but modernising village community will be lost. In the same vein, Basu criticized Anthropologists for not far cared to undertake fieldwork to ascertain the situation on the ground level, independent of political propaganda, media reports, and public outcry to understand the concerned people's perception about loosing of land and livelihood.

Through this article, Basu appealed to the Anthropologists, to take a position on real-life problems to earn social recognition. In the last few lines of this article, he said "I earnestly hope that the Anthropologist of tomorrow can prepare themselves to be proud partners of 'mankind in the mass towards the control of its affairs, locally and globally'.

I am reminded of one incident, sometimes during the first week of December 2009. Basu was recovering from a serious cardiovascular ailment in a city-based nursing home. He requested the consulting doctor to release him from the nursing home as soon as possible because he has many unfinished works to complete. He said to the doctor "I have to write for the land looser people of Nandigram and Singur...... I have to write against the police atrocities and the state against these land losers......I have to join the protest movement of the civilians". I was a witness to this conversation. Basu's wish was not fulfilled; he passed away for the heavenly abode on December 12, 2009.

The above narratives perhaps strongly establish Basu as a Humane Anthropologist.

IX

Professor Basu was a Fellow of Royal Anthropological Institute, an Active Member of the International Association for Human Biologists, a Life Member of Indian Anthropological Society, Founder Member of Sasanka Sekhar Sarkar Society for Human Sciences and INCAA, and founder fellow of West Bengal Academy of Science and Technology and Founder Member Centre for Interdisciplinary Studies on Human Development (CISHD), Kolkata.

Basu was very candid to his scholars. After qualifying for the UGC Junior Research Fellowship, I decided to join ISI for my doctoral programme. I approached Basu to be my supervisor for the doctoral programme. He agreed to supervise me but, categorically said: "Well, I can supervise your Ph.D. thesis, but in turn do not expect me to help you in getting a job". In another incident, I requested Basu to be the co-author of my research papers. He politely refused my wish and said "At this stage of my life, I do not want to take co-authorship. As a teacher, I must correct your research article. At most, you can acknowledge me in your article". After the submission of my thesis, I was desperately looking for a job opportunity. My senior colleagues at the Indian Statistical Institute, who was very affectionate to me tried to create a position in the institute as Junior/Senior Technical Assistant. Their idea was to get me initially inducted into that position and later in a scientific position. When they approached Basu with this proposal, he gently discouraged them. He knew very well that in ISI, it would not be possible for any scholar to switch over from a technical position to a scientific position. Interestingly, Basu called me one day and cleared his stand on this issue.

During the post-retirement days, I got the opportunity to spend quality time with Basu. We used to discuss various issues ranging from his experience in attending selection committee meetings to the contemporary state of Anthropology in India and the globe, my prospective postdoctoral project to his dislikes in the functioning of ISI to the atrocities of state. These were indeed some enriching experiences for me. If I search deep into my memory lane, I am sure to come across many incidences that reflect his persona. For example, the University Grants Commission, at a one-time point had stopped sending fellowships to the UGC sponsored research scholars who were working in ISI, including that of mine. When Basu came to know about it, he offered me financial assistance to meet my fieldwork expenses. Again, in a fatherly attitude, he did not hesitate to caution me when he used to found my activity (which is not related to academics or him personally) unacceptable to him. Basu considered all his scholars as close family members; and like the head of the family, he always stood beside them as a solid rock.

Basu was a great connoisseur of classical music, literature, art, and paintings, especially that of Van Gouge. Many of us do not know that Basu was a great Philanthropist. He was a generous sponsor of many organisations that served for the cause of humanity and used to help many destitute whom he knew personally.

Basu was soft-spoken, polite, compassionate, and humble, but had a strong personality and determination. He was a scholar par excellence, revered by the Anthropological fraternity and a great mentor of many of us. Basu always wanted to keep himself away from the limelight. In one word, Amitabha Basu was an institution! I consider myself very fortunate for getting associated with him. His demise is a personal loss for me.

In the end, I reiterate what I stated at the very beginning of this write-up. The world view of Amitabha Basu, which is also his political philosophy, was strongly embedded in his life and works.

Acknowledgements: I would like to express my sincere gratitude to all the scholars, especially to Professor T.B. Subba for giving their critical observation on the manuscript.

Bibliography

Baker, PT. 1989. Introduction. In A. Basu and R. Gupta (Eds): *Human Biology of Asian Highland Populations in the Global Context*, pp. IX. Indian Anthropological Society, Calcutta.

Basu, Amitabha 1971. 'Intrinsic rate of natural increase among the Pahira'. *Social Biology* 18: 195-199.

Basu, A. 2003. 'Trends in biological anthropology'. In GC. Ghosh and TB. Subba (Eds): *Anthropology of North-East India, A Text Book*, Orient Longman, New Delhi.

Basu, A. 2006. 'Social unrest: some personal observation and reflection'. In Ajit K Danda, S.B. Chakrabarti, and Arbainda Basu (Eds): *Social Unrest*, Indian National Confederation and Academy of Anthropologists, Calcutta.

Basu, A., Gupta R, and Mukhopadhyay B, 1984. 'Anthropological Demography of Populations of the Eastern Himalayas'. In J. R. Lukacs (Ed): *The People of South Asia*, pp. 343-364. Plenum, New York.

Basu, Amitabha 1969. 'Digital anomaly among the Pahira'. *Man* 4: 274-276.

Basu, Amitabha 1969. 'Pahira: A populational genetic study'. *American Journal of Physical Anthropology* 31: 399-416.

Basu, Amitabha 1974. 'Anthropology in search of a purpose - the test case of the Pahira of Manbhum'. *Indian Museum Bulletin* IX: 17-24.

Basu, Amitabha 2009. 'An Anthropologists look at Anthropology in the contemporary social scenario'. In Bapukan Choudhury and Pradip Jyoti Mahanta (Eds): *The World of B.M. Das*, pp. 290-306. Assam Academy for Cultural Relations, Guwahati.

Basu, Amitabha and Biswas SK, 1980. 'Is Indian anthropology dead/dying?' *Journal of Indian Anthropological Society* 15: 1-4.

Basu, Amitabha and Chakrabarty Mita 1996. 'Formulating "Good Questions" half the work is done: Qualitative data and the anthropological approach Nutritional/health research'. In R. Khogsdier (Ed): *Contemporary Research in Anthropology: A Felicitation Volume in the Honour of Aloke Kumar Ghosh,* pp. 29-38. Commonwealth Publisher, New Delhi.

Basu, Amitabha and Namboodiri Kadambari K. 1971. 'The relationship between total ridge count and pattern intensity index of digital dermatoglyphics'. *American Journal of Physical Anthropology* 34: 165-173.

Basu, Amitabha and Namboodiri Kadambari K. 1975. 'Social history and bio-anthropology in Haiti, West Indies'. *Anthropologie* 13: 149-158.

Basu, Amitabha, Gupta Ranjan, and Bhattacharya Kalyan K. 1980. 'A demographic study of Mirpur: A village in coastal Midnapur district, West Bengal'. *Journal of Biosocial Sciences* 12: 227-234.

Basu, Amitabha, Gupta Ranjan, and Mukhopadhyay B,1984. 'Anthropological Demography of Populations of the Eastern Himalayas'. 10.1007/978-1-4899-5001-7_16.

Basu, Amitabha, Gupta Ranjan, Robert E. Ferrell, Robert C Elston, Roberts DF., and Mukherjee DP. 1993. 'Panel discussion on genes, environment, and disease', In PP. Majumdar (Ed): *Human Population Genetics*, pp. 315-319. Plenum Press, New York.

Basu, Amitabha, Mukhopadhyay Susmita, Majumder PP, Roy Subrata K., Mukhopadhyay Barun, Bharati Premananda, and Gupta Ranjan 1987. 'Food practices in contrasting populations: an anthropological study of the Sherpas, Lepchas, Oraons, and Mahishyas of West Bengal'. *Social Science Information* 26: 847-868. https://doi.org/10.1177/053901887026004007.

Basu, Amitabha, Namboodri K, Weitkamp LR, Brown WH, Pollitzer WS, and Spive MA. 1976. 'Morphology, serology, dermatoglyphics, and microevolution of some village populations in Haiti, West Indies'. *Human Biology* 48: 245-269.

Basu, Amitabha, Roy Subrata K., Mukhopadhyay Barun, Bharati Premananda, Gupta Ranjan, and Majumdar Partha P., 1986. 'Sex bias in intrahousehold food distribution: roles of ethnicity and socioeconomic characteristics'. *Current Anthropology* 27: 536-539.

Bharati, Premananda, and Basu Amitabha, 1990. 'Fertility, mortality, and maternal anaemic status in a village population of West Bengal, India'. *Annals of Human Biology* 17: 331-335. 10.1080/03014469000001102.

Majumder, Partha P, Gupta Ranjan, Mukhopadhyay Barun, Bharati Premananda, Roy Subrata, Masali Melchiorre, Sloan AW, Basu Amitabha. 1986. 'Effects of altitude, ethnicity-religion, geographical distance, and occupation on adult anthropometric characters of eastern Himalayan populations'. *American Journal of Physical Anthropology*. 70. 377-393. 10.1002/ajpa.1330700312.

Mukhopadhyay, Barun 2010. 'In Memorium (1938-2009)'. *Collegium Anthropologicum* 34: 341-342.

Mukhopadhyay Susmita 1998. 'Role behaviours among urban women as revealed by time allocation'. *Collegium Anthropologicum* 22: 241-246.

Piplai, Dipak 2018. 'Ek Nritatiker Kotha' (in Bengali). In Arup Roy (Ed): *Bigyan Sadhanay Bangali*, Milemishe, Kolkata.

Ray, Subha 1997. *Socioeconomic Concomitants, Health and Well Being of Two Social Groups Inhabiting a Squatter Settlement in Calcutta*. Unpublished Ph.D. thesis in Anthropology. University of Calcutta, Calcutta.

Ray, Subha 2012. 'Anthropology today: Addressing the need of the hour'. *The Eastern Anthropologist* 65: 289-304.

23

D.K. Bhattacharya and his Contributions to Prehistoric Anthropological Studies in India

Geetanjali Devi

Dibyendu Kanti Bhattacharya, best-known among the community of Anthropology and Archaeology as Prof. D.K. Bhattacharya served as a Professor of the Department of Anthropology, Delhi University until his retirement. Besides, Prof. Bhattacharya worked as an ad-hoc Lecturer in the Department of Anthropology, Lucknow University just after completing his Ph.D. Prof. Bhattacharya was the son of Mr. Jitendra Mohan Bhattacharya and Mrs. Manorama Bhattacharya born on the 28th of June, 1939. He had seven siblings - five brothers and two sisters. His father was a Sanskrit teacher in Bengali Boys' High School at Delhi where Prof. Bhattacharya studied as well. It is known that Prof. Bhattacharya had been suffering from asthma and breathing difficulty from the time when he was five years old. One day he heard his father murmuring to his mother that he would not stay alive for long and as such he must be permitted to do whatever he desired. However, he did not let this incident affect him or weaken him rather he stood strong and became the person whom we all know as Prof. D. K. Bhattacharya. Even years late, during his intense asthma attack, he never restricted himself from teaching, research, and fieldwork.

Prof. Bhattacharya was very passionately coveted to undertake activities for the prosperity of the land and the people which found its way when in May 1958 he happens to run away from home to join the Bhoodan movement initiated under Acharya Vinoba Bhave in 1951. His genuineness to serve the people made him continue the movement for six months. But, this act of him had to be faced with trouble in acquiring admittance to the M.Sc. course at the University of Delhi. Nonetheless, he accomplished M.Sc. with a specialisation in Physical Anthropology in his post-graduation from Delhi University. He was awarded Ph.D. from the University of Delhi for his research work on serological and some morphological studies among the Anglo-Indian in the year 1964.

"My Journey with Anthropology" in *The Eastern Anthropologist* (2015), is an exemplification of Prof. Bhattacharya's academic voyage. Prof. Bhattacharya vividly depicts the challenges and admires the events and individuals that immensely contributed to making his voyage unforgettable. Prof. Bhattacharya looks up to the incident when he had to move to Social Anthropology to pursue his post-doctoral research. The incident is such that in 1964 he applied for a CSIR post-doctoral fellowship on the topic: "Inheritance and Functioning of Amino Isobutyric Acid in Human Urine Excretion" which required a photo densitometer and his laboratory had no photo densitometer. Therefore, with a letter from his Head of the Department, Prof. P.C. Biswas, Prof. Bhattacharya went to meet Dr. Talwar of AIIMS if he could use their photo densitometer to which Dr. Talwar replied this was stupid research and such research has no value. Hearing this Prof. Bhattacharya felt humiliated and sent a resignation letter to CSIR and the next day applied for the UGC Post-doctoral fellowship on the topic: "Social Contours of the Anglo-Indians of India". After hearing the topic, his social anthropology professor called him to his room, locked the door from inside, and said "Do not flirt with a subject you're not trained in". He just completed one fieldwork for Bombay Anglo-Indians and prepared a paper for the journal *Race* published by the Institute of Race Relations, London which was later on reprinted in a book on minorities edited by Prof. Kathelene Rose, USA.

Prof. Bhattacharya still inspires the beginners as well as the research scholars of Anthropology with his works like, "Prehistoric

Archaeology" and "An Outline of Indian Prehistory". His journey from one specialisation to the other is quite an enthralling happening that finds substance in "My Journey with Anthropology". Once, a post was advertised in Delhi University with the essential qualification of Physical Anthropology and an ability to teach Archaeology. He applied for the post, got selected, and joined in December. Initially, he was asked to take racial history classes for four months. Then, in May, his HoD sent him to Prof. H.D. Sankalia (1908-1989) at Pune to learn Archaeology which became the turning point of his life. During those days, Prof. Bhattacharya would stay with his classmate and friend Prof. K.C. Malhotra in a quarter allotted to Prof. Malhotra in the Deccan College campus. Early in the morning, Prof. H.D. Sankalia would take him to the riverbank of Mula-Mutha in Yerwada and after touching the ground would say: "you see, this is the actual gravel of the second pluvial that I was talking about". Prof H.D. Sankalia also asked his artist Mr. Dalvi to make a model of the river section in a portable box with a glass cover so that Prof. Bhattacharya can take the model to Delhi to help him in teaching his students. He was moved by the devotion of a teacher, Prof. H.D. Sankalia. Within two months of his stay in Pune, he was confident enough that he can teach Indian Prehistory and had collected many tools from the sites that he surveyed.

After coming back to Delhi he made some changes in the existing syllabus by incorporating fieldwork as a part of the practical. Arranging fieldwork in Prehistory was not a trouble-free task as such fieldwork is away from human habitation where there is no place to stay, no guarantee of food and water. Within nearly twenty years he and his students could collect tools from all the periods of Palaeolithic, Mesolithic, and was at a position that the same could be donated to many colleges and universities.

Prof. Bhattacharya remained a DAAD postdoctoral fellow in Germany. In 1971, when he got selected for this fellowship, the then HoD, Prof. I.P. Singh asked him the notes of his lecture so that the teacher who gets appointed during his leave vacancy can teach with the help of his notes and within twenty days Prof. Bhattacharya wrote the entire course of European, African and Indian Prehistory. These notes later got published in the form of a textbook in the year 1972 during his absence with the help of Prof. Singh. Thus, he became the author of a textbook at the age of 32 years which became widely popular among the degree students of Bihar, Orissa, and West Bengal. He returned from Europe in the year 1974 and published a book entitled *"Palaeolithic Europe*" in 1978 for which he was awarded a D.Litt. This book contained his research work and his visits to different sites and museums. It was because of this fellowship that he had got a chance to work with Professor Francois Bordes (1919-1981) who was the Director of a Quaternary Research Center in Bordeaux. He stayed there for two months and acquired a great deal of knowledge after which he published a book on European prehistory from Humanities Press, USA. He was awarded D.Litt. on this work.

He was the first non-white to write a book on the Palaeo-history of the Europeans. He always argued to relate Archaeology to Physical Anthropology and Cultural Anthropology. He developed the "nutcracker" model proposed by David Pilbeam as the cause of the evolution of the hominid into a lecture entitled: "*Kahani ek dant kee*" (The story of a tooth). Later on, with the growing popularity of the lecture, the UGC created a twenty-two minutes video of this lecture.

Prof. Bhattacharya got an opportunity to visit many archaeological research centers in the UK, Denmark, Sweden, Austria, Norway, and Switzerland during the fellowship in Germany. He got appointed to the post of Reader in 1985 and the post of Professor in the year 1991 in the Department of Anthropology, University of Delhi. Madhya Pradesh, Bihar, and Jharkhand up to West Bengal were the states where he conducted extensive archaeological research.

He also linked palaeolithic archaeology with human biocultural evolution and argued for the unusually huge increase of borers and eyed needles in Europe during Upper Palaeolithic. According to him, the man changed to daytime hunting during this period which led to the loss of body hair and an increase of sweat pores in them. Therefore, they adopted to cover themselves with animal skin to fight with cold winters. Hence, to work with animal skin required tools like raclette and borers or eyed needles. The absence of these types in tropical areas like India further proved this point.

Prof. Bhattacharya was really worried about the growing disregard and contempt getting reflected within the branches of Anthropology.

Once he tried to convince his colleague that Prehistoric Archaeology deals with culture and the expression of litho-culture is often used by pre-historians. Prof. Bhattacharya in an article entitled "Rethinking in Indian Anthropology" published in *Anthropologist* (2000) depicted his concern that one day the specialised branches of the subject Anthropology would become unrecognizable to each other as they are facing a problem of segmentation. According to him, Anthropology should work out a formula where most recent advances in biological and sociological aspects can be united to devise new research strategies. He said that the impact of specialisation has created a vast gap within the sub-disciplines of Anthropology that we are not able to address the real issues. He emphasised that in the future, researches should be conducted in a manner where a population is considered not only as a product of genetic combination but also as a product of society and history.

His credentials of the sub-disciplines of Anthropology reflect in the beautifully penned down articles of him. Prof. Bhattacharya in the article "Anthropology in Prehistoric Archaeology: The Indian Scene", published in the *Journal of Human Ecology* (2000) argues that India is still following the Geo-zoological methods and techniques of 1840-1870. He showed his deep concern over the division of prehistoric cultures in India which he calls an "over-simplistic", "lubbocki", "lubbockian straight jacket" approach. His attempt to look into the archaeology of aging found a place in the article "Old Age in Prehistory" in the *Journal of Human Ecology* (2001). Concerning human evolutionary studies, he provides the example of Olduvai remains and remarked (2000:107): "If we have to in this manner inflate our genus Homo we are still underestimating the actual species diversity of hominids over the past two to three million years." "Anthropology and Social Health" (2001) is Bhattacharya's endeavour of understanding the speedy growth in incidence of social evils owing to factors such as rapid urban growth and break down of the joint family system.

In a foreword by H.D. Sankalia in the book titled, *"The Emergence of Culture in Europe"* published by B.R. Publishing Corporation, Delhi, Prof. Sankalia writes: "Dr. Bhattacharya, to my mind, is the first Indian who has made a first-hand study of the material collected in various countries of Europe and brought the information together in this handy volume for us. That he is India trained and acquainted with Indian problems makes him catch the "wavelength" of Indian students in a much better way than a European author of a similar book could have achieved".

Prof. Bhattacharya along with his research student Dr. Manoj Kumar Singh did excavation at a Lower Palaeolithic site called Kondapeta in Andhra Pradesh. Prof. Bhattacharya remained the President of the Anthropology and Archaeology Section of the 86th Indian Science Congress Association meeting held in the year 1999 at Chennai. On a sponsored programme of Millennium Ecosystem Assessment for his contribution as coordinating author of Cultural Services, in the year 2003, he visited Indiana University, USA; Frankfurt in Germany, and the Czech Republic. Here are names of a few of the Universities and Institutes in India where Prof. Bhattacharya delivered invited lectures: (a) Panchanan Mitra Lecture at Asiatic Society in 1993; Dharani Sen Memorial Lecture at the Department of Anthropology, Calcutta University in 1997; D.N. Majumdar Lecture at Lucknow in 2003 and J.S. Bhandari Memorial Lecture in 2015 at Lucknow.

Prof. D.K. Bhattacharya had a keen association with many national organisations and institutes, such as the University Grants Commission, Indira Gandhi National Centre for Arts, New Delhi; Anthropological Survey of India; member on the board of examiners of many Indian Universities. He supervised eight research scholars for their Ph.D. programme at Delhi University.

References

Bhattacharya, DK. 1978. *The Emergence of Culture in Europe*. B.R. Publishing Corporation, Delhi.

Bhattacharya, DK. 2000. 'Anthropology in prehistoric archaeology: The Indian scene', *Journal of Human Ecology,* 11,1:23-31.

Bhattacharya, DK. 2000. 'Future prospects of human evolutionary studies', *The Anthropologist*, 2, 2:107-111.

Bhattacharya, DK. 2000. 'Rethinking in Indian Anthropology'. *Anthropologist* 2, 1:1-5.

Bhattacharya, DK. 2001. 'Anthropology and social health', *The Anthropologist*, 3, 3, 195-199.

Bhattacharya, DK. 2001. 'Old age in prehistory', *Journal of Human Ecology*, 12, 4: 301 – 305.

Bhattacharya, DK. 2015. 'My journey with anthropology'. *The Eastern Anthropologist*, 68, 1:29-34.

Ghosh, A. 2018. 'Professor Dibyendu Kanti Bhattacharya'. *Indian Anthropologist*, 48,1: 93-97.

Singh, MK. 2014. 'Bhattacharya, Dibyendu Kanti'. In C Smith (Ed): *Encyclopedia of Global Archaeology*. Springer, New York.

Srivastava, VK.2019. 'In Memoriam Professor D.K.Bhattacharya'. *The Oriental Anthropologist* 19, 2: 338-342.

Internet sources

https://link.springer.com. Retrieved on 02/03/2020 at 4:00 pm

https://serialsjournals.com. Retrieved on 02/03/2020 at 2:45 pm

https://www.jstor.org/stable/26633118. Retrieved on 01/03/2020 at 1:00 pm.

24

A Man before his Times: Vardesh Chander Channa

Subhadra Mitra Channa

Vardesh Chander Channa was affiliated with the Department of Anthropology, University of Delhi both as a teacher and as a student. He taught in various capacities from the year 1975 to the year 2005 at this institution, to which he has made a lasting contribution, both in terms of his academic inputs and in terms of institution building.

The Early Phase

Dr. Channa came from a background that set him somewhat apart from most of his colleagues. Born in an affluent business family he had received his primary education from Welham's Boy's School in Dehradun and then from Mayo College in Ajmer. He did B.Sc. from St. Stephens before joining M.Sc in Anthropology. He, therefore, had strong foundations and was known to be teaching his students good English as well as good anthropology. He studied French at Delhi University and the Alliance Francais. He was fluent in French and was able to read Levi-Strauss in original, an author, over whose works he had considerable command. At the same time, he took pride in his mother tongue and was among the few people I know who could read Gurmukhi.

He did his Ph.D. under Prof. P.C. Biswas, also the founder of the anthropology department at Delhi. At that time, specialisations in anthropology were rare and Prof. Biswas, was a practitioner of both branches of anthropology, Physical as well as Social. Vardesh Channa, specialising in social anthropology, did one of the first urban fieldwork in anthropology when most anthropology was being done in rural and tribal areas. The field area for his research project was the historic old city of Delhi. For those not familiar with the geography of Delhi, this is the walled city built by emperor Shah Jehan in the 17th century having particular social geography typical of the cities of North India, under Islamic rule. The urban neighbourhoods are largely demarcated by caste and social ranking, which coincided at the time the city was built. The rich and upper castes lived in large spacious houses called Havelis while the lower castes, serving the upper class/caste were huddled in small demarcated enclosures.

The native population of Delhi comprises of the Aggarwals, or the trading castes, the Gour Brahmins or priestly castes, and the Kayasthas and the Khandelwals, scribes and literary persons, who were the bookkeepers and accountants at the Moghul courts. In the pre-partition days, aristocratic Muslims lived in this area and an array of lower caste service providers, both Hindus, and Muslims. While the upper castes and wealthy Muslims had spacious quarters known as Havelis, the lower castes were crammed into Katras that are small clusters of one-room tenements around a common courtyard.

The Aggarwal, a caste group of middle to wealthy merchants is a closed and introverted community. They are not amenable to being interviewed or interrogated as they like to keep their wealth and community secrets under wrap. They are also pure vegetarians and follow purity pollution norms quite strictly. The walled city is also a very conservative area where changes are slow to take place. Each Aggarwal family lives separately in their enclosed homes so that unlike what we normally find in a village situation, it is not likely that several persons can join in an interview. It was, therefore, not an easy task to go from house to house, trying to take interviews and to persuade them to open up and give relevant information. Vardesh Channa had to make great efforts to establish rapport from house to house and to interview people singly in their shops and homes. In this enterprise he was however helped by young residents of Old Delhi, who all became eminent anthropologists later in life; Prof. Vinay Srivastava, Prof. Nikhilesh Kumar Aggarwal, and Prof. Charusmita Sharma (Gupta). These young enthusiasts became his voluntary assistants, and he generously coached them in anthropological theory.

As he would jokingly tell, the Aggarwals are a very secretive and introverted community and would never have agreed to be interviewed and studied, except that many families considered him to be an eligible bachelor and a potential son-in-law. Although a Punjabi, he was an Arora, a Baniya (trader) caste of Punjab. Bonds of likeness were established, as he projected himself as a businessman and coming from a trading family, in fact, lineage. His father had come from Punjab at the age of 12 and then become an assistant to Sardar Sujan Singh, one of the architects of New Delhi, and later became a highly successful contractor and businessman. Dr. Channa was also running a laundry shop and doing business while studying. His father had passed away when he was only 15 years old and as a teenager, he had been faced with numerous litigations and had to fight many court cases to retain his properties. The trading community of Aggarwals could relate to him and he would share his family narratives with his informants. His work remains one of the few ever done on a *Baniya* community. Much later when another researcher had tried to study the Marwaris of Delhi, she was denied permission for her study by the caste panchayat, after many bouts of negotiations.

In those days there were no computers and no online access to study material and books. As I have already mentioned, Vardesh Channa had mastery over the French language and was a member of the Alliance Francais, from whose library he read Levi-Strauss, Marcel Mauss, and Emile Durkheim, Louis Dumont, etc, in their original versions and then gave informal lectures to his young colleagues and later formal lectures to his students. Since Prof. Biswas had retired long before he could finish his thesis and was also not an active supervisor because of his ill health and relative less expertise in cultural anthropology, Dr. Channa had to struggle on his own to develop the theoretical framework and do analysis on his own. In the process and helped by his keen reading habits, he developed the concept of caste identity and continuity, which was a breakthrough in an era when identity studies were practically unknown. Most people were still working within the structural-functional framework and limited to the study of social change at the outer limit.

The work among the Aggarwals indicated to him the importance of caste, not merely as a structural phenomenon, the approach that was predominant among Indian anthropologists in those times but as an ongoing process of identity. Most cultural practices of the Aggarwals were directed towards preserving and continuing this identity, that was the core of their social existence. He focussed on their kinship and religion, the institutions informing the core caste (or jati) values and norms. However, there was another dimension that was covered by Dr. Channa, namely gender. Although in the late sixties, when he began his research, there were no signs of any gender or feminist studies in India, he turned his attention on the women, not only from the outside, as objects but also as narrators of their experiences. His inclusion of the life history of a young Aggarwal woman, in her own words, was a methodological innovation, not known by many scholars in India, at that time. He not only recognised that the world of women was different from that of men, he also included their stories in their voices.

In 1975, he received his Ph.D. degree from Delhi University, and almost immediately began to teach, although in an ad hoc capacity. Only three other teachers were teaching social anthropology at the department of anthropology, Delhi University at that time, two of them without a doctorate. The addition of Dr. Channa to the teaching faculty was a great boon for the students who opted for social anthropology in that period.

While discussing academics, it is customary to speak about their teachers and mentors, but unfortunately, the early stage of anthropology often left scholars without mentors as there were few people to teach and often not of their specialisation. Dr. Channa was largely a self-made scholar. But there was one person who had taken him under his wings and helped him chart out a possible academic career. Those who have known Prof. I. P. Singh have also known him to be an exceptional human being. During his long stint as Head of the Department, he had invited many renowned foreign scholars to the department. Always Vardesh Channa would be asked to escort them as among all the others at that time he was most proficient in spoken English (also French) and had impeccable etiquettes and manners. From Chie Nakane, Frederick Barth, Stanley Freed, and his wife and many others who visited the department, every time an eminent social anthropologist came, he was asked to accompany them and entertain them. After our marriage, I became an additional party and we often had these scholars come over and eat at our house, and we also took them around for fieldwork or other visits. It was an opportunity that was also not lost. In the days of no internet and no google, personal interactions were a great opportunity to learn and both of us took every advantage of learning from these scholars.

Teaching career

Vardesh Channa had a brilliant but relatively short teaching career. He always carried a futuristic vision and was a pioneer in introducing the department of anthropology to several new courses in Cultural Anthropology, Psychological Anthropology, and Ecological Anthropology were his visions for the future. He also taught his students Industrial Anthropology and Development Anthropology, two new fields of inquiry introduced by him. At that time anthropology in India was dominated by the British School of structural-functionalism. He was among the first, apart from Prof. J.D. Mehra, to introduce the various sub-disciplines of American cultural anthropology to the Department of Anthropology. While Prof. J.D. Mehra had introduced Medical Anthropology and Political Anthropology, Dr. Channa introduced several others out of which his favourite was psychological anthropology. It was not an easy task but he meticulously searched and read through all available material on psychological anthropology and also collaborated with colleagues from the Psychology department of Delhi University to co-teach with him on this course. He ordered various psychological tests and even opened a laboratory, for which there was no space in the department, and these precious tests were housed in a classroom.

But lack of space was more than compensated by the enthusiasm of his students who were very happy to learn a new branch of cultural anthropology. Ecological anthropology was introduced into physical anthropology but Dr. Channa also introduced it as a dimension of cultural anthropology and with a great deal of commitment, created an excellent syllabus that continues with modifications even today. Ecology emerged as a strong point of specialisation in the department at Delhi along with Medical Anthropology and was never discontinued. One of his early students, now a Vice-Chancellor, Prof. Patnaik recalled how he would push the students to read original books and make frequent visits to the library. He said that Dr. Channa gave him an assignment on 'logic of inference' and told him to go ahead, saying, 'yes, you can do it'. Patnaik was cloistered inside the library for several days trying his best to do what at that time seemed to him an impossible task. 'But today I can appreciate how Dr. Channa pushed his students to excel, to reach beyond their presumed capabilities'. Many of his students are today holding high positions, but invariably they remember his contribution to their grooming with gratitude.

As part of his accomplishments as a cultural anthropologist, Dr. Channa was an accomplished fieldworker. In those days, fieldwork was done in the traditional style, with the students and teachers staying in the field, close to the people they studied and not in air-conditioned hotels or guest houses as is becoming the trend. Most groups started from Delhi with bag and baggage without having much idea of where to stay and what they would experience in the field. There was very little sense of insecurity and things were far more peaceful and safer than as they are now. One would get down at some small station, look around and contact the local people, would get some accommodation, cook one's food, and generally rough it out.

Dr. Channa was a master negotiator and had great people skills. I remember once I had accompanied him for fieldwork and we had taken about thirty students in a passenger train with no reservation, going to Himachal Pradesh. On way, while passing through some small towns, a group of rowdy boys forcibly entered the train compartment and began to behave roughly. The many girls in the group were petrified. But Dr. Channa was very calm and collected. Instead of getting rough or trying to confront the rowdy elements, he began to talk to them in a friendly manner. The boys had snatched his cap and were initially very hostile. But with continued talking, he was able to calm them down and they soon became his ardent fans. Not only did they return his cap and generally apologized for their misbehaviour, but they also left the train peacefully at the next station. While leaving they, again and again, told him how impressed they were with him and his advice.

At the same time, Dr. Channa was very sensitive to the sufferings of the marginal and the downtrodden whom he met in the field area. In one of his papers, he has written so poignantly about the old couple whose fields were overrun by boulders because of some road-building activity. He writes about the negative aspects of dehumanised development plans. He would also try to help people in whatever ways he could, including his students, many of whom developed life long affectionate and enduring relationship with him. Even today I meet some of them who tell me how they were inspired to continue in anthropology only because of his influence. He was specifically concerned with those he felt were socially or otherwise marginalised. He would always look out for the weak ones in his brood of students and take special care of them.

How he conducted fieldwork also taught his students the real meaning of fieldwork in being immersed in the field. He never encouraged them to fill up forms and get obsessed with numbers but to get immersed in the field. Again, he advocated for the phenomenological approach long before it entered into the syllabus of anthropological teaching in India. For example, he would tell his students, 'you have achieved real rapport if you can sleep in your informant's house.' In the village, he would often lounge on a cot in someone's house, apparently relaxing but keeping all his senses alert. He would often say that an anthropologist is never bored, for where ever they are, true anthropologists are always doing fieldwork; for they are constantly observing in whichever situation they find themselves. Much later, at an American Anthropological Association meeting in Washington D.C, I had the chance to listen to Renato Rosaldo, who narrated and analyzed an experience that he had at an airport when a flight delay was announced. A Middle-Eastern woman who did not know any English went into panic mode thinking the flight had been cancelled. He gave a detailed anthropological description of the entire situation as well as his analysis based on it. In another instance, Homa Hoodfar, the Canadian -Iranian anthropologist, who spent some time in an Iranian prison, had related how she managed to survive her prison sentence, by pretending she was doing fieldwork in the prison. I was reminded of Vardesh Channa saying that anthropologists are always doing anthropology, where ever they may be.

While on Departmental fieldwork with students, there was one more principle he always followed. He contributed to his food expenses. He would tell me that the fieldwork expenses are borne by the students, by their contributions, why should I eat from their money?

But fate dealt him a very cruel blow. This brilliant and compassionate fieldworker had to face a great disaster when one student drowned in a pond, while on fieldwork with him, in Bastar. Sensitive as he was, he was unable to take the shock and was psychologically depressed for several years after that. This took a toll on his teaching as well as prevented him from going for fieldwork for some years. It was only around 1987 that he was again able to successfully carry out fieldwork with students again.

Research guidance

Dr. Channa would not easily take a student on for guidance of research, either M.Phil or Ph.D. but those that he did take, have remained ever attached to him for the stimulation that he gave to them and his extreme involvement in their work. To him, a research student was not just someone you got over with and add to your C.V. To him each student's research was his own, and he became deeply involved with the project. It was perhaps for this reason that he was averse to take on too many students at one time. He preferred to have one or two devoted students, and he would devote himself to them.

With his great enthusiasm in teaching and promoting psychological anthropology, one of his students, now a brilliant anthropologist in her own right, Prof. Nita Mathur, produced the first thesis based on psychological anthropology, on the innovative topic of how dance is used for the socialisation of children among the Tamil Brahmins of Delhi. This was another thesis on urban anthropology and today Prof. Mathur is a renowned urban anthropologist working on consumer cultures in the city. However, when I discussed this with Prof. Mathur, she pointed out that the original topic was not meant to be a dance. The original idea of research was to understand why the Tamil Brahmins were so over-represented in bureaucracy and were extremely successful as administrators. It was an attempt to relate culture to personality and dance only came into the picture when preliminary studies revealed the importance of dance in the socialisation process of the Tamil Brahmins. He had the habit of discussing topics threadbare with the students and then left them to find their way. He regarded his role as a teacher to be that of a stimulator and supporter but never to spoon-feed the student.

He would always develop a personal equation with his students, especially the research scholars and it was common for them to drop in at home and have food and long discussions with him. At times, if they were doing local fieldwork, he would accompany them on fieldwork. Inevitably they became and remained members of an extended family, forever.

He was always ahead of his time in choosing topics for research. He would always pick up a book that he thought was pointing to a new direction in anthropological studies. As in those days, there was no internet, that came long after, books and journals were the only means of getting to know the global academic trends and he was constantly trying to learn what were the new trends and what new things he could teach. But even though he was teaching before the internet and e-teaching, as it is being done today was in vogue; he had an idea that it was the future of education. According to Prof. Patnaik, he taught them about the importance of technology in the future of anthropological research, telling them that computers will play a significant role in anthropological methodology.

Although he was not my guide, my supervisor being Prof. J.D. Mehra; he was the person to introduce me to my field area in Old Delhi. While doing fieldwork for his research on the Aggarwals, he was also keenly observing and interacting with the other communities in this area. He became friendly with a Dhobi (washerman) who asked him as to why he was not studying their community. He was also much intrigued as an anthropologist to know that they were a small community of a few hundred members who only married within their own '*biradari*' or sub-caste. He realised that it was a ready-made field so to say and one that would provide a unique opportunity for an anthropological study. He accompanied me on my initial field trips but never interfered later with my academic freedom. Later I did my fieldwork and research independently and it was one unwritten rule that although we discussed among ourselves neither of us intervened or influenced the other's work. While he was initially interested in religion and caste I was interested in economic anthropology and later in gender. But much later I too became engrossed in religion and caste but from a very different perspective.

Publications

One sentence that he had told me had left an indelible impression on my mind, he had told me that what we write remains forever. He said that no matter what positions we hold, what lectures we give, or what meetings we attend; these are for the moment only. A few years hence people forget. But writings remain forever. Even today we remember Malinowski and Tylor, for what they wrote. He was very fond of reading, a voracious reader but was very careful in his writing. He had the habit of fully analyzing his data, be very clear in his mind about what the outcome was to be before he would write anything. He would always like to see every aspect of the data fall in place. Everything must be explained. Most of his academic work was done before the era of post-modernism. His writings however did reflect the subjectivity and narrative style of later postmodern writings although he was a meticulously objective analyst.

His first book was based on his Ph.D. thesis on the Aggarwals and the second on Hinduism, where he had used the data on the practice of religion that he collected during the long time spent in Old Delhi while doing his Ph.D. Yet he conducted much fieldwork to collect data meticulously for his second book as well. Since it was written several years after our marriage, we went to attend every Hindu festival for one year to Old Delhi. During that period, it was as if we had suddenly turned religious. Not only did we attend every festival, but we also collected pictures of gods and goddesses and read the texts of Tulsidas's Ramayana and Mahabharata. Many of the ritual bhajans and shlokas were translated into his book.

As I have mentioned before, Dr. Channa was deeply involved in gender issues as he was extremely critical of the patriarchal values of

Indian society. He truly believed that women were equal in all respects and that they should be given every opportunity and also respected. A large number of people preach, but very few practice. A part of it was due to his very western upbringing in early childhood. He had admired the British and other foreign school teachers at Welham and they remained his ideals as well as the values of self-reliance and masculinity as projected by the western value system.

With his values he always found the practice of dowry to be abhorrent. He always believed that a man should live by the money he earns and not try to eke it out of his father-in-law or wife's family. More than a social evil, acceptance of dowry to him was a way of self-depreciation. A way in which a man would demean himself. While doing research among the Aggarwals he was exposed to the systematic dowry give and take practiced by them. He was so distressed that he spent a lot of effort to decipher the causes of dowry and its effects. The research that he did was published as a paper in the journal Human Organisation and remains one of the most read articles on the subject.

In her book *What Anthropologists Do?* Veronica Strang has quoted extensively from this paper. Stanley and Ruth Freed had also quoted from his book on Hinduism in their volume on religion in Shanti Nagar, their several volumes on one village in India. Although he had written relatively few papers and books, Vardesh Channa, remains one of the most quoted Indian authors.

When he was struck by a hereditary disease and became unable to do much academic work, he was planning to write a book on 'How to Change People'. The reason that he gave for such a project was the harassment that he was facing from some colleagues in the Department of Anthropology, Delhi University. As told to me by his student, Prof. Nita Mathur, he was not as perturbed by this harassment as he was curious to know the reasons for it. Always a strong believer in the scientific method, he believed that one can cure anything, provided one knew the cause of it. Therefore, his book on changing people was directed towards the higher goal of transforming negativity into positivity.

Another reason for his not writing too much was that he only wrote if he thought he had something original to say or when he thought he had arrived at some relevant conclusion about his data. Unlike many other scholars, he was never bothered to write only to increase the numbers on his bio-data. In many ways, he was indifferent to worldly achievements.

Personal life

Vardesh Channa was a political person and would be always clear about his political ideologies. He belonged to a party called the Swatantra Party that mainly consisted of upper classes of members, who believed in equality, freedom, and liberty for all, in quite the true sense. I do not know about others, but I know for sure that Dr. Channa wholeheartedly believed in the principles of being liberal and humane. Two topics never entered the conversations in our house, differences based on caste and religion, and sexual or gender inequalities. We had friends belonging to all communities and we would visit them, participate with great sincerity in all their rituals, be it in a Church or a mosque. His best friend was Christian and we often attended church services and addressed his parents as mummy and daddy. We had many Muslim friends and my daughters grew up, asking for Idi on the occasion of Eid. He was a very good friend in need and went all out to help friends and neighbours. During the riots that erupted after the assassination of Mrs. Indira Gandhi, his first concern was to rush to the houses of his Sikh friends to check if they were alright. For his political activities, he mixed wholeheartedly with the Jatavs and other scheduled caste communities that lived in the back lanes of Regarhpura in Karol Bagh in New Delhi, which was our home. There never was any mention of caste or religion in our household. Vardesh Channa came from a family of Arya Samaji's who did not believe in any of the orthodox Brahmanical tenets of Hinduism. Another reason for the liberal outlook was their original home on the North-West Frontiers that according to him bordered on the salt ranges of Afghanistan. Although deeply spiritual and religious, his mother was also extremely liberal in her outlook and had little belief in empty rituals and superstitious beliefs. He never made any distinction between rich and poor and all who were considered friends, were welcome to food and drinks at his house.

He was generous to the extreme when it came to helping others. But he never liked to spend on his self. He had impeccable taste in clothes and appearance but never wished for the excess of anything. If he thought two sweaters were enough, no one could persuade him to buy a third. Later in life, he would refuse to take gifts from his daughters, saying he did not like extravagance.

We always experimented with food, and most of our spare time was spent together in the kitchen trying to cook a variety of dishes from across the world. I remember he once came home beaming with a winemaking book under his arm. But despite much labour and effort, winemaking was an art we never managed to master.

Since he believed in true gender equality, he spent a great amount of time in the kitchen, mostly trying to make exotic European dishes. Once, a great deal of experimentation had gone into making French Onion Soup. Sometimes we were very lucky and dishes turned out perfectly, sometimes they did not. He was particularly proficient in making soufflés and puddings that he decorated and presented very well.

As I have emphasized, he always practiced what he preached. When our second daughter was born, he arrived at the nursing home, carrying a bottle of champagne and flowers for the doctor. She was taken aback, as most people in India mourn the birth of a second daughter, and told him that she did not accept gifts. But he persuaded her saying that he was so happy that he wished her to share in his happiness. He never expressed any wish to have anything else than the daughters that he had. My daughters were very surprised when they realised that many other girls they came across at school and college told them about being discriminated against as compared to their brothers. Or parents of daughters complaining about not having a son. After growing up they realised how liberal their parents were in bringing them up. They had never been told that girls don't do this or girls don't do that. As a consequence, since they had nothing to rebel against, they grew up home birds. They had no incentive to go out since they were never told not to.

Even now they prefer to stay home and experiment with cooking! Some things do run in the family.

The impact on anthropology

The Department of Anthropology at Delhi University is considered among the premier institutions of anthropology in India. The students from this department have been making their mark in anthropology, far and wide and although many of our students went abroad, all have done well in the field of social anthropology. With just three or four teachers in social anthropology at one time, how did they manage to not only teach but also to keep their students up-to-date and well versed in global developments in anthropology. All the teachers of social anthropology always consulted the latest books and journals and kept themselves and their students informed of the global trends. Dr. Channa was greatly enthusiastic about the library and spent much time there. With the help of Prof. S.L. Malik, they had coded and systematised the entire departmental library that still is classified according to their codes.

The constant introduction of new ideas and new topics has kept the department ahead in all fields of anthropology as the introduction of Psychological Anthropology and Ecological Anthropology by Dr. Channa indicates. He also developed the fields of research methodology keeping in mind the latest trends. The students were already becoming aware of debates on the subjectivity of social anthropological research, the use of network theory, and the use of psychological testing, from the seventies at the department. The active participation of students and teachers in the regularly held departmental seminars is another aspect of teaching that was followed by most teachers. But above all, the regular and rigorous training in fieldwork remained a highlight for years to come.

Some Important Publications

Books

Channa, VC, 1979. *Caste Identity and Continuity,* B.R. Publishing Corporation, Delhi.

Channa, VC, 1984. *Hinduism: A Cultural Profile of the Gods, Goddesses, Rituals, Romance and Fables in today's Hinduism*, National Publishing House, Delhi.

Van Willigen, J, and VC. Channa 1991. 'Law, Custom, and Crimes against Women: The Problem of Dowry Deaths in India' In J. McDonald (Ed): *Human Organisation* Reprinted in *The Applied Anthropology Reader*, pp. 116-30, 2002, Allyn and Bacon, Boston.

Index

B

C

D

E

F

J

K

L

M

N

T